Automation in Communication

By drawing on multiple examples from healthcare, religion, service encounters, and poetry, Lionel Wee presents rich insights into the use of automation in communication through a posthumanist lens.

As communication becomes increasingly automated, the use of automation creates significant conceptual challenges for ideologies about language, beliefs about the nature of language, as well as assumptions about the roles that interpretation, anthropomorphism, and folk theories of mind play when language is used in communication. This book unravels the ideological implications of automation in communication and provides a new theoretical ground to address the major issues raised by automation. Wee discusses the importance of thinking carefully about how we identify and distinguish the roles of speaker and hearer. He also argues that we need to re-evaluate our understanding of the relationship between language and community.

This book will be vital to students interested in studying the intersections of AI, language, and communication, as well as researchers working in communication studies, linguistics, and the broader sociology of language in the age of technological change.

Lionel Wee is a Provost's Chair Professor in the Department of English, Linguistics and Theatre Studies and Dean of the Faculty of Arts and Social Sciences at the National University of Singapore. He sits on the editorial boards of the *Journal of Sociolinguistics, Applied Linguistics, English World-Wide, Sociolinguistic Studies, Multilingual Margins,* and *Studies in World Language Problems.*

T0384848

Routledge Studies in Sociolinguistics

For more information about this series, please visit https://www.routledge.com/Routledge-Studies-in-Sociolinguistics/book-series/RSSL

Automation in Communication

The Ideological Implications of
Language Machines

Lionel Wee

Routledge
Taylor & Francis Group

LONDON AND NEW YORK

Designed cover image: © Getty Images

First published 2025
by Routledge
4 Park Square, Milton Park, Abingdon, Oxon OX14 4RN

and by Routledge
605 Third Avenue, New York, NY 10158

Routledge is an imprint of the Taylor & Francis Group, an informa business

British Library Cataloguing in Publication Data
A catalogue record for this book is available from the British Library

ISBN: 9781032741611 (hbk)
ISBN: 9781032732237 (pbk)
ISBN: 9781003467922 (ebk)

DOI: 10.4324/9781003467922

Typeset in Galliard
by Taylor & Francis Books

Contents

Acknowledgments

The ideas in this book have benefited from conversations, presentations, and seminars with many different colleagues over the years.

I would also like to thank the National University of Singapore for research support, without which this book would not have been possible.

Finally, I wish to acknowledge that extracts from the following publications are reproduced here with minor revisions:

Wee, L. 2015. "Mobilizing affect in the linguistic cyberlandscape: The R-word campaign." In *Conflict, Exclusion and Dissent in the Linguistic Landscape*, edited by R. Rubdy and S. Ben Said, 185–206. Basingstoke: Palgrave Macmillan.

Wee, L. 2021. *Posthumanist World Englishes*. Cambridge: Cambridge University Press.

Wee, L. 2021. *The Communicative Linguistic Landscape*. London: Routledge.

1 Machines Are Talking ... But Are They Actually Speaking?

Introduction

We use language to transmit ideas, express emotions, craft identities, write poetry, among many other communicative activities. But as studies of styling (Coupland 2007; Wee 2015) remind us, language is just one among the many different resources that are used when we communicate. For communication to take place, language works in concert with other resources such as gesture, dress, posture, setting. And increasingly, 'other resources' also includes automation.

This book is about the use of automation in communication. It is an undeniable fact that various technological advancements ranging from relatively simple computer programs to highly developed artificial intelligence (AI) are coming to be more and more involved in our communicative activities. In this introductory chapter, I present some examples to give us a concrete sense of what it means to be saying that communication is becoming automated. I show that even an apparently simple case – such as when a sign at a carpark indicates to drivers the number of lots that are vacant – already raises challenging questions about how to understand the communication that is taking place. The questions only gain in complexity as we move on to consider automation that involves even more sophisticated and interactive programs, such as chatbots, echoborgs, translation apps, and of course, ChatGPT. Machines are indeed talking, and in many cases, the talk is not merely ancillary to the communications between humans. Oftentimes, humans and machines work in concert to produce a message that is to be conveyed. In yet other cases, humans are communicating with and even getting advice and comfort from machines. In cases such as these, are the machines in fact not just talking but actually speaking? The latter term implies intention rather than mere vocalization.

There is, however, a pervasive preconception that the notion of 'speaker' has to be tied to personhood and to being human. This is even though ideas about what it means to be a person or to be human are by no means straightforward and free of ideological assumptions. It is the (human) speaker who is presumed to have an intention to communicate. This is what leads that person *qua* speaker to produce an utterance, one that supposedly reflects their communicative intent. We will see, however, that the use of automation creates

DOI: 10.4324/9781003467922-1

significant challenges for such a preconception. There are also other preconceptions embedded in how we think about the processes that underpin communication that are just as problematic. The use of automation requires, for example, that we think more carefully about how we identify and distinguish the roles of speaker and hearer. It also requires that we re-evaluate our understanding of the relationship between language and community. I discuss these problematic preconceptions in the first part of the chapter before bringing in examples that involve automation.

The discussion in this chapter leaves us with the question highlighted in the title. The remainder of the book shows how these ideological issues can be coherently addressed.

Preconceptions of Language and Communication

The various ways in which communication can be automated raise interesting problems for deeply entrenched ideas about language and communication, in particular, for what Duranti (1992) calls 'the personalist view of meaning' and what Goffman (1981) calls 'the traditional paradigm for talk'. It is worth noting, however, that even before automation enters the picture, both the personalist view of meaning and the traditional paradigm for talk have already been subject to major criticisms. The introduction of automation exacerbates the existing problems with these two ways of thinking about communication while raising new ones as well.

I start with a discussion of some of the oft noted problems for the personalist view of meaning.

The Personalist View of Meaning

There is a pervasive assumption that an analysis of language and communication should place primary emphasis on the individual human speaker's intentions. It is the individual human who has the capacity for intent, including a communicative intent. This intent is assumed to be fully formed within the individual who then uses language to communicate this intent of theirs. A typical example might be a speaker who first has a clearly formed desire for a cup of tea. This speaker consequently utters 'I'd like a cup of tea' with the intention of conveying this specific desire. Duranti (1992, 26) refers to this as the 'personalist view of meaning' because the fully formed intent is assumed to originate from inside the individual speaker before it is externally communicated.

The personalist view of meaning has been criticized, primarily from a linguistic anthropological perspective, for not giving sufficient attention to cultural and contextual factors. The main thrust of the criticism is threefold: One, communication is far more interactive than has been recognized so that the hearer often plays an active role in (co-) constructing the meanings of communicative acts. Two, it is not always or even often the case that a fully formed intention precedes the act of communication. It has been noted, for instance, that communication is often routinized so that speakers act in ways that reflect a particular habitus (Bourdieu 1977). Greetings ('Hi', 'How are you?', 'Hello') are a prime example of such routinized communicative behaviour. But even if we return to our example about requesting for a cup of tea, the speaker who says, 'I'd like a cup of tea' may not actually be thinking specifically about tea in any deliberate or intentional manner but could be asking for a cup of tea simply because (as far as this speaker's upbringing or cultural background is concerned) a cup of tea is what one usually has at this particular time of day. Alternately, the speaker may not actually want a cup of tea at all but is only trying to be polite to their host. Also, perhaps just as frequently, speakers retrospectively construct their intent in the light of how their communication was interpreted, where this construction of intent is often also a jointly undertaken discursive enterprise. In other words, rather than intent preceding and driving communication, the construction of intent is itself the outcome of a collaborative communicative achievement. For example, consider the following exchange that occurs an hour after the speaker has consumed the cup of tea.

HOST: Ah, you look much better. Are you feeling more relaxed now?
SPEAKER: Yes, thanks for the tea. I guess I really must have wanted that cup of tea even though I actually didn't feel like it at the time.

And three, the centrality given to speaker intention is unjustified especially if this is presented as a general claim about how communication works. This is because cultures vary greatly in the degree to which speaker intention can be even considered a relevant variable in meaning construction. I do not wish to deny that personalist construals of meaningful acts do occur in social life. However, it is 'not the *only* route and furthermore in some contexts the dispreferred one' (Duranti 1992, 44; italics in original). The danger with philosophical accounts that define intention in personalist terms is that they risk elevating one possibility for meaning construal to the status of a universal.

In this regard, two particular works are worth noting. The first, Duranti (1992), through a detailed investigation of the Samoan *fono* (formal meeting), demonstrates that, in some cultures at least, the main concern is the allocation of responsibility rather than the reconstruction of speaker intention. In the case of the *fono*, speaker intention is even considered irrelevant since responsibility is distributed on the basis of the actual consequences of what was said rather than any intention the speaker may have had. In one of Duranti's examples, an orator had, some weeks earlier, announced to the village that a newly re-elected official would be coming to present some goods to the village assembly. Considerable resources were thus spent on preparing for this high-level event. However, when the event failed to materialize, the orator was, in the course of a *fono*, considered responsible for having embarrassed the village regardless of whether he had in fact intended to do so or not. The punishments considered by the members of the *fono* included a heavy fine and even expulsion from the village. As Duranti (1992, 33) puts it:

This means that in Samoa a speaker must usually deal directly with the circumstances created by his words and cannot hide behind his alleged original intentions.

The second work, Du Bois (1992), investigates the nature of communication in acts of divination and illustrates that, in such cases, it is possible for communication to take place with neither speaker intention nor speaker responsibility present. One of the examples discussed by Du Bois (1992, 54) is the Sixteen Cowrie divination of the Yoruba of Nigeria, where a diviner first shakes a basket containing sixteen cowrie shells. Depending on the number of shells that come out facing up, different figures are named. Associated with each figure are sets of divination verses, which the diviner proceeds to recite until the client finds one that seems relevant to their particular situation. Du Bois' contention is that divination gives us a clear case of meaning without intention (56):

> Regarding intentionality, clearly these utterances are outside the control of their utterer in at least two respects. First, they are traditionally specified texts, memorized from the oral teachings of a senior diviner over the long years of study required to master such a large corpus of divination texts. Second, the verse that the diviner utters on a particular occasion is specified by the aleatory mechanism of the cowrie toss, whose result is quite outside the control of the diviner. Although the client selects among the several verses presented the one which he or she considers relevant to the case, what is relevant for our purposes is that the diviner's recitation is governed by an aleatory mechanism.

Language is certainly being used communicatively in the case of the Sixteen Cowrie divination, but the use does not reflect any specific intention emanating from within the speaker/utterer. This is because the speaker neither controls the selection of the set of verses nor their meanings. The set of verses is determined by the tossing of the cowrie shells. And it is the client who ultimately decides which specific verse is most relevant to their situation. Du Bois therefore concludes that 'a striking characteristic of divinatory language is that it is capable of going beyond suppression of intention to the actual elimination of speech-actor responsibility' (52).

What these two examples demonstrate is that the personalist view of meaning in communication is highly limited, privileging a culture-specific and anthropocentric view of individualized personhood, intention, and communication (Cameron 2000a, 2000b; Foley 1997, 264).

The Traditional Paradigm for Talk

In addition to the personalist view of meaning, there are also problems with what Goffman (1981, 130) calls 'the traditional paradigm for talk'. In this traditional paradigm, talk is treated as being essentially dyadic. It is understood as an oral face-to-face conversation that takes place between a speaker simpliciter and a hearer simpliciter. However, Goffman points out that, absent further qualifications, the use of terms such as 'speaker' and 'hearer' is highly problematic.

In his discussion of footing, by which he means the various ways in which participants to a communicative event can align themselves, Goffman (1981, 129–130) notes that the terms 'speaker' and 'hearer' tend to prioritize oral communication to the point where other channels of communication such as visual cues, touch, and writing may all be downplayed or perhaps even neglected. But these other channels should not be treated as being secondary to the aurally conveyed linguistic message, as though they only and always serve to merely supplement it. After all, an accompanying gesture can influence or even override the understanding of the linguistic message. Eye-rolling, for instance, indicates that the individual finds the message to be too ridiculous to be taken seriously. Smiling, when delivering what might otherwise be considered an insult, may signal that what is actually intended is good-humored teasing.

Moreover, approaching our understanding of communication in terms of a 'hearer' without further deconstructing the term ignores the fact that a ratified participant may not be paying attention despite being the intended recipient of the message (as in the case of a 'hearer' who happens to be daydreaming). Likewise, 'hearer' also fails to give due cognizance to those situations where a non-ratified participant (such as an eavesdropper) may in fact be listening very carefully. What counts as a 'hearer', according to Goffman, can be much more nuanced than the term itself suggests and, by extension, is more complicated than what the traditional paradigm for talk is able to recognize and account for.

Goffman also makes the point that the traditional paradigm, with its dyadic presumption, has no place in its account for an 'audience', that is, a group of individuals who are ratified participants in the sense of being allowed to be present at a communicative event but who are not actually expected to be actively involved in the production of the utterances that constitute the communicative event. Nevertheless, depending on the nature of the communicative event in question, some audiences may be expected to be more active than others. An audience at an orchestral or theatrical performance is generally expected to remain quiet during the performance itself but it is also expected to applaud *as a group* at the end of the performance. An audience at a lecture, on the other hand, can actively participate in the discussion but usually only if questions or comments are invited from the audience. In such situations, an individual audience member may temporarily function as 'speaker' should he or she happen to be selected by the lecturer or, if one is present, by the moderator (note that the role of 'moderator' is itself yet another way in which a participant can align to a communicative event, one that is distinct from 'speaker', 'hearer' and 'audience').

And perhaps most famously, in his discussion of 'production formats' (Goffman 1981, 145; see also Chapter 3), Goffman deconstructs what it means to be a 'speaker' by pointing out that the person who is delivering a message (i.e., the person who actually does the talking) may not necessarily be the one who composed the message or even the one whose views and ideas are being represented. Goffman's main point is that agentive responsibility for what is being said or produced can be distributed and so does not always reside with the speaking entity (see Chapter 3 again for further discussion). For example, a spokesperson for a company is a speaker but this person is actually speaking on behalf of the company rather than in their personal capacity. In contrast, someone expressing anger is presumably speaking on their own behalf even if they may be upset about someone else's predicament.

But even though Goffman's points about the need to look beyond a simple dyadic model of communication are well taken, he, too, has the same problem as the personalist view when he privileges the speaker over the hearer. As Goodwin and Harness Goodwin (2003, 225) note, there is a 'marked asymmetry' in how Goffman treats the speaker and hearer. The former is 'endowed with rich cognitive and linguistic capacities, and the ability to take a reflexive stance towards the talk in progress' while the latter is 'left cognitively and linguistically simple' (Goodwin and Harness Goodwin 2003, 225). The basic and unquestioned assumption, even for Goffman, is that communication always begins with the speaker and that speaker's intention *qua* human individual. However, there is a need to recognize that the hearer, too, makes an active contribution toward the construction and unfolding of the exchange, one that is in fact far more consequential than that of the speaker. Appreciating the significance of the hearer becomes particularly important when looking at communication involving automation. This is because while there remain questions about whether robots and apps are actually endowed with intelligence or sentience, there is no doubt that how a particular communicative activity is understood depends very much on the willingness of a hearer to anthropomorphize the speaker – and it is from this willingness that other considerations follow such as the attribution of communicative intent. This willingness can vary regardless of whether the speaker is recognizably human or not. This is because the decision as to whether some entity should be treated as indeed human is a deeply ideological one. As Pennycook (2018, 2–3) points out:

> … humanism has also been consistently blind to human difference. Despite its claims to describe a common human condition, humanism has long been both exclusionary – it was never a category that included everyone – and specific to a particular version of humans.

It is on such grounds that some, such as Braidotti (2013, 16), take up a specifically anti-humanist position, asking why, as a woman, she would want to be a member of a category (human) that has been so consistently exclusionary: 'I am none too fond of Humanism or of the idea of the human which it implicitly upholds'. Humanism generally assumes a fixed universal commonality for all humans, and as many critics of this position have remarked, this position was all too often Western, Educated, Industrialized, Rich and Democratic (WEIRD) (Heinrich, Heine, and Norenzayan 2010). We might add White, Male, and Straight to that list.

Put in broad terms, the adoption of a human-centric perspective – a perspective that is by no means universally understood or accepted – is main reason why both the personalist view of meaning and the traditional paradigm of talk have no principled way of accounting for the presence and involvement of non-human participants. This is obviously a key point that needs to be addressed if the role that automation plays in communication is to be properly and seriously considered. As we now see, these problematic preconceptions regarding language and communication are also carried over to the more specific pragmatic notions of speech acts and the Cooperative Principle, both of which also privilege the intention of the individual human speaker.

Speech Acts and The Cooperative Principle

Speech acts are considered 'staples of communicative life' (Green 2021), and, in this regard, Austin (1962, 1) argues that 'many utterances which look like statements are either not intended at all, or only intended in part, to record or impart straightforward information about the facts.' Instead, utterances constitute speech acts, whose illocutionary intent and perlocutionary effects depend on the existence of conventionalized procedures, where 'certain words' are uttered by '*certain persons* in certain circumstances' (Austin 1962, 14; italics added). The default assumption that speech acts involves 'persons' is echoed by Searle when he speaks of 'human communication' as 'trying to tell someone something' (Searle 1969, 47):

> Human communication has some extraordinary properties, not shared by most other kinds of human behavior. One of the most extraordinary is this: If I am trying to tell someone something, then (assuming certain conditions are satisfied) as soon as he recognizes that I am trying to tell him something and exactly what it is I am trying to tell him, I have succeeded in telling it to him.

Similarly, Grice's (1957) notion of 'nonnatural meaning' takes as its point of departure the proposition that a human speaker communicates an effect to their audience by, in part at least, getting the audience to recognize the speaker's own intention to produce such an effect (Grandy and Warner 2020). A number of modifications to Grice's original formulation – the details of which need not detain us here – have led to its incorporation into speech act theory (Searle 1969), relevance theory (Sperber and Wilson 1995), as well as more recent attempts to refine Grice's own claims concerning the calculability of implicatures (Récanati 1993; Saul 2010).

More pertinently, the view of communication undergirding the works of Austin and Grice relegates the hearer to the relatively passive role of simply trying to decipher or reconstruct as accurately as possible the speaker's intention. Also, speaker responsibility, insofar as it is even an issue of discussion (rather than being dismissed under the rubric of 'perlocutionary effects') is essentially treated as a function of speaker intention. That is, speakers are held responsible for the resulting effects of their communicative acts to the extent that they intentionally chose to engage in the act despite the fact that they foresaw, or can be reasonably expected to have foreseen, its consequences (though see Duranti's discussion of the *fono*, above). Thus, as Oishi (2006, 1–2) points out:

> Austin presented a new picture of analysing meaning; meaning is described in a relation among linguistic conventions correlated with words/sentences, the situation where the speaker actually says something to the hearer, and associated intentions of the speaker … Austin formulated a method to describe a sentence in terms of the speech situation where it is uttered: by means of associated linguistic conventions, the speaker, with an associated intention, actually performs an act to the hearer, which induces a certain response from the hearer.

Likewise, Grice's (1975, 45; italics added) Cooperative Principle is formulated from the perspective of the speaker, 'Make *your* conversational contribution such as is required, at the stage at which it occurs, by the accepted purpose or direction of the talk exchange in which *you* are engaged'. The Maxims of Quality, Quantity, Relation, and Manner are all typically then understood as maxims that the speaker should, all things being equal, attempt to observe. The starting point for both Austin and Grice, then, is the speaker and that speaker's communicative intent. Even though the hearer is expected to work out various implicatures, as Grice acknowledges, this is an activity that the hearer carries out based on what the speaker utters, which thus characterizes the hearer's responsibility as one of recovering as accurately as possible what the speaker intended by their contribution. It is clear that by focusing on speaker intention and by viewing communication as involving a dyad of speaker and hearer, both Austin and Grice are drawing on the presumptions found in the personalist view of meaning and the traditional paradigm of talk. And this means that concepts such as speech acts, Cooperation, and Maxims, are vulnerable to the same issues that plague the personalist view and the traditional paradigm. This is not to suggest that the concepts from Austin and Grice are irrelevant. Speech acts, Cooperation and implicatures continue to be used in analytical work (Bäckström 2020; Bayat 2013; Buchanan 2013; B. Clark 2021; Janssens and Schaeken 2016), and because of this, we need to take a position on whether these notions ought to be considered at all applicable when trying to account for the use of automation. In this book, I show how they can and should be recontextualized within an approach to pragmatics that gives greater emphasis to the role of the hearer and, in particular, to the hearer's willingness to anthropomorphize the entity that they are interacting with (see especially Chapters 4 and 5).

At this point, with these issues in mind, we can move on to consider some actual examples of automation in communication.

Are 'Friends' Electric? Five Examples

'Are "Friends" Electric?' is a 1979 song by Gary Numan and the Tubeway Army. The song describes a world where machines provide various services to humans and the title, in particular, refers to a robot prostitute (Simpson 2014). The following examples demonstrate that machine 'friends' are in fact far more ubiquitous and less sensationalistic than the one referred to by Numan and, because of this, are linguistically actually more interesting.

Example 1: The Carpark

I start with a relatively simple example though we will quickly see that its simplicity belies the complexity of the issues involved. Consider the by now ubiquitous use of automated signs at carparks to indicate to drivers if a carpark is full and, if not, just how many empty lots are actually available (Wee 2021a). Thus, a driver who is approaching a carpark may variously encounter a sign with a message that reads 'Carpark full' or '86 lots available'.

The automated sign at the entrance to the carpark is obviously intended to be communicative, having been programmed to take note of the number of cars that are already present in the carpark and to convey in real time the relevant information (i.e. how many lots are still empty) to drivers who may be thinking of parking their cars there. In a multi-storey carpark, drivers may even be told of how many available lots are actually distributed over the different levels (e.g. 'Level 3, 24', 'Level 4, 35'). All this raises the question of how we are supposed to conceptualize the communicative acts coming from the carpark. Note that we are not at this point talking about the Turing Test or Searle's Chinese Room puzzle (see the following chapter for discussions about these). Rather, the question that confronts us is a much more basic one about how to analyse the pragmatics of the communication that is taking place.

Presumably, we wish to avoid anthropomorphizing the carpark sign and thus to avoid attributing intentions to it. Unfortunately, things are not quite so simple. There is no doubt that the driver is necessarily engaged in some sort of inferencing so as to process the information provided by the carpark sign. From the driver's perspective, what sort of inferencing is taking place when the 'interlocutor' happens to be a machine as opposed to another human being? Here, anthropomorphic reactions are certainly not uncommon. For example, we have all had moments when we rail against our desktops. Or when we get frustrated with the spellchecker on our mobile phones, when it insists on correcting a piece of text that contains a neologism. A more extreme and dramatic example would be the case of the woman using a club to attack a robot (Yen 2023). And we also admit – after calming down – that these acts of venting are irrational since we do not actually expect our desktops to react to our anger. Likewise, a driver who notices that there are in fact empty lots available, even though the sign says 'Carpark full' will most likely assume that the machine is faulty rather than conclude that it has any intention to deceive. Thus, there are presumably differences in how interactions with a machine are being conceptualized by the human participant as compared with interactions involving a fellow human being. But what exactly are the differences and what would be the theoretical implications that follow? And would those conceptualizations change as the machines increase in sophistication (see Examples 2 and 3 below)?

For now, let us move on to the other side of the interaction, as it were. The occasional tendency to anthropomorphize behoves us to ask whether it at all makes sense to assert that the machine is producing speech acts and being Cooperative in Grice's (1975) sense of the term, and concomitantly, whether it is perhaps even observing particular Maxims. For example, given that the machine has been programmed to convey information in a syntactically and lexically restricted manner, would we want to suggest that the brevity of its message shows that it is observing the Maxim of Manner? Certainly, we would want to acknowledge that whoever programmed and installed the machine intended for it to be useful and that its usefulness includes conveying the relevant information in as brief and clear a manner as possible. So, Grice's ideas might be still applicable if we treat the communication as coming from the programmer. However, this position is not without problems of its own, for at least two reasons.

The first reason is this. Bringing in the programmer into the pragmatics of the carpark communication event so as to justify the applicability of Grice's ideas assumes that the programmer is yet another human being. Qua human being, it is then unproblematic to attribute to this entity the kinds of intentions and goals ordinarily discussed in relation to Grice. However, in the case where the communicative technology has been created by a computer program, then the same questions about how to understand the communicative pragmatics arise once again. This latter scenario is not as farfetched as it seems because machines are already capable of writing their own code (Galeon 2017). In such cases, there is no recourse to an actual human being, one to whom the received understandings of speech acts and the Cooperative Principle might be attributed.

The second reason arises from the fact that even when a human programmer can be traced, we still need to separate the intentions of that programmer from the intentions (if any) of the program. This is because the specific information being conveyed on any given day and time about the state of the carpark (e.g., the actual number of lots available on specific levels or whether the entire carpark is full) is not something that the human programmer would likely be aware of. The information is gathered and conveyed via sensors that are independent of the programmer (which is of course the whole point of the programming). So, whatever information is being communicated to the driver at any particular moment is information that the program (but not the programmer) would have access to. Which brings us back to the question of how to understand the pragmatics of the communication, when the driver is being informed of the state of the carpark. If our stance here is that the Gricean notions of Cooperation and the associated Maxims, as well as Austinian speech acts, are not at all applicable, what then are the available conceptual alternatives?

Example 2: The Chatbot

Let us move on to our second example. A chatbot is a piece of software that conducts a conversation via auditory or textual methods. Such programs are often designed to simulate, with varying degrees of sophistication, how a human would behave as a conversational partner. Chatbots are typically used in customer service. Some chatbots use fairly advanced natural language processing systems, but many of the simpler ones merely scan for keywords within the input from the human interlocutor and then provide a reply that has been already prefabricated by selecting from an existing database. The provided reply is selected based on the number of matching keywords from the human interlocutor's input.

Here is an example of a chatbot, from the Development Bank of Singapore (DBS). The bank's website has a picture of a computer screen with smiling features and the speech bubble 'Do you need any help?' The picture is clearly intended to suggest that the DBS chatbot has some human-like features but it is by no means intended to deceive anyone into thinking they are actually dealing with another human (unlike the echoborg example below). A click on the speech bubble brings up the following introduction:

> Hi, I'm DBS digibot! You can ask me questions about DBS products and services, or get help with your accounts and cards.
> What can I help you with?
> Can you tell me what is preferred payment plan
> Fee waiver for my Card / Cashline
> How to apply for Personal Loan?
> My card is damaged, I need a replacement
> View your deals and offers
> Or just type your question in the chat

If one were to enter the query 'How do I apply for PayNow?' (PayNow is a mobile payment system), the following response crops up:

> You can register for PayNow via DBS iBanking, iWealth or your digibank app. During registration, you will be asked to (1) select the DBS/POSB account that you want to link to your selected PayNow Proxy (mobile number and/or NRIC/FIN number), and (2) set a PayNow Nickname for your registration.
> Please note that you will need to register for PayNow first, before you can receive funds into your DBS/POSB bank account via PayNow.

Clearly, the DBS chatbot is much more interactive when compared with the carpark sign. It can handle a wider range of (banking related) topics, and its responses can also be more individualized, allowing it to handle (within limits) fairly specific inquiries from individuals about the bank's products and services. As mentioned, visitors to the bank's website are under no illusions that they are dealing with a fairly sophisticated computer program rather than interacting with another human being. Nevertheless, the greater level of interactivity that the chatbot is capable of arguably gives the question of how to analyse the pragmatics of an interaction involving automated communication even greater urgency and significance. We need to ask, for example, about the kinds of language and communicative ideologies that guide and inform the ways in which humans interact with much more responsive programs. Such ideologies may or may not be different than those that guide and inform human-to-human interactions. That is, as programs get increasingly sophisticated – consider for example, Amazon's Alexa or Apple's Siri – we have to consider if the ideologies involved might actually start to approximate those that inform human-to-human interactions. Despite the importance of these questions, we currently have very little idea about the details of the ideologies involved and how to accommodate such ideologies in our conceptualizations about language and communication.

Example 3: The Echoborg

Our third example involves the concept of an echoborg. Whereas in the first two examples, the human interlocutors are under no illusions that they are dealing with computer programs, an echoborg represents an interesting twist, one where the human speaker is used to extend or supplement the communications that are coming from an artificial intelligence. Specifically, an echoborg is a person whose utterances and gestures are determined to varying degrees by the communications that originate from an artificial intelligence program. An echoborg is a kind of cyranoid (the latter term is clearly inspired by Rostand's play *Cyrano de Bergerac*). A cyranoid is defined by Corti and Gillespie (2015, 30) in the following manner:

> A cyranoid is created by cooperatively joining in real-time the body of one person with speech generated by another via covert speech shadowing. The resulting hybrid persona can subsequently interact with third parties face-to-face.

As Corti and Gillespie (2015, 30) observe, 'naïve interlocutors perceive a cyranoid to be a unified, autonomously communicating person ...' In the case of an echoborg, the artificial intelligence is joined with a human surrogate such that the latter then becomes the public and human face of the former. Lamb (2015) provides a succinct description of what might happen with echoborgs:

> AIs use human surrogates or "echoborgs" to speak their words and socialize with humans. The living, breathing avatar simply recites the computer's words at the conference table, serving as a humanizing conduit for an inhuman will.

The interactional goal here is to give the illusion that one is communicating with a fellow human being when in fact the communication originates from an artificial intelligence. The human with whom one is apparently communicating is really working at the behest of the artificial intelligence. Echoborgs can be useful. For example, some individuals might feel more comfortable if they think they are interacting with another human even though the kinds of information and advice they want might be better and more efficiently provided by an artificial intelligence.

This 'synching' of a human front with an artificial intelligence raises conceptual issues such as the nature of speakerhood. Who exactly is speaking under such a condition where the activity of speaking is distributed over more than one entity? Is it the human extension or is it the artificial intelligence, or is such a binary approach misguided? Even if we were to decide, say, that the human extension is properly the speaker, we would still need to explain how we intend to understand the role played by the artificial intelligence. In this regard, it should be recalled that Goffman (1981) addresses the question of how to understand the dissociation of the message from those who designed the message. In his references to the production format, he separates the roles of principal, author, and animator (see above). Goffman's insights provide a promising the conceptual base for getting a handle on these questions, though they are not without problems (see the next chapter).

Example 4: The Translation App

Our fourth example comes from a BBC travel show, where an English speaker travelled across China using a translation app on his mobile phone to communicate with the locals. His English utterances were translated by the app, with varying degrees of communicative success into Mandarin, which would then play the translated version for his Chinese interlocutors. We have to seriously consider the possibility that the Mandarin 'spoken' by the app by the phone is not the same Mandarin as that spoken by the Chinese interlocutors that he encountered. The differences in some instances may be negligible so that the exchanges were successfully conducted. Yet, in other cases, the apparently nonsensical output led to laughter from the interlocutors, presumably because they were aware that they were not dealing with the speaker alone but a combination of the speaker and his translation app. Thus, we have to consider that the English-speaking traveller is actually a kind of Mandarin 'speaker' when using the app, so that the app becomes an (occasional) extension of the speaker, a hybrid entity that we might characterize as a linguistic cyborg.

Unlike the echoborg, where a human happens to be supplementing the communication activities of an artificial intelligence, the travel app is the converse. It represents a relatively more familiar case of technology being used to extend or supplement the human speaker's communicative intentions. The phenomenon of the cyborg reinforces the need to address the question of how to understand what is happening when the act of communicating is distributed across human and non-human entities.

Example 5: ChatGPT

While it is not inaccurate to describe ChatGPT as a chatbot, its sophistication and immense generative power has, since Open Artificial Intelligence created it in November 2022, made it highly controversial. ChatGPT has been described as 'groundbreaking' and a 'game-changer' (Frankiewicz 2023), with the potential to 'revolutionize a number of industries' (Kaufmann, quoted in Patterson 2023). It therefore deserves to be discussed on its own.

ChatGPT's ability to produce songs, essays, poems, and hold lengthy conversations has made educational institutions aware of the need to develop policies on its use in student work. Jobseekers are known to use it for writing CVs (Christian 2023), and it has been 'credited as the author or coauthor of more than 200 paperbacks and e-books in Amazon's bookstore' (Nolan 2023). As Nolan (2023) reports:

> One paperback where the bot is listed as a coauthor, "ChatGPT on ChatGPT: The AI Explains Itself," was described as having been "written entirely" by the AI bot. The Kindle version of the book is free but a paperback costs $11.99.
> Another popular genre is children's books written by ChatGPT and illustrated by other AI programs. Ammaar Reshi, a product-design manager at a financial-tech company based in San Francisco, told Insider he wrote and illustrated a children's book in 72 hours using ChatGPT and Midjourney.

According to Haleem, Javaid, and Pratap Singh (2022, 3):

> ChatGPT differs from previous AI models, as it can write software in many languages, debug code, break down a complicated subject into manageable chunks, prepare for interviews, draft essays ... ChatGPT can produce texts that sound like human speech in an informal setting and perform basic tasks. ChatGPT aims to create a cooperative AI system that can produce language that is helpful, engaging, and contextually relevant.

We should of course be wary of the hyperbole surrounding ChatGPT, especially if, as this book will show, gradations of anthropomorphism mean that attributions of intelligence and even sentience to the AI program are but more extreme versions of ideological propensities that are already immanent to the conduct of communication.

Choi's (2023) point that ChatGPT can be argued to exhibit 'artificial general intelligence' is, however, well-taken. Unlike highly specialized chatbots (such as Example 2 above) that appear in specific contexts to perform only dedicated functions, the sheer variation of tasks that ChatGPT is able to perform gives it the appearance of general intelligence – something that we would like to assume is the province of humans. It is this general ability do just about anything and everything that makes ChatGPT such a noteworthy development in the use of automation in communication. Here is a form of automation that can (apparently?) dispense with the need for human collaborations. The impression that it can communicate entirely on its own accord raises the question of whether it is 'almost like a new intellectual species' (Choi 2023), one that is perhaps on par with or even superior to humans.

This brief discussion of five examples – and as will be amply demonstrated in the rest of this book, many more examples are easily found – has highlighted some of the key questions that arise when we turn our attention to the increased use of automation in communication. It should be clear the personalist view of meaning, the traditional paradigm for talk, speech acts, and the Cooperative Principle – at least as these are usually understood – are all ill-equipped to handle the presence of automation in communication because they are based on questionable assumptions.

In particular, there are three major issues raised by automation. One, we have to recognize that the boundaries that constitute the speaker are porous so that individuating the entity that we call 'the speaker', even the human individual speaker, is by no means a straightforward matter. Relatedly, we also have to avoid placing too much emphasis on the human speaker's communicative intent. Two, we need to give greater attention to the role of the hearer in interpreting the communicative event. In particular, we have to take seriously the idea that it is the hearer who decides whether or not to attribute communicative intent to a speaker – and this conceptual shift is highly consequential and significant for how we go about understanding the pragmatics of communication. Three, once attention is shifted to active role of the hearer, then the issue of automation in communication has to be recognized as being a matter of understanding the factors that would encourage a hearer to anthropomorphize an automated entity.

Organization of this book

This book is organized as follows. The next chapter builds up the theoretical framework for understanding automation in communication. Chapter 2, *Laying the Groundwork: Posthumanism, Boundaries, and Assemblages*, outlines how answers to the communicative conundrums raised by automation for our ideologies about language and communication might be arrived at. Posthumanism takes seriously some of the key issues that arise when trying to understand the role of automation: agency cannot simply be presumed to be the province of human participants, and greater recognition needs to be given to the presence and participation of nonhuman interactants. The chapter ends by emphasizing that agency is not only 'unlocalizable'; it is also distributed across assemblages of both humans and things.

With the framework of posthumanism in place, Chapters 3, 4 and 5 then respectively tackle the three issues mentioned at the closing of the preceding section. Chapter 3, *The Death of the Speaker*, shows how, with the introduction of automation, the issues of speaker agency, boundary and intention become even more intractable unless a posthumanist orientation is adopted. The main issue regarding speaker agency is that agency is distributed rather than localizable within a putative speaker. The issue with speaker boundary is that the boundary that delimits the speaker does shift, and accommodating these shifts requires an appreciation of the properties of assemblages. And the main issue regarding speaker intention is not it does not exist; instead, it is how to situate intention in relation to distributed agency and shifting boundaries. The overall argument from this chapter is that the speaker has to be relegated to a much less important role in communication than has been traditionally the case. Instead, it is the hearer that needs to be given much greater importance and consideration.

Which bring us to Chapter 4, *A Hearer-Based Pragmatics*. This chapter further develops the implications in the preceding chapter our understanding of language and communication. The hearer is an active participant whose role is not merely that of recovering the message from the speaker by trying to reconstruct the latter's intention. The hearer has to first of all recognize that there is indeed a speaker present and from there, decide on just what kind of speaker they are interacting with. This includes deciding what kinds of capacities to attribute to the speaker and consequently, how to construe the message that is emanating from that speaker. These are non-trivial matters that follow from more fundamental considerations such as whether to bestow personhood and intentionality, and concomitantly, a mind, to the speaker – considerations that, ultimately, depend on how the hearer frames the communicative event in question.

Chapter 5, *Gradations of Anthropomorphism*, discusses a range of examples, from food delivery apps to healthcare and religious communication, to make the point that any attempt to seriously account for the role of automation has to acknowledge that there are gradations of anthropomorphism involved. In religious communication, for example, if worshippers are to feel that their spiritual needs have been met, the automated entity must not only be seen as a mere conveyor of information; it needs to be construed as providing legitimate guidance that takes into consideration the concerns of an individual worshipper. The key point being emphasized is this: anthropomorphism is an interpretive move on the part of the hearer, that is, it is the hearer that decides whether or not to attribute humanlike qualities to the interlocutor, and from there, decide what kinds of speech acts are being performed so as to generate the relevant implicatures. This chapter, then, explains the implications of such gradations of anthropomorphism for our understanding of language and communication. It shows that Cooperation and speech acts need to be viewed from an assemblage-theoretic perspective. It is how the assemblage has been put together that encourages the hearer to anthropomorphize (or not) an automated entity.

Chapter 6, *Creativity and Heritage: Two Elephants in the Room*, further takes up the complex and admittedly sensitive issues that are raised by the widespread use of automation. There are uncomfortable questions – uncomfortable particularly from the perspective of modernity – for how to evaluate the implications of automation for what we think of as linguistic creativity, and linguacultural heritage. Both linguistic creativity and linguistic heritage tend to be uncritically conceptualized in human-centric terms. However, given the existence of AI-generated poetry and the use of AI to help with the production of creative writing, we have to ask how much credit automation has to be given for the works that are produced. This is not just about the credit that should be given (or not be given) in relation to individual pieces of work; it is also, over time, about how we cumulatively understand the notion of linguacultural heritage and the role of AI in this heritage.

The penultimate chapter, *Towards Posthumanist Organizations*, emphasizes the importance of developing posthumanist organizations to help resolve some of the issues raised in the preceding chapters. Especially in highly diverse societies, where there is a wide variety of languages and dialects, contestations over which language or dialect ought to be given official recognition or used under what circumstances can emerge. Given the resources and power available to organizations, it is not uncommon to rely on them to help resolve the complex issue of managing ethnic and linguistic diversity. However, organizations tend to succumb to assumptions of modernity, which treat language as a stable entity with clear boundaries, one that bears a historically continuous relationship to its speakers. This leads to a hardening of boundaries between different ethnolinguistic groups, a presumption of unambiguous linkages between a given group and a particular language – all as a consequence of the orientation of organizations towards modernity. Organizations have to wean themselves away from this orientation that, by default, tends to inform their approaches to ethnolinguistic complexity. In contrast, an organization that is posthumanist in orientation will treat such boundaries as historically contingent and flexible, and it will recognize its own complicity in the construction of any assemblage. Posthumanist organizations are thus needed regardless of the issue of automation. By the same token, this chapter shows that posthumanist organizations are also better able to accommodate the increasingly complex roles that automation is playing in the societal use of language and communication.

Chapter 8, *Assemblages and the Emergence of Language from Communication*, closes the book by extrapolating from the arguments presented thus far to more general implications for theorizing about language and communication. Language is shown to be an assemblage that emerges from a wider assemblage of communicative practices. Different ways of constructing the linguistic assemblage are therefore possible. This raises the question of whether the only available epistemological stance towards these different linguistic assemblages has to be that of radical relativism, where there is no viewpoint from which one might evaluate the plausibility and desirability of one linguistic assemblage over another. Radical relativism would suggest that we cede any attempt at all to exert epistemic authority. This chapter shows how epistemic authority can remain both relevant and necessary.

2 Laying the Groundwork
Posthumanism, Boundaries, and Assemblages

Introduction

We saw in the preceding chapter examples of how automation can insert itself into communication in a variety of ways. It can take the form of a separate interlocutor, with varying degrees of sophistication as to its communicative abilities (as in the carpark sign and DBS chatbot examples). It can act in concert with a human individual, where the latter supplements the messages that are emanating from the former (as in the case of the echoborg), or, conversely, it can serve as a communicative aid so that the messages emanating from a human interlocutor are conveyed to the intended addressees (as in the case of the travel app). And in the case of ChatGPT, it even becomes a question of whether there is anything that a sufficiently sophisticated AI cannot do. These examples, with many more easily attested, as the following chapters will show, raise uncomfortable yet important questions for the ways in which language and communication are often assumed to work – questions that cannot be adequately addressed without revisiting and re-evaluating taken-for-granted ideological assumptions. In particular, we need to avoid the importance that has been traditionally given to the speaker's intention. We should also not be locked into the assumption that the speaker is necessarily human or even the idea that the speaker can be unproblematically treated as being clearly separate from and independent of any communicative aids that they might utilize.

This chapter argues that posthumanism provides the groundwork for how the preconceptions regarding language and communication can be fruitfully and coherently revised so as to take into account the presence of automation. In brief, posthumanism rejects the idea that objects and entities come with stable and pre-existing boundaries that 'define' what they are. Instead, boundaries are always being constructed and reconstructed via assemblages. A consequence of this focus on assemblages is that agency and intention, particularly the former, must be treated as distributed rather than localized 'within' an individual human actor.

In what follows, I elaborate on these points to explain just what posthumanism is. This will set the scene for how we can actually go about reconceptualizing our assumptions regarding language and communication.

DOI: 10.4324/9781003467922-2

Posthumanism

According to Barad (2007, 136), posthumanism 'eschews both humanist and structuralist accounts of the subject that position the human as either pure cause or pure effect, and the body as the natural and fixed dividing line between interiority and exteriority'. In other words, posthumanism questions the very things that traditional views of language and communication tend to take for granted: that there are self-evidently and unproblematically identifiable entities known as human individuals; that the lines or boundaries that separate one human individual from another, as well as from the environment or tools that these individuals may use, are equally self-evident and unproblematic; and finally, that causal actions begin with these self-evidently existing human individuals.

Where posthumanism is concerned, identifying what constitutes the individual human actor and concomitantly, the boundaries that separate this actor from other actors or from the tools that they might use; and locating causation as emanating from within this individual human actor – all these are by no means conceptually or empirically unproblematic. It is, as posthumanism recognizes, no simple matter trying to decide what constitutes the individual human actor nor is it any less of a challenge trying to unambiguously locate agency and causation within the actor that has been so constituted. It is, however, important to stress that posthumanism does not deny that humans exist. But what it does is to caution us against taking what counts as the human individual to be a stable and unchanging unit. Moreover, it warns us against uncritically privileging the activities of the human individual in trying to understand the world. Such activities include communicative events, of course, and in this regard, posthumanism is wary of taking as unquestioned the assumption that communication necessarily stems from an individual speaker's well-formed intention. Concomitantly, posthumanism is careful not to treat communication as always or necessarily traceable to or grounded in an individual human's activity. As Pennycook (2018, 6) explains:

> Posthumanist thought thus questions the boundaries between what is seen as inside and outside, where thought occurs and what role a supposedly exterior world may play in thought and language. Posthumanism is best seen not so much as an identifiable philosophy, a fixed body of thought, but rather as an umbrella term, a navigational tool for understanding a present undergoing massive change, a way of responding to the need to rethink what it means to be human following both 'onto-epistemological as well as scientific and bio-technological developments of the twentieth and twenty-first centuries' (Ferrando 2013: 26). Posthumanist 'doesn't presume the separateness of any-"thing", let alone the alleged spatial, ontological, and epistemological distinction that sets humans apart.'

> (Barad 2007, 136)

Before continuing further, it may be useful at this point to identify two broad lines of inquiry that come under the umbrella of posthumanism. One line, which we might call the 'ecolinguistics' tradition, aims to transcend the human so as to encompass all living beings and the natural world. The International Ecolinguistics Association, for example, defines "ecolinguistics" as a field which "explores the role of language in the life-sustaining interactions of humans, other species and the physical environment" (International Ecolinguistics Association, n.d.). According to Stanlaw (2020, 1), their aim is twofold, both theoretical and applied: First, they want "to develop linguistic theories which see humans not only as part of society, but also as part of the larger ecosystems that life depends on." The second aim is more pragmatic: it is to show "how linguistics can be used to address key ecological issues, from climate change and biodiversity loss to environmental justice." Chen (2016), Pennycook (2018), and Mendes (2020) are some of the works that come under this tradition.

The other line of inquiry, which we might think of as the 'cyborg' tradition, looks at the implications of Artificial Intelligence and biopolitical technologies for what it means to be human. As regards this latter 'cyborg' tradition, Rose (1998, 4–5, citing Haraway 1991; italics mine) elaborates with the following examples:

> A whole variety of practices bearing upon the mundane difficulties of living a life *have placed in question the unity, naturalness and coherence of the self.* The new genetic technology disturbs the naturalness of the self and its boundaries in relation to what it termed, tellingly, its 'reproduction' – donating sperms, transplanting eggs, freezing and implanting embryos, and much more. Abortion and life support machines, together with the contentious debates around them, destabilize the points at which the human enters existence and fades from it. Organ transplants, kidney dialysis, fetal tissue brain implants, heart pacemakers, artificial hearts all problematize the uniqueness of the embodiment of the self, not only establishing 'unnatural' links between different selves via the movement of tissues, but also making all too clear the fact that humans are intrinsically technologically fabricated and 'machinated' – bound into machines in what we term normality as much as in pathology. No wonder that one image of human being has so rapidly disseminated itself: the cyborg (Haraway 1991). *This image of the human as a cybernetic organism, a nonunified hybrid assembled of body parts and mechanical artifacts, myths, dreams and fragments of knowledge, is just one dimension of a range of conceptual challenges to the primacy, unity and givenness of the self.*

Thus, this other line of posthumanist inquiry focuses more on the implications of technological changes and their adoption, in particular, for how such developments challenge commonly held assumptions about the naturalness of what it means to be a human being.

Both lines of inquiry are posthumanist in that they problematize the centrality that has traditionally been given to human agency and the taken-for-granted status of the human individual as the unit of such agency. Nevertheless, as should be clear, it is the 'cyborg' tradition that is the focus of the present book.

On The Porosity of Boundaries

Haraway has influentially used the cyborg as a metaphor for understanding the development of humanity, science and politics: 'So my cyborg myth is about transgressed boundaries, potent fusions, and dangerous possibilities' (2016, 14). In particular, Haraway (2016, 20) wants to draw attention to the artificiality of boundaries, to the contingent nature of inherited dichotomies that have come to be treated as sacrosanct.

She identifies three crucial boundary breakdowns: (i) between human and animal; (ii) between animal-human and machine; and (iii) between the physical and the non-physical (10–12). It is worth discussing these three boundary breakdowns in some detail because they all, in one way or another, bear on issue of automation in communication that this book is concerned with.

Between human and animal

Regarding the boundary between human and animal, Haraway notes that 'language, tool use, social behavior, mental events—nothing really convincingly settles the separation of human and animal' and 'many people no longer feel the need for such a separation; indeed, many branches of feminist culture affirm the pleasure of connection of human and other living creatures' (10). Indeed, the establishment of this boundary starts with the insistence (rather than the demonstration) that there must be something that indubitably separates human from animal. And it is from there that various candidates are offered as practices or properties that clear mark this boundary.

Language, as Haraway notes, is one such commonly suggested candidate. However, despite continued claims that language is specific to the human species, most notably by Chomsky and his adherents, the evidence and arguments in favour of this position are at best suspect. Chomsky has consistently insisted that humans possess a language system or organ that is species-specific. Animals may communicate, but Chomsky has always asserted that they do not have language because they lack the relevant linguistic system (Anderson and Lightfoot 2004, ix; Chomsky 1976, 1986, 1993; Cook and Newson 1996, 107). However, this argument is problematic given claims made by Chomsky himself.

The language faculty that he is interested in ('I-Language') is only incidentally related to language. According to Chomsky (2001), it would have been entirely possible for this same language faculty to be linked up to other kinds of systems, such as, for instance, the digestive system, in which case this faculty would still exist but there would not be anything produced that we might recognize as or consider to be language. It remains unclear whether under these circumstances the 'I-Diges-tion' would be of any interest to the generative program though the answer would still appear to be 'Yes' given Hinzen's (2006, 21) observation that Chomsky:

> ... even envisages the fantasy of some crazy scientist who has discovered the neural basis of how our brains store information about linguistic structures

and rewires our brains so that the cognitive system of language outputs not to the performance systems to which it factually outputs now, but to others, which use human linguistic structures for a different purpose, such as loco-motion. *The moral of the story, I suppose, is that if our human language system might in principle be used quite differently than we use it now, then it does not, as a system of knowledge described purely formally, intrinsically relate to its factual use.*

Consequently, to even describe the cognitive system in question as a *language* system or a *language* organ is very much a misnomer. It is a system or organ that is incidentally linguistic because it just happens to be connected to performance systems that are traditionally considered as related to language *from an E-Language perspective.* Thus, despite Chomsky's dismissal of its importance, it is really only because of the existence of E-Language that the generative program even finds itself in the business of studying language at all. For Chomsky, it is the underlying system itself, assumed to exhibit formal computational properties and that is only incidentally language-related, that is the actual target of investigation. This formal computational system may in principle be linked up to locomotive, digestive or other systems, but it is the formal computational properties of this system, assumed to be invariant, that the investigative energies within the Chomskyan research program are really directed towards.

However, if the putative linguistic system is only contingently linked to parti-cular performance systems in humans and could in principle be or have been linked to locomotive or digestive systems, then how can we be so sure that the same abstract computational system is not also present in other species, but it just so happens to be linked to other systems that preclude us from recognizing its existence? The generative program is unable to answer this question in any meaningfully empirical sense; it is really only an article of faith that the formal computational system that supposedly underlies human language cannot also be found in other species.

In this regard, it is worth noting that Tomasello (2010, 2014) provides an alter-native view to the Chomskyan picture, one that is much more plausible and com-pelling. Tomasello argues that human communication is fundamentally linked to cooperation and sociality. The latter, in turn, require the establishment of shared intentionality and common ground. Thus, instead of treating language as something that exists apart from communication and moreover, as something that only inci-dentally happens to be used for communication, Tomasello's argument (contra Chomsky) is that language emerges from communication itself (see Chapter 8).

Between animal-human and machine

In the case of the boundary between animal-human and machine, Haraway (2016, 11) observes that the boundary was much easier to sustain when machines were less sophisticated, that is, less autonomous, which is no longer the case (as we have already noted in the preceding chapter):

But basically machines were not self-moving, self-designing, autonomous. They could not achieve man's dream, only mock it. They were not man, an author to himself, but only a caricature of that masculinist reproductive dream. To think they were otherwise was paranoid. Now we are not so sure. Late twentieth-century machines have made thoroughly ambiguous the difference between natural and artificial, mind and body, self-developing and externally designed, and many other distinctions that used to apply to organisms and machines.

The increased sophistication of machines, especially as regards their use in communication is of course the key focus of this book. It is pertinent at this point to bring up both the Turing Test and Searle's (1980) Chinese Room puzzle.

In Turing's original formulation, a machine and a human interlocutor are each hidden from view, and they are individually engaged in conversation with another human interlocutor, a judge. The goal of the judge is to try to determine which of the two entities that they have been interacting with is a machine and which is a human. Should the machine succeed in 'fooling' the judge, then the machine can be said to have passed the Turing Test or what Turing (1950) calls 'The Imitation Game'. Churchland (1995, 234) discusses various problems with the Test, such as that it is too lenient (it allows behaviours that don't really reflect intelligence), it is too strict (it omits animal intelligence, which may not be captured in the use of ordinary language). More interesting, however, are the following two points. One, Churchland (1995, 233) notes that in some cases of the Test, judges actually mistook a human interlocutor for a machine. This is relevant because, as Churchland (1995) points out, at least one reason why one of the humans was mistaken for a machine was because his communicative style, 'brief to a fault, simple sentences, lucid logic – happened to fit the public's stereotypical or prototypical image of how a computer is supposed to behave'. In fact, as machines become better at approximating 'stereotypical' human behaviour, the onus is less of the machine trying to fool the judge than on the human participant trying to convince the judge of their humanness (Christian 2011).

The second point is this. Turing's test was predicated on a sharp distinction between human and machine. Human and machine are separated and are judged individually. The human communicates with the judge as does the machine. There is no consideration of hybrid or cyborg entities such as the echoborg or a human using a translation app. In other words, the presumption of the animal-human and machine boundary, or in this case, human and machine boundary, leads to the thinking that human and machine are pitted against each other. In contrast, the increased use of automation in language and communication requires that we focus on the complex and interesting ways in which human and machine can work in concert. In the case of the echoborg, for example, we need to address questions such as these: Who exactly is the speaker under such a condition where the activity of speaking is distributed over more than one entity? Is it the human extension or is it the artificial intelligence, or is such a binary approach misguided?

The Turing Test asks whether a sufficiently sophisticated machine might be able to imitate human interaction to the point where it becomes impossible to distinguish between man and machine. In contrast, Searle's (1980) Chinese Room argument is specifically focused on the manipulation of formal symbols by an information-processing system. Searle's argument asks us to consider the following scenario: an individual (someone with no knowledge of Chinese) is placed in a room and follows a rule book on what Chinese symbols to present as outputs in response to Chinese inputs. Searle asks whether – even if we allow that this individual performs the task to the point of actually passing the Turing Test – this person can be said to actually understand Chinese. Searle's argument is aimed against what he characterizes as the 'strong AI' position (which would claim that such symbolic manipulation constitutes actual understanding) as opposed to the 'weak AI' position (which would treat the manipulation as merely simulating understanding). For our purposes, it is important to note that Searle's argument is specifically directed against the philosophical view known as computationalism (Searle 1992, 44), where the mind is viewed as an information-processing system operating on formal symbols. Because of this, Searle's Chinese Room argument is not actually aimed at AI in general. It applies only to computers that engage in formal symbolic manipulation rather than, say, those that work on neural nets and are capable of machine-learning.[1]

The issues raised by the Turing Test (and, to a lesser extent, Searle's Chinese Room puzzle) are nevertheless relevant to the question of how to approach the pragmatics of communication when machines are involved. As we have seen, the pragmatics of communication is typically approached from the perspective of the speaker, in particular, that speaker's communicative intent. Thus, how to discern speaker intent and relatedly, intelligence, understanding, and personhood, are issues that are raised by Turing and Searle.

But these issues take on a far different complexion once we approach things from the perspective of the hearer. We will see that there are gradations of anthropomorphism (Chapter 5), depending on how communicatively interactive the automation happens to be. And importantly, this gradation of anthropomorphism requires not a privileging of speaker intent but, instead, of hearer interpretation. Once the focus shifts to prioritizing the hearer's perspective, then the important question is not whether the hearer can successfully distinguisher a machine from a human interlocutor (à la Turing) or whether the symbol manipulator truly understands the symbols they are manipulating (à la Searle). Instead, the question is now about the kinds of conditions or situations might encourage a hearer to treat their interlocutor as being intelligent, sentient, etc. In the case of Searle's thought experiment, the focus now is not on the symbol manipulator trapped in the Chinese Room. Rather, it is on how the hearer who sits outside the Room apprehends the entire configuration or 'assemblage' (see below) that comprises the Room, the symbol manipulator within, and the series of symbols that are being displayed for the hearer's benefit.

Between the physical and the non-physical

The boundary between the physical and the non-physical relates to the issue of materialization. Haraway (2016, 12–13) points out that:

> ... the boundary between physical and nonphysical is very imprecise for us ... Modern machines are quintessentially microelectronic devices: they are everywhere and they are invisible ... miniaturization has changed our experience of mechanism ... Contrast the TV sets of the 1950s or the news cameras of the 1970s with the TV wristbands or hand-sized video cameras now advertised. Our best machines are made of sunshine; they are all light and clean because they are nothing but signals, electromagnetic waves, a section of a spectrum, and these machines are eminently portable, mobile ...

In the specific case of language and communication, this amounts to questioning the relationship between language and materiality. Language cannot be treated as an abstract invariant system that exists independently of how it is materialized. It might perhaps be suggested there is a difference between communication and language *per se*. Such an insistence on separating language from the conduct of communication, however, presumes rather than demonstrates that a clear and unproblematic distinction can be made between language itself as a relatively stable phenomenon and the material communicative processes that actualize it. On this account, it is as though the role of the latter was merely that of realizing the former: language qua abstract and stable phenomenon is supposedly left unaffected by how it might be variously materialised – and this includes the involvement of automation in communication. In contrast, a materialist view of language avoids a presumption that language exists in a realm that is somehow independent of its various manifestations (Shankar and Cavanaugh 2017). I return to this issue of the materiality of language in Chapter 6.

Boundaries and Assemblages

We might at this point ask whether some accommodation for the porosity of boundaries as well as the presence of automation is already available from, say, Goffman's (1981) ideas about footing and production formats. This is because, as we saw in the preceding chapter, Goffman clearly wants to question simplistic understandings of what it means to be a speaker or hearer. If such an accommodation is already available, then we might have to concede that the appeal to posthumanism is unnecessary. As I now show, Goffman's ideas still require some nuancing because they tend to assume that the entities occupying the roles are typically human. And the nuancing that is required for Goffman's ideas takes us in the direction of posthumanism.

While Goffman is keen to emphasize that the roles relevant to an understanding of communication are much more varied than has been acknowledged by the traditional distinction between 'speaker' and 'hearer', there are nevertheless two problems with his approach. One is that his approach is too human-centric, treating the source of the communication (especially where 'principal' or 'author' are concerned) as ultimately human. The other is that he does not sufficiently consider the increasingly complex and even integrated ways in which different entities can work together communicatively.

Let us begin with the issue of human-centricity. Perhaps the closest we come to finding some accommodation for nonhuman interlocutors is in Goffman's notion of animator. Let me therefore say a bit more about what it means to be an animator. This is an issue that Goffman himself considered and reconsidered over the course of his research and it is of especial relevance to our investigation of automation in communication. Goffman (1974, 523), rather restrictively, initially considers the animator to be necessarily human, and he uses the term 'figure' instead to describe the various inanimate objects that the human animator might utilize to emit or transmit the message so as to effect or complete the act of communication. But he later abandons this distinction between (human) animator and (non-human, inanimate) figure (Goffman 1981, 144; see also Manning and Gershon 2013, 112), referring to the animator as a 'talking machine.' However, when Goffman elaborates on the animator, his prime example is that of the human speaker's own vocal cords. This is to drive home the point that the animator is a recognizably distinguishable aspect of what is typically thought of as the speaker. Consider, in this regard, Goffman's (1981, 144; italics added) comment that the vocal cords of the speaker serve as a 'sounding box' in much the same way as a loudspeaker system or a telephone:

> His is the sounding box in use, albeit in some actual cases he can share this physical function with a loudspeaker system or a telephone.

Even though he acknowledges that things such as a loudspeaker or a telephone are also working in similar ways to the vocal cords (and hence are functionally also animators), he really only uses these mechanical examples to illustrate his point that the speaker's vocal cords are performing a distinct role from, say, the speaker's mind – which presumably performs the roles of principal and animator. Thus, it is no surprise that Goffman describes the role of a loudspeaker system or a telephone as one of 'sharing the physical function' of the speaker's vocal cords. This is because he makes the assumption that the message should always be ultimately emanating from a human speaker. This assumption is perhaps understandable given that one of Goffman's aims in discussing production formats is to highlight problems with the traditional paradigm of talk (as we saw in the preceding chapter). However, the introduction of automation raises the question as to whether it is always the case that a message can be traceable to a human source.

Consider, in this regard, the carpark sign, the simplest of the five examples that were discussed in Chapter 1. The sign is at the very least an animator since it is ultimately the entity that the driver encounters and that provides the latter with the requisite information concerning the number of parking lots available.

However, there is no human actor who can be said to occupy the role of principal, author or even animator so as to ground the communicative event. Obviously, the driver finds the communicative event meaningful in that relevant information is being conveyed. But as we noted, the specific information that is being conveyed at any given moment concerning the state of the carpark, that is, the actual number of available lots, is not something that the programmer (human or otherwise) would be aware of. This means that even the contents of the message (and not just how the message is being phrased or how the message is ultimately being conveyed) are not traceable to a human principal. In the case of the echoborg, it is the AI that is both author and principal, and it is the human that is the animator. And in the case of ChatGPT, the AI is all three: author, principal and animator.

For less dramatic examples, consider also the installation of maps and directional information on mobile phones, which means that more individuals are using their phones for navigation purposes. Here, it is arguably the phone that is principal, author and animator all at once, since it provides the directional information, either in text or spoken mode. It may of course be contested that the phone is really only the animator, and it is the navigation app that is the principal and perhaps author as well. Both possibilities cannot be ruled out prima facie. This is because deciding between them depends on whether we consider the app to be part of the phone or not. That is, once an app has been installed into a phone, should it now be treated as part of the phone, or should it still be considered a separate entity? The answer that we give depends on how we construe the 'boundary-conventions' (Shapin and Schaffer 1985, 342; cited in Latour 1993, 16) of the phone. There is no a priori way of establishing these boundary-conventions that does not require an acknowledgement that the boundaries are socially constructed. Hence, the term 'conventions'. In other words, any attempt to treat the boundaries as objective entities, to argue that they exist independent of any act of social construction, is a serious mis-construal of what the boundaries are. Which brings us to the second problem with Goffman's approach: the need to recognize the complex ways in which different entities can work together communicatively.

What Shapin and Schaffer (1985) refer to as 'boundary-conventions' are, from a posthumanist perspective, better thought of as assemblages. In posthumanism, the socially constructed nature of boundaries is given theoretical weight via the concept of assemblages. Bennett (2010, 23) succinctly describes assemblages as 'ad hoc groupings of diverse elements.' While assemblages are organized, this organization is not static but changeable. For example, if we focus on an individual human speaker, we may (following Goffman) treat the vocal cords as the animator and the rest of the speaker as principal and author. Or should it just be the speaker's brain that is principal and author? At the same time, however, if we want to focus on the fact that this individual happens to be serving as a spokesperson for a company, then the entire individual will now be treated as the animator with the company as the principal and author. This example, including the uncertainties about how to demarcate the rest of the individual speaker from the vocal cords merely reinforces the point that assemblages do not pre-exist the processes by which boundary-conventions come to demarcate the contours of a particular assemblage.

An assemblage is best understood as a contingent mix of practices and things, where this contingent ensemble of physical and non-physical objects – broadly characterizable as 'semiotic' – is distinguished from yet other contingent ensembles in being 'selected, organized, stratified' and hence demarcated from an otherwise endless flow of circulating signs (Deleuze and Guattari 1987, 406). Assemblages are organized and ordered, but this organization and order is contingent and changeable. Possibly the most significant advantage of thinking in terms of an assemblage is that it allows us to recognize the roles that boundedness, order and organization play in the ontology of an entity even as it at the very same time insists that we acknowledge that what constitutes the boundaries, order and organization – and hence, what counts as the entity itself – can be multiple, contested and shifting. This is because assemblages are always in the process of 'coming together and moving apart' (Wise 2005, 77).

A good illustration of what an assemblage is provided by Latour (Hazard 2013, 66, italics added):

> According to Latour, the NRA's (National Rifle Association) braying insistence that "guns don't kill people, people kill people" is premised on more anthropocentric understandings of agency that treat material things such as guns as diligent *instruments of human volition*. Latour contends, on the contrary, that once a person picks up a gun, she or he is not quite the same person as before. Guns, among other things, when connected with humans, make up *new networks or assemblages that embolden or enable certain kinds of actions*, specifically killing. (One would not use the barrel of a gun to arrange a bouquet of roses, after all.) ...
>
> According to Latour, when a person kills with a gun, it is not only the person who kills. It is the larger assemblage that kills. Its murderous agency is distributed across its many parts including a finger, a trigger, a bullet, a human brain, violent films, and so on. *Agency is always complex agency, unlocalizable and distributed across assemblages of both humans and things.*

In the example above, Latour neatly illustrates the problem with restricting agency to human actors such that non-human entities are seen as mere 'instruments of human volition'. The person who is holding a gun has agency in a way that is different than a person not holding gun – even if both have the desire or intention to kill. The combination 'person + gun + intention to kill' constitutes a new network or assemblage that allows for some types of actions over others. Thus, there are multiple and changing assemblages depending on, for instance, whether the person is holding the gun or whether the gun is stored in a safe away from the person. These different assemblages ('person + gun' or 'gun + safe' or even 'person + safe') involve different arrangements of entities with the potential for bringing about different effects. Taking this insight seriously means recognizing that agency is not only 'unlocalizable'; it is also 'distributed across assemblages of both humans and things'[2] – a point that we will return to shortly.

The concept of an assemblage has proven extremely useful in urban studies, for example. It provides a conceptually valuable way to think about the city, one that both recognizes and explains why different ways of understanding the city are in fact unavoidable. Consider, for instance, the following description of Los Angeles, taken from a popular travel website (Time Out Group 2016):

> Precisely what constitutes Los Angeles is a matter for interpretation … Los Angeles County contains 88 incorporated cities, each with its own jurisdiction; among them are Santa Monica, Beverly Hills, Culver City, Pasadena and Los Angeles itself. To add to the confusion, some areas (for instance, East LA and Marina del Rey) are unincorporated, under the jurisdiction of Los Angeles County but not the city. While West Hollywood is an independent city, Hollywood is just one of many neighborhoods in the city of Los Angeles.

These points are elaborated upon by Purcell (2002, 105), who stresses that it is by no means at all clear or uncontroversial as to what actually constitutes the city:

> The politics of scale literature makes clear that scales (such as the urban) are not pregiven or self-evident; rather they are socially produced through political struggle … For example, clearly 'Los Angeles' would involve more than just the municipal jurisdiction. The limits to the city would likely extend to the urbanized area of the city. But how extensive would these limits be? Would residents of Tijuana be considered residents of Los Angeles? According to what criteria?

Struggles over how to define the city are struggles over how to assemble and reassemble the city in ways that reflect different and changing interests. The city is, in other words, is an urban assemblage. The understanding of what the city is can vary according to the particular way in which the urban assemblage is being constituted. Crucially, there is no objectively independent way to understand the city apart from the specific and multiple assemblages that characterise it. There is no 'real' city that exists independent of these assemblages – an absolutely crucial point that needs to be consistently kept in mind. These points apply no less to the study of communication. Our understanding of who or what the speaker and hearer are cannot be separated from the assemblages that we identify as constituting the boundaries of a communicative event.

Three Important Properties of Assemblages

The first thing to appreciate about assemblages is that they are material signs and that they can also trigger other signs into self-organizing. In developing their ideas about assemblages, Deleuze and Guattari are cognizant of work in complexity theory,[3] which shows that some physical and biological systems can be triggered by environmental factors into self-organizing. This is an insight that Deleuze and Guattari take seriously but they do so by emphasizing the historical and political dimensions of complex systems (Bonta and Protevi 2004, 4):

> Signs are no longer limited to linguistic entities that must somehow make contact with the natural world, and sense or meaning need no longer be seen as the reference of signifiers to each other. Rather, the 'meaning' of a sign is a measure of the probability of triggering a particular material process.

In other words, signs do not merely represent or refer as though the semiotic not only occupies a non-material realm and, worse still, a non-material self-enclosed system, that must then somehow try to establish a connection with the material world. The semiotic includes the material. So, signs can have material effects on other signs by initiating a process of assembling with the result that other signs are then ordered. Note that this is consequential in that a sign must be understood to not only have material effects, it also goes against a strict understanding of the autonomy of signs as constituting self-contained and sharply bounded systems. This, too, is why Deleuze and Guattari recognize the need for 'mixed semiotics', the idea that there are multiple regimes of signification which do not necessarily fall into neatly demarcated and consistently separable systems (Bonta and Protevi 2004, 8; Deleuze and Guattari 1987, 119).

Deleuze and Guattari (1987, 174, 306) use the terms 'deterritorialization' to describe the process by which elements of an extant assemblage dissemble and go on to form a new assemblage or 'reterritorialize'. They distinguish between 'relative deterritorialization' and 'absolute deterritorialization' (1987, 142, 510). In relative deterritorialization, the self-organization follows the patterns that have already been conventionalized. With relative deterritorialization, then, the new assemblage is largely similar to or a reproduction of its earlier counterpart. In contrast, in the case of absolute deterritorialization, the self-organization exhibits the system's ability to depart from established patterns or templates, thus demonstrating a capacity to bring about transformations or novelties. Needless to say, when we look at language and communication, we will find a mix of relative and absolute deterritorialization.

The second thing to appreciate is that the constituent parts of any assemblage are themselves assemblages. Indeed, this is what makes Deleuze and Guattari's notion of an assemblage so radical. That is, 'any particular assemblage is itself composed of different discrete assemblages which are themselves multiple' (Haggerty and Ericson 2003, 608). This radicalness arises from the realization that things which are typically assumed to have an internal unity and thus (by virtue of this unity) a built-in or naturally endowed boundary – such that this boundary serves to externally and 'naturally' distinguish one thing from some other – are, in fact, heterogeneously constituted internally. There is neither 'a primordial totality' nor 'a final totality' (Deleuze and Guattari 1987, 42). By extension, then, the boundaries that we otherwise often take for granted as unproblematically bestowing 'thingness' are themselves contingent. This is the point made in the preceding chapter in the discussion about navigation apps and whether or not an individual human speaker can be treated as an animator. Recall that if the speaker happens to be acting as a spokesperson for a company, then the relationship between the two is such that the speaker is the animator with the company being the principal and author. But if we focus on the individual spokesperson, then it is also possible to identify the vocal cords as that individual's animator.

The third follows from the preceding point. Precisely because the component parts of an assemblage are always in the process of being assembled and reassembled, the relation between the parts is one of exteriority rather than interiority. A relation of interiority assumes that the 'component parts are constituted by the very relations they have to other parts in the whole' and 'a part detached from such a whole ceases to be what it is, since being this particular part is one of its constitutive properties' (DeLanda 2006, 9). Component parts derive their existence from being members of the whole, so that the latter is attributed an ontological significance greater than the former (as in structural functionalism). In contrast, the notion of an assemblage demands that we instead acknowledge and give greater focus to relations of exteriority. Relations of exteriority make no assumptions about the sacrosanct relationship between a component and the assemblage that it happens to be part of. A component can always be detached from an assemblage and 'plugged into a different assemblage in which its interactions are different' (DeLanda 2006, 10–11). Relations of exteriority therefore emphasize that the component parts only bear a contingent relationship to the assemblage. It should be clear that relations of exteriority follow from taking seriously the nature of assemblages. This is because if assemblages are themselves the results of bringing together a heterogeneous collection of objects, then we have no grounds for assuming that this collection of objects should fit each other in any *a priori* manner such that their relation to the resulting assemblage is one of interiority.

Agency as Distributed

The importance given to the notion of assemblages demonstrates that posthumanism takes seriously the idea that agency cannot simply be presumed to be the sole province of human actors not least because the idea of an individuated human entity is itself neither stable nor unproblematic. Agency needs to be recognized as distributed, and what we see or think of as a cause-and-effect relation is always dependent 'on the collaboration, cooperation, or interactive interference of many bodies and forces' (Bennett 2010, 21). This willingness to accord agency to all forms of matter, in Bennett's terms requires recognizing that anything – worms, a dead rat, gunshot residue – can be an 'actant' (6). By 'actant', Bennett wants to emphasize that any entity or phenomenon has 'vibrant materiality': it has the capacity to make a difference in the world because it can have an effect, as a result of which they then affect the various assemblages that they may be part of. We saw this in Latour's example of the gun, where the person holding the gun, the bullet, the human brain, among other, are all potentially actants. Conversely, the term 'actant' then is intended as a reminder not to accord agency only to human individuals. Agency is not an autonomous property residing within an individual; agency is feature of the assemblage and because of this, it has to acknowledged as distributed rather than localized. Thus, Bennett points out that (112–113):

> My 'own' body is material, and yet this vital materiality is not fully or exclusively human. My flesh is populated and constituted by different swarms of foreigners... the bacteria in the human microbiome collectively possess at least 100 times as many genes as the mere 20,000 or so in the human genome... we are, rather, an array of bodies, many different kinds of them in a nested set of microbiomes.

This leads Bennett to emphasize 'distributive agency', which she explains 'does not posit a subject as the root cause of an effect', and which she contrasts with traditional views that treat agency as 'an advance plan or an intention' (31). Indeed, 'a lot happens to the concept of agency once nonhuman things are figured less as social construction and more as actors, and once humans themselves are assessed not as autonoms but as vital materialities' (21). This is because 'an actant never really acts alone. Its efficacy or agency always depends on the collaboration, cooperation, or interactive interference of many bodies and forces' (21). Thus (32):

> ... there are instead always a swarm of vitalities at play. The task becomes to identify the contours of the swarm, and the kind of relations that obtain between its bits... this understanding of agency does not deny the existence of that thrust called intentionality, but it does see it as less definitive of outcomes. It loosens the connections between efficacy and the moral subject, bringing efficacy closer to the idea of the power to make a difference that calls for a response.

Bennett's reference to 'the contours of the swarm' is, of course, an acknowledgement of the need to think in terms of assemblages, and the issue then becomes one of understanding the relations between the various 'bits' of an assemblage. This, as we noted in the preceding section, requires accepting that this relation is one of exteriority rather than interiority.

Another important point to note is that thinking in terms of assemblages does not mean rejecting the reality of intention. As mentioned in the preceding chapter, I am not denying that personalist accounts of meaning exist. Rather, my concern is when the personalist account assumes the status of a universal and default explanation of how agency and causality work. In this regard, Bennett rightly points out that a posthumanist perspective does not deny the existence of intentionality but, critically, it treats intentionality as 'less definitive of outcomes.'

What this means is that we can continue to insist that the individual human actor has an intention to act. But rather than simply assume that intention exists within the individual actor, it is more relevant instead to look into how and under what circumstances the hearer is prepared to attribute or deny intention to a speaker. Such a move avoids the ontologically problematic stance of assuming that intention bears a causal relation to acts, including acts of communication. Instead, it has the advantage of recognizing that attributions of intention to a speaker or, conversely, denying such intentions or even treating intentions as irrelevant, are all reliant on the ideological assumptions that the hearer brings to the communication event.

Conclusion

This chapter has provided a detailed discussion of posthumanism, and in so doing, outlined how some of the issues raised by the presence of automation for our preconceptions about how language and communication work might be resolved. When a communication emanates from an AI program, for example, and the human speaker responds, it is not atypical to simply try to locate communicative intent and agency within the human speaker. But in doing so, traditional accounts have little or nothing to say about the role of the program.

In the absence of any conceptual adjustments, we are left with two options, both of which are equally problematic. One option is for us to continue to ignore the presence of automation. This is a stance that is surely unsustainable as automation becomes increasingly pervasive in communication, and it takes on ever more interactive and constitutive roles regarding the messages that are being composed. This option effectively abdicates any scholarly responsibility for trying to provide some intellectual account for how to understand the linguistic and communicative implications of automation. The other option is for us to simply bite the bullet and attribute the same kind of communicative intent to the program. But this, too, is highly unsatisfactory since we need to acknowledge that not all forms of automation are equally sophisticated nor is automation being used in the same way all the time. This second option would also collapse any differences between a program and a human speaker, which is surely also an unsatisfactory move. We thus need to be attentive to how programs can, in under the right conditions, encourage the hearer to elide any difference between human and machine. In addition, as Du Bois's (1992) example of divination demonstrates, we also need to allow for the fact that communication can take place with an entity even if there is no communicative intent is being attributed.

The point is that modifications need to be made to our preconceived ideas about language and communication. Posthumanism provides valuable signposts as to what these needed adjustments might be, particularly the importance it accords to assemblages, the recognition that anything is potentially an actant, and the acknowledgement that agency is distributed. The next chapter begins the work of fleshing out in detail the necessary ideological adjustments based on posthumanist insights.

Notes

1 A related criticism is Hubert Dreyfus's 1972 argument that computers cannot do what humans do because the latter, unlike the former, make use of unconscious processes informed by real-world experiences rather than rely on formal symbols. Somewhat ironically, Dreyfus's ideas have been credited with inspiring the 'sub-symbolic' shift in AI research towards connectionism and information retrieval, and away from a focus on the formal manipulation of symbols. See, for example, Crevier, *AI: The Tumultuous History* (1993).

2 Latour's work, particularly his work on Actor-Network Theory (ANT) has at times been characterized as non-representational, which, if true, would make it difficult to reconcile the ideas in ANT with a focus on implicatures, speech acts and ideologies.

   However, it is important to note that Latour (and for that matter, Deleuze) does not actually reject representations. As Farías (2010, 7) notes, 'ANT makes out of Deleuze's philosophy of creation an empirical project focused on the generative capacities of actor=networks and new entities (objects, technologies, truths, economic actors) and dimensions (times, spaces) brought into being'. Indeed, Latour is in fact less concerned with dismissing mental concepts as irrelevant than with insisting that, where agency is concerned, human and non-human entities are conceptually treated on equal footing. Indeed, he rejects the dichotomy between 'mentalist' and 'materialist' explanations (Latour 1986, 28), making clear that the problem is to avoid 'autonomizing discourse' so that connections between 'nature, society and discourse' are not lost (Latour 1993, 64). And his (Latour 1999) discussion on distributed cognition is precisely not to reject mentalism but to challenge a compartmentalization that insists on separating thought ('inside') from the world ('outside').

3 The influence of complexity theory in linguistics itself is nothing new (Larsen-Freeman 2008, among others). What I want to emphasize here, however, is less complexity theory than the nature of assemblages.

3 The Death of the Speaker

Introduction

In the first two chapters, I discussed how highly pervasive preconceptions about language and communication continue to remain influential and problematic, and I indicated that a posthumanist approach can help direct us towards resolving the problems associated with them. One of the major issues that I highlighted is the assumption that what has traditionally been treated as the speaker is actually a complex entity so that trying to demarcate the boundaries of what we can consider to be the speaker is no simple matter. There are, as Goffman makes clear in his discussion of production formats, different ways of being a speaker: one can be an animator, a principal, or an author, or some combination of the three.

What we will see in this chapter is that automation brings into relief the fact that even the recognition of these different production format roles is not sufficient if the complex issues relating to speaker agency, speaker boundary and speaker intention are not taken into serious account. In particular, once agency is understood to be distributed within an assemblage and, furthermore, once it is acknowledged that the boundaries of an assemblage can shift, then we have to ask, how relevant is it to be privileging the speaker's intention when it comes to understanding communication?

The title of this chapter is obviously a riff off Barthes' (1986) highly important essay, *The Death of the Author*. In that essay, Barthes questions the coherence of trying to pin down the definitive meaning of any piece of text by focusing on the intentions and goals of the individual author, considering this a foolhardy enterprise (49–50; italics in original):

> The *author* is a modern character, no doubt produced by our society as it emerged from the Middle Ages, inflected by English empiricism, French rationalism, and the personal faith of the Reformation, thereby discovering the prestige of the individual, or, as we say more nobly, of the 'human person'.

The character of the author, Barthes argues, is a modern construct. It is an ideological effect of certain modernist assumptions concerning the integrity and

DOI: 10.4324/9781003467922-3

identifiability of individuals, and these, the intentionality and creativity that can be attributed to such a character. He, however, goes on to point out that (52–53):

> We know now that a text consists not of a line of words, releasing a single 'theological' meaning (the 'message' of the Author-God), but of a multi-dimensional space in which are married and contested several writings, none of which is original: the text is a fabric of quotations, resulting from a thousand sources of culture.

That is, even if we wish to assert that a piece of text is produced by a single individual, the sources that this individual drew upon in producing the text are unavoidably multiple in nature. It is therefore difficult to credit an individual author as being *wholly* responsible for a given text because all texts draw upon multiple sources. Even when we shift our focus to the reader of the text, each reader is creating anew their own specific interpretation of the text so that the writer comes to exist anew each time a reader reads the text. Given that even the same reader may not interpret the text in exactly the same manner when reading it on different occasions, Barthes' argument about the problem with trying to pin down a single and stable textual meaning and moreover, a meaning that must be traceable to and privileges the author's intention cannot be ignored. As Tearle (2021; italics in original) puts it:

> In the traditional view, the author is like a parent, who conceives the text rather as a parent conceives a child. The author thus exists before the novel or poem or play, and then creates that literary work.
>
> But in Barthes' radical new way of viewing the relationship between the two, writer and text are born simultaneously, because whenever we read a literary work we are engaging with the writer *here and now*, rather than having to go back (to give our own example) four hundred years to consider Shakespeare the Renaissance 'author'. 'Shakespeare', as the writer, exists now, in the moment we read his works on the page in the twenty-first century.

While Barthes may have been talking primarily about literary texts, his points – that trying to attribute to an author a singular creativity that then becomes a paramount criterion in how to understand the text is an exercise in foolhardiness; and correlatively, that there can never be a final, definitive interpretation of a text – apply to language and communication in general. With automation, we will see that there is an even greater need to 'distance' the Author from the text (Barthes 1986, 53). Such a move clearly goes again much of the speaker-centredness that is a characteristic of our traditional ways of understanding language and communication. It is the argument of this chapter that the primacy that still tends to be accorded to the speaker must, indeed, be removed.

This chapter is organized as follows. I begin with a critical discussion of Goffman's production format, where I will suggest that even though the three roles identified by him are useful, what we need to do, in order to account for the use of automation, is to delink them from the notion of speakerhood. That is, while we should be prepared to identify roles such as the animator, the principal and the author,[1] there is no reason to assume that these are necessarily speaker-related roles. Such a move, we will see, confers certain benefits. It will allow us to more easily recognize that there are complexes of animators, complexes of principals and complexes of authors – yet another important advantage when dealing with automation. Acknowledging the presence of complexes is, of course, entirely consistent with the posthumanism emphasis on assemblages. Whereas the first half of this chapter deals with the issue of delinking, the latter half of is given over to the matter of speaker intention. Here, I argue that while the reality of intention need not be denied, in the context of assemblages, intention plays a much smaller and less deterministic role in how assemblages work.

The Production Format of the Speaker

We have seen (Chapter 2) that in his discussion of the problems associated with the traditional paradigm of talk and, in particular, the problem with treating the speaker as an unanalysed unit, Goffman (1981, 145) brings in the concept of the 'production format', where he proposes to distinguish between the animator, the author and the principal.

To recapitulate, the principal is the entity whose ideas and views are being conveyed via the language that is being used or produced. The author is the entity who composes the text and who is thus responsible for the specific choice of words or more broadly, the design of the message. The animator is the entity through which the message is actually emitted or conveyed. By deconstructing the speaker into the principal, the author and the animator, Goffman therefore makes the important point that what has hitherto been treated as a simple individual unit, the speaker, actually conflates very distinct communicative roles. To elaborate, Goffman recognizes that the entities that make up the speaker can be distributed across these different roles. In some cases, all three roles converge so that the entity that speaks or writes the message is also responsible for the actual words being used in the message and the message also happens to reflect that very same entity's point of view. This is the default assumption in the traditional paradigm of talk, where, for example, if Speaker A says 'I am cold', it is assumed that the words are chosen by the speaker and these words reflect that speaker's actual state of being cold. Speaker A is, in this case, simultaneously author, principal and animator. The roles can diverge, however, as when, for example, a pop singer performs a song composed by someone else. In that case, the singer is the animator, the composer is the author, and (given that the song would typically represent a fictionalized scenario) the principal would be the fictional persona from the 'song-world'. Thus, the principal of a song about heartbreak would the song-specific persona whose heart has been broken. A key point to keep in mind as the discussion in this book progress is that the introduction of automation into communication challenges this default assumption. Increasingly, it is important to *not* assume as a default that all three production format roles are conflated. Instead, our default assumption will have to be that the responsibility for a piece of text is distributed across a number of distinct entities, some of whom are automated.

That having been said, there are nonetheless a number of significant issues with Goffman's description of the production format. For him, an animator is still a type of speaker, as is a principal and an author. In other words, Goffman still treats these as the ways in which different types of speakers should be distinguished because 'A person frequently enacts all of these different speakers at the same time' (Manning 1992, 171). Recall that the notion of a speaker for Goffman is very much tied to that of being a person. Goffman, by insisting that these production format roles are different ways of being a speaker, is still continuing to link the roles to a human being. This is the criticism that was made in the preceding chapter, that Goffman's approach remains highly anthropocentric rather than recognizing that nonhuman entities are also actants.

This is a problem because the insistence on tying these roles to speakerhood does not allow us to account for the many different ways in which automation figures in communication. This problem, if unaddressed, leaves us with the following conceptual quandary. We can persist, with Goffman, in treating the roles of animator, author and principal as different ways of being a speaker. But we then also need to explain just where or what is this person that these roles must ultimately refer to. Or we can delink the still very useful roles of principal, author and animator from that of the speaker. These roles are indeed highly relevant to analysing communication but I want to suggest that there is no actual need to presume that the roles must in any consistent or predictable way always be traceable to a person qua speaker. Such a presumption, we saw, exists only because Goffman starts with the traditional paradigm of talk and he aims to critique the notion that communication can be understood as involving a simple dyad of (human) speaker and (human) hearer. The presence of automation, however, requires not only that we accept that the traditional paradigm of talk of problematic; it also behoves us to jettison the assumption that communication necessarily involves speakers, especially if by the use of this term we are referring to human interlocutors.

As the carpark example (see Chapter 1) demonstrates, what we have is a case of an animator with no human actor to ground the communication. In addition, this is an animator that is arguably also the principal and the author of the messages that are being presented to various drivers. But even if we agree that the carpark sign is all three (principal, author and animator), we should not be required to concede that this makes the carpark sign a speaker. Delinking the three roles from that of the speaker allows us to do this. Assuming we agree that 'speaker' requires some degree of anthropomorphism, then the question of whether the carpark sign is to be considered a speaker will have to be decided on a different basis: whether there is in fact any anthropomorphising going on. And this latter issue, as we will see over the next two chapters, is really up to the ideological assumptions that the hearer (in the case of the carpark example, the hearer is the driver) brings to the communicative event. So, once we delink the roles of the principal, the author and the animator from that of the speaker, we can still recognize these roles as being relevant to the production format of a communicative event but we are not obligated to go on and assume that there must always be some kind of a speaker involved, much less a person who is acting as a speaker. The following two examples show how such a move provides a neat conceptual advantage when dealing with automation in communication.

Consider, as our first example, the electronic greeting that the Singaporean coffee chain Toastbox gives to its customers (Wee 2014, 62). The electronic register where the Toastbox employee takes a customer's order and collects payment has been configured so that it does not only display the amount to be paid; it also displays the greeting 'Welcome to Toastbox. I'm Ella.' This is a case of synthetic personalization (Fairclough 2001, 52), where an attempt has been made to personalize the organization's relationship with its customers by giving the impression that what is actually a generic interactional script has been individualized so that each customer feels they are being treated in a manner that is highly personal. As Fairclough points out, individuals who interact with organizations often feel (with some justification, it has to be said) that they are little more than generic entities who are all treated in much the same manner. Synthetic personalization, as an interactional strategy, aims to mitigate this concern (with varying degrees of success, obviously) by making these individuals feel that the organization sees them as individuals with unique characteristics and deserving of personalized attention. In the case of Toastbox, this admittedly half-hearted attempt at synthetic personalization takes the form of a personal greeting from Ella. The hope, presumably, is that customers will feel they are interacting with a specific individual rather than just any Toastbox employee, and moreover, an individual who is friendly and welcoming. Hence, the use of the name and not surprisingly, a female name. As Hultgren (2009, 8; see also Cameron 2000a, b) notes that there is a tendency for service sector work to be seen as feminized work:

> In the service sector, organizations have been quick to realize that they can capitalize on women's presumed 'natural' skills. In an increasingly saturated market where businesses compete on service, they want employees who are willing to serve the customer, who can create rapport, show a personal interest in the customer, offer empathy and understanding, and women, at least stereotypically, seem to fit the bill.

Unfortunately, however, different employees (including employees of different genders) are on duty, and the greeting itself is not changed frequently enough, if at all. Since it is unlikely that Toastbox has many employees all of whom happen to be named "Ella," the greeting itself clearly lacks plausibility and sincerity. This is because the greeting is clearly dissociated from the individual who happens to be manning the register at any particular moment. Which means that the greeting is clearly not coming from the human individual – even if we wanted to treated the individual as the principal and author, and the register as the animator. Rather, it is a programmed greeting that is coming wholly from the register itself.

This is a transparent attempt at synthetic personalization, and its lack of plausibility and sincerity is nevertheless relatively inconsequential for Toastbox. In this regard, it is instructive to understand the reason why this is so. As I have pointed out elsewhere (Wee 2015), organizations are set up or established with very specific goals in mind, and they are oftentimes even expected to state these goals in the form of vision and mission statements. The goal(s) motivating the creation of the organization constitute its primary purpose. A university, a hospital, and a fast food restaurant all have different primary purposes (respectively, education, health care, selling food). At the same time, many organizations also participate in ancillary activities (sometimes described as "corporate social responsibility"). The ancillary activities are where an organization sites its obligations to ethical regimes that may not figure as part of its primary purpose. Yet, that very sense of obligation is indicative of the organization's awareness that these other ethical regimes represent values that the organization needs to be at least seen as upholding.

As an automated greeting, the use of 'Welcome to Toastbox. I'm Ella' does not impact in any significant way on either Toastbox's primary purpose (serving food and drinks) or any of its ancillary activities (e.g. Toastbox welcomes customers with service dogs and is committed to reducing the use of plastic as part of the organization's move towards sustainability). This is not to say that there are absolutely no consequences. Customers may note this use of an automated greeting as a lack of attention to operational detail on the part of the organization. But it is not clear that there are more substantive effects beyond this. Even so, it is nevertheless worth noting that Toastbox has subsequently changed its greeting. The 'Ella' greeting is no longer in operation. Instead, its registers carry greetings like 'Welcome to Toastbox. I'm R2-Cashier1' The first part is still a greeting obviously. But the second part, rather than attempting to present itself as an individual named 'Ella', identifies the greeter more impersonally by a numbered designation, in this case, Cashier Number 1 of Cash Register Number 2. Regardless of whether the earlier version created any public comment or outcry, the fact that Toastbox decided to make a change is clear indication that the organization became at some point aware of the (admittedly minor) problems with the 'Ella' greeting, and decided to opt for something that would be less connected to a particular human. The identifier 'R2-Cashier1' is neither associated with any specific gender nor is it tied, unlike a personal name, to any distinct individual.

The Toastbox box example is a case of automation being used to greet customers. The use of the first person pronoun ('I'm Ella/I'm R2-Cashier 1') makes it clear that Toastbox, the organization, wants the cash register to be construed as the entity that actually conveys the greeting to the customers. That is, Toastbox intends the register to be seen as performing the act of greeting. While the organization itself can perhaps be described as the principal of the greeting and the programmer the author, it is the cash register that is undoubtedly the animator. Given that it is the cash register, qua animator, that customers encounter, should it also be considered a speaker, in this case, an animator-speaker perhaps? However, we have to ask, in what sense are we at all looking at a speaker? As mentioned earlier, the notion of a speaker typically implies person-hood and with that, the capacity for an intention to communicate. In the case of a human animator, such as a singer or a spokesperson speaking on behalf a company, the intention presumably would be to sing the song well or to repre-sent the company's position accurately. Can any such intention (e.g. to provide accurate and instantaneous information to drivers entering the lot) be attributed to the cash register? In this case, however, it is unlikely (though certainly not impossible) that a customer would treat the cash register has having the intention to greet. This differs from the greeting that might come from a human service staff. A customer may, in this case, accuse the staff of being rude or insincere – accusations that point to the presumption that the human greeter has a commu-nicative intent. But similar accusations are not likely to be levelled at the cash register – which goes to the point that the production format roles identified by Goffman need to be dissociated from that of the speaker.

This point gathers even greater force when we move on to consider our second example, which has to do with the increased use of automation in call centres. As automation becomes more widely used by call centres, there is shift from script-ing to programming. Call centres have long been a topic of interest in socio-linguistics especially following Cameron's (2000a) seminal work, which focuses on how call centre operators are required to follow scripted interactions. These are interactions developed and prescribed by the companies that they work for. They are intended to optimise the work of call centres (so that the operators can respond to as many calls as possible within a short period of time) and to present the companies in the best possible light (the operators are trained to answer calls in a friendly voice, to appear welcoming even if they are exhausted from having dealt with many calls already). Cameron points out the level of detail that com-panies might script the linguistic behaviours of the call centre operators, noting that there are guidelines on what specific speech acts and address forms to use, stipulations regarding voice quality, and even reminders to avoid gaps and over-laps in managing turn transitions. For example, among the checklist of items that a call centre supervisor may use to evaluate the operators' performance are the following (Cameron 2000a, 332):

SMILING: Does the member of staff answer the phone with a smile?
PITCH: The depth of pitch in the staff's voice will determine the degree of sincerity and confidence associated with the message that they are giving the caller.

As she notes, despite the vagueness surrounding something like 'depth of pitch', checklists such as these are used to in 'both formal appraisal and more informal regular coaching of individual operators by their supervisors' (333). In addition to the vagueness of some the evaluation criteria, there are aspects of the call centre operators' interaction that may be prescribed, even though these are not actually within the operators' control. Thus, the reminder to avoid conversational gaps and overlaps poses a particular challenge for the operators. This is because, unlike, say, the phrasing of questions (which can be incorporated into a script), the management of turn transitions relies also on how the callers themselves behave in the course of a conversation (332).

Subsequent works on call centres have largely followed this focus on how call centre operators' communication practices are regulated (Holtgrewe, Kerst, and Shire 2002; Hutchinson, Purcell and Kinnie 2000; Hultgren 2009). For example, Hultgren (2009) looks into how the agency of call centre operators is affected by the codification and enforcement of rules governing their language use as employees. Critiquing the work that has taken place primarily within the Conversational Analysis framework, Hultgren argues that there tends to be an assumption that call operators have agency in accomplishing their interactional goals (14). In contrast, Hultgren notes that 'the tendency by call centres to intervene in their employees' use of language is arguably one of the most important principles around which the work in call centres is organized' (1) and the phenomenon of scripting in particular demonstrates 'the unprecedented extent to which call centres teach, prescribe, codify and enforce rules for a vast array of employees' linguistic behaviour' (3).

Keeping the foregoing in mind, we can now look at an example of the use of automation in call centre communication. The following example is from the DBS Bank's Singapore customer service.

Good morning. Welcome to DBS Bank. For English, please press 1 …
[In Mandarin: 'For Mandarin, please press 2'. No other language choices are available. If neither 1 nor 2 is pressed, the system will say 'Sorry, information has not been entered'. Then, the language options are again repeated.]
For lost card and suspected fraudulent transaction, press 9.
To report automated voice call or phishing SMS, press 7.
Alternatively, please continue to hold.
[Pause of about 6 seconds]
Dear customers, the GST voucher payout has been credited to eligible customers who have linked the NRIC to PayNow. You may check your bank account via Digibank. For eligible customers who have not linked their NRIC to PayNow, the GST voucher payout will be credited to your bank account by 30 June. For more information, visit gstvoucher.gov.sg.
[Pause of about 3 seconds]
Please enter your NRIC, debit or credit card number or your phone banking user id followed by the hash key.
[Pause of about 3 seconds]
If you are not an existing customer, press 1.
[After 1 is pressed …]
For lost card and suspected fraudulent transaction, press 1. Fee waiver request, press 2. Cards and cashline application status, press 3. Rates and

branch information, press 4. Self-service option using phone banking PIN, press 5.

For customer service officer assistance, press star zero.

There are three things worth noting about the automated communication. The first is that it is not easy to get to speak to an actual human operator. The opportunity to speak to a customer service officer is only made available after extensive navigation of the various options that the automated menu presents. And even then, the decision to speak to a human operator is indicated by pressing star zero. Presumably, the combination of star zero (as opposed to a number) reduces the chances that the caller might through sheer luck accidentally press a button that would enable them to come into actual contact with a human operator.

This leads to the second point. The way in which the automated communication is organized, with its extensive menu of options, seems deliberately intended to dissuade the caller from accessing the customer service officer. Being able to finally access this individual requires a not insignificant degree of patience and persistence on the part of the caller. The key thing to understand here is that the automation is not merely a supplement to the human customer service officer. The organization in question, in this case, DBS Bank, is trying to shift the responsibility for handling call centre duties, particularly those that are relatively routine in nature, to the automated program. The human service officer is supposed to be the last resort, entering the picture only when the automated program is unable to handle the needs of the caller. This point is reinforced by the fact that when there is a high volume of calls, the caller does not even have the option of holding and waiting for a human operator to be available. The menu suggests to the caller that they may want to 'chat with our digibot' or visit the bank's website – and then proceeds to end the call.

The third is this. Because the caller is forced to navigate the menu before encountering a human assistant, and because the navigation tool available to the caller only involves pressing specific buttons on their phone, the organization is thus able to tailor the menu to allow it to include 'extraneous information', that is, information that are not necessarily related to reasons why a person might be calling. For example, in the extract above, the automated communication also includes information about the payout of a GST (Goods and Services Tax) voucher. This refers to the Singapore government's issuance of cash to help lower- to middle-income Singaporean families with their household expenses. The bank here is part of the mechanisms for disbursing the funds from the government to eligible Singaporeans. Its inclusion of an announcement regarding the GST payout is more part of a public service rather than directly related to its primary purpose. Hence, the automated communication directs callers with queries about the voucher to the government's website ('visit gstvoucher.gov.sg'). The use of automation thus gives the organization even greater control over the interaction than were it to use human operators. This is because it can include other pieces of information (advertisements, public advisories) that may not be directly relevant to why someone might be calling. Callers often have no choice, however, but to listen to these other pieces of information before they can get to the menu options and, if needed, ultimately to a human operator. Human operators are made available only after the menu options that lead to yet further automated responses have proven unhelpful.

If we assume that the call centre programme is a relatively basic one (e.g. callers press menu buttons to indicate their requests and preferences in response to a restricted set of options presented to them), then (as with the Toastbox example) we are looking at an automated animator. Once again, the question before us is whether it is possible to trace this automated animator to a speaker. Given the highly restricted and scripted nature of the interaction, there is no way for a caller to present their concerns in a more nuanced or idiosyncratic. It is only if the menu options already programmed into the automated animator fail to sufficiently address the caller's concerns can there then be recourse to an actual human operator or speaker. The automated call centre programme, even if it is relatively more interactive than the Toastbox cash register, is therefore still not a speaker. Crucially, it is not possible to treat the automated programme as an extension of the human operator, as Goffman wants to do when he treats the vocal cords as a part of a human speaker. This is because, if the menu options do indeed help to address the caller's needs, then there is absolutely no need to bring in the human operator at all. And as we have seen, it is indeed the hope of the bank that most of the time, this will indeed be the case: the human operator's involvement is unnecessary.

Complexes in Production Formats

Delinking the production format roles from speakerhood provides us with yet a further advantage. We need not separate out those roles that are linked to a person from those roles that are not. For example, we need not privilege a person's vocal cords as being a different kind of animator from, say, a loudspeaker system or a telephone (cf. Goffman 1981, 144; see Chapter 2). Thus, rather than suggest that the vocal cords are a kind of animator-speaker while the loudspeaker system and the telephone are 'just' animators, we can simply treat all of them as animators. This is extremely useful because it allows us to recognize that animators – with the same argument applying to principals and authors – can work in complexes.

To return to one of Goffman's own examples, in a case where a person is using a loudspeaker or a telephone so that they are then able to better communicate their message to a wider audience or to someone located some distance away, what we have in effect is a complex of animators working in concert ('loudspeaker + vocal cords' or 'telephone + vocal cords'). Someone who is using the loudspeaker system to project a telephone conversation will effectively be using at least three animators that are working together ('loudspeaker + telephone + vocal cords'). These animators are doing different things, of course, which is the reason why there is a need for a complex of animators rather than just one. The vocal cords that carry the speaker's voice, are not easily interchanged with some other person's vocal cords, and because of this, serve to index the individual speaker's personal contribution and participation in the communicative event. In contrast, a loudspeaker system or a telephone is used for amplification (in the case of the former) and transmission across long distances (in the case of the latter). They are also typically used by different individual speakers and are, as a consequence, less personally connected to specific individuals. In other words, a loudspeaker or telephone is typically used *in conjunction with* vocal cords whereas the converse does not hold. So, rather than just noting that loudspeakers, telephones and vocal cords all are possible animators, what we have in effect is an array of animators that are working together. And if a lecture, for example, is being broadcast or televised to a wider audience, then there can be even more elaborate complexes of animators being integrated to work in concert. For example, a live CNN report on the summit preparations for the 2019 meeting between Donald Trump and Kim Jong Un in Hanoi, Vietnam, featured a conversation between a news anchor based in Atlanta, Georgia, USA, and a reporter located in Hanoi. This live conversation was made possible via an constellation of broadcasting technologies that allowed both audio and video content to be dispersed not just between the two conversationalists but to a worldwide audience of viewers. Indeed, one might posit that *all* forms of mediated communication necessarily involve sets of animators working together.

Authorial complexes, too, are not uncommon. We tend to think of a single-authored book or article as having just one author. But in Goffman's terms, it is the principal who presents his/her ideas in the book or article. The author, from the production format perspective, is the entity responsible for the wording of a text. So, the principal is certainly also an author in this sense (unless the principal has completely abdicated the writing to a ghost-writer). However, so is the copy-editor, who makes suggestions about spelling and phrasing. And once we consider texts that are multimodal (e.g. advertising copy), different parties may be involved in making decisions about wording, about the choice of relevant images, and even about the formatting and placement of texts vis-à-vis images. Given this book's focus on the use of automation in communication, we have to therefore ask whether a spellcheck program should not also be treated as an author. At the very least, it is part of an authorial complex since the program alerts us to words that may be wrongly spelled and even suggests possible alternatives.

These two factors – that nonhuman interlocutors have to be given due consideration when communication is being studied, and that there can be complex combinations of authors, animators and principals – bring us back to the post-humanist arguments that boundaries are porous and shifting, that it is important to recognize the 'vibrant materialities' of actants, and that agency is distributed. Therefore, it is extremely importantly that we be mindful of how the boundaries that go into marking an assemblage are constructed. All these issues, it should be clear, do not mean that Goffman's ideas about footing and production formats are without value. His fundamental point about the need to deconstruct simplistic understandings of 'speaker' and understand how they are distributed over entities performing different roles in communication is in fact more relevant than ever. But it does mean that, unlike Goffman, the roles of author, animator, and principal should not be necessarily tied to that of a speaker at all. This delinking of the principal, the author and the animator from the speaker is entirely consistent with posthumanism. This is because it serves to draw attention to how assemblages – in this case, communicative assemblages – might be constructed. The principal, the author and the animator can still, of course, be linked to speakerhood, and they can, as in prototypical cases of communication, still be conflated to form the speaker but, crucially, they need not be. Furthermore, letting these other roles, in particular, author and animator, become independent of the notion of speakerhood, also help to recognize them as actants alongside the human participants.

By way of summarizing the discussion thus far, we see, then, that the boundary of what constitutes the speaker, following Goffman, indeed shifts and is distributable across the three production format roles. Importantly, however, we have made the argument that speaker agency is only contingently present because these three roles do not necessarily imply the presence of a speaker. When automation is being used, there is undoubtedly some communicative activity going on, but whether or not to the existence of this communicative activity further justifies invoking the presence of a speaker is really something that is dependent on the construal of the hearer.

All this leaves us with the issue of how to situate speaker intention, an issue to which I now turn my attention.

The Contingency of Intentions

Let me start with a caveat. I have suggested that the presence of a speaker is contingent upon the hearer's willingness to accept that an entity worthy of being recognized as 'a speaker' is indeed present and relevant to a given communicative event – an argument that will be developed in the next chapter. It therefore follows that a discussion of speaker intention will, likewise, be dependent on the hearer's willingness to recognize the presence and relevance of any such intention.

In the discussion in this section, I consider cases where a speaker is accepted by the hearer to be present, and where, furthermore, speaker intention is indeed acknowledged to present. Interestingly, however, we will see that the hearer may consider speaker intention to be irrelevant to how the communicative event is to be construed. This, once again, reinforces the point to be developed in Chapter 4, that we need to be more seriously engaged in a hearer-based pragmatics as opposed to one that is speaker-based.

We know by now that it is the presumptions associated with the personalist view of meaning that accords prime importance to the speaker's intention in grounding a communicative event. That is, it is assumed that in order for communication to be meaningful, a speaker must have an intention to communicate something, and it is up to the hearer to do their best to understand or recover what this something happens to be. An example we considered was when a speaker utters 'I'd like a cup of tea, please' to convey their specific desire for a cup of tea. The job of the hearer is then to interpret the utterance as reflecting that desire, and depending on the specific details of the context, decide whether or not to act in a manner that meets the speaker's desire.

As a problem with this primacy accorded to speaker intention, we discussed Duranti's (1992) example of the Samoan *fono* (formal meeting), which showed that, in some cultures, the main concern is the allocation of responsibility rather than the reconstruction of actor intention. In that example, an orator was being punished for having embarrassed his village by claiming that a newly re-elected official was coming to visit. The failure of the visit to actually take place was considered sufficient grounds by the members of the *fono* to punish the orator, regardless of whether the orator intended to misled or whether he was himself the victim of misinformation. But lest the Samoan *fono* example be dismissed as 'exotic' and not truly reflective of how communication 'actually' takes place, consider the fact that in Western societies, particularly in response to instances of hate speech, there is a growing willingness to focus on the perlocutionary effects of such speech regardless of whether any offense was intended by the speaker.

Take, as an example, The R-Word campaign, which was initiated in 2004 by the Special Olympics International Board of Directors to eliminate the use of the word 'retarded' (and its morphological variants). While the original impetus for the campaign came from the request by Special Olympics athletes to "update the movement's terminology from 'mental retardation' to 'intellectual disabilities'," the campaign expanded its scope in 2008 from the Special Olympics community to include the general public when it decided to "combat the inappropriate use of the R-word in common usage".[2] The campaign's slogan is "Spread the word to end the word." In discussing this campaign, we will pay specific attention to the divergence between illocutionary intent and perlocutionary effect, since a key feature of the campaign's argument is that the R-word is hurtful regardless of the speaker's intention.

The overwhelming concern for the campaign's advocates is that the use of the R-word is deeply hurtful. This can be seen in the campaign's claim that the R-word's negative connotations serve to perpetuate a negative (and hence, inaccurate) stereotype about people with intellectual disabilities. Thus, consider the following extracts from the campaign's website (bold in original, the shift between upper and lower case 'R/r' is in the original as well):

(1) When they were originally introduced, the terms 'mental retardation' or 'mentally retarded' were medical terms with a specifically clinical connotation; however the pejorative forms, 'retard' and 'retarded' have been used widely in today's society to degrade and insult people with intellectual disabilities.

Today the r-word has become a common word used by society as an insult for someone or something stupid. For example, you might hear someone say, 'That is so retarded' or 'Don't be such a retard.' When used in this way, the r-word can apply to anyone or anything, and is not specific to someone with a disability. But, even when the r-word is not said to harm someone with a disability, it is hurtful.

(Accessed August 8, 2011)

(1) provides a historically sensitive account of how the R-word has gone from being a specialist term to one that is widely used, and has, as a consequence, acquired a pejorative connotation. Because this pejorative use of the R-word is often aimed at people with intellectual disabilities, this is why it needs to be eliminated. (1) also describes uses of the R-word towards people who are not intellectually disabled as well as things – to which the attribute is irrelevant in the first place. The claim here is that even such uses of the R-word are "hurtful," presumably because these help to continue the perpetuation of negative stereotypes about people with intellectual disabilities.

The focus on the emotional effects of the R-word motivates the campaign's "eradicationist" position (Hill 2008, 57), where the goal is to "end the word." The campaign's eradicationist position suggests that there are almost no occasions on which the use of the R-word might be considered acceptable, appropriate, or even tolerable. The presumption here is that the very use of the word is hurtful. Thus, consider the following two examples, all taken from the campaign's website (accessed August 8, 2011). The first example is shown in (2), where the campaign's website celebrates the fact that on October 5, 2010, US President Barack Obama signed into federal law a bill known as Rosa's Law:

> (2) Rosa's Law, which takes its name and inspiration for [sic] 9-year-old Rosa Marcellino, removes the terms 'mental retardation' and 'mentally retarded' from federal health, education, and labor policy and replaces them with people first language 'individual with an intellectual disability' and 'intellectual disability.' The signing of Rosa's Law is a significant milestone in establishing dignity, inclusion, and respect for all people with intellectual disabilities.

It seems obvious that the drafters of the various federal policies had no intention to insult or degrade when they used the R-word. And it is not really specified if anyone has found the experience of reading federal policies that contain the R-word to be hurtful. Nevertheless, because these policies do contain the R-word and because readers of the policies may feel insulted or degraded, the R-word, according to the campaign, must be removed.

The second example is shown in (3). Among the many links that the campaign's site provides under its 'News' section is a link to a news article from US Weekly (2010). (3) is an extract from that article (italics added):

> (3) When Jennifer Aniston used the word "retard" in a *Live! With Regis and Kelly* interview in August, Peter Berns, CEO of The Arc (a nonprofit advocacy group for those with intellectual and developmental disabilities), told US Weekly her usage of the term was "extraordinarily offensive and inappropriate."

"Frankly, someone in her position ought to know better," Berns said of Aniston, 42. "She is using language that is offensive to a large segment of the population in this country... *Even if [the word] wasn't intended to insult them, that is the effect of it.*"

Berns' statement makes clear that illocutionary intent is indeed irrelevant so that even calling Aniston's utterance a gaffe (Hill 2008, 88) is not enough to excuse her use of the R-word. The concern is specifically with the perlocutionary effect of insulting "a large segment of the population." This perlocutionist ideology contrasts significantly with the personalist ideology (Rosaldo 1982). Hill (2008, 38) points out that the latter holds that "the most important part of linguistic meaning comes from the beliefs and intentions of the speaker," and observes that a problem with the personalist ideology is that it has sometimes been used to "insulate" speakers from accusations of racism, on the grounds that a speaker may have only been ignorant or insensitive (111). In this way, the personalist ideology sometimes errs on the side of being too lenient or kind, by allowing speakers to get away with racist remarks mainly because it is difficult to determine a speaker's actual intentions. In contrast, the perlocutionist ideology goes to the other extreme. Since speaker intention is no longer a relevant consideration, there is no excuse that would be acceptable for using the R-word.

Let us now look at a case where intention is indeed being attributed to an automated entity. In the following example, the potential for anthropomorphism is exactly what researchers are relying on when robots are being used to help children who have autism learn how to socialize. Weir (2015) describes one such experiment, where a child with autism is in a room with his mother. A humanoid robot is also present. The child backs away from the robot, and in response, the robot 'hangs its head and whimpers' (Weir 2015, 42). The child then moves closer, and the robot responds with 'smiles, happy sounds and a cascade of bubbles' (42). As Weir points out, the hope is 'that robotic systems can help the children learn valuable social skills such as imitation, taking turns and maintaining joint attention with another person' (42):

> And there's evidence that happens. As Scassellati and Mataric describe in a recent review, a variety of studies have reported that kids with autism will look from the robot to a parent and back again, or excitedly point out some feature of the robot to an adult or another child (*Annual Review of Biomedical Engineering*, 2012). In their excitement, the children seem to naturally seek out those joint displays of attention that are so important for social interaction.
>
> (Weir 2015, 42)

The child's response to the robot is a demonstration that the child is interpreting the whimpering as a non-linguistic speech act, in this case, a request by the robot to not be left alone. When the child moves closer to the robot and the latter then responds with 'happy sounds', this reinforces for the child the notion that the child did indeed interpret the robot's request correctly. This final example drives home the point that ultimately, it is the hearer's willingness to attribute intention that has to be given greater prominence in our understanding of communication.

Conclusion

In this chapter, I have argued that there is a need to distance the role that the speaker plays in communication. This is not to suggest that the speaker is completely irrelevant. Rather, the problem with traditional approaches has been that the speaker has been treated as an identifiable single and stable entity, and moreover, an entity whose intention should be privileged in understanding how communication unfolds.

This chapter has instead shown that, especially with automation, Goffman's ideas regarding the production format are not only relevant, they actually do not go far enough in delinking the roles of animator, principal and author from that of the speaker. I have therefore called for such a delinking, showing that there are conceptual benefits that accrue from such a move.

This 'death of the speaker', so to speak, leaves us with the question of what, then, a reconstituted approach to the pragmatics of communication should look like. As this chapter has also indicated, it is the hearer who actually decides whether a speaker is present at all in the communication that they (the hearer) are apprehending, and concomitantly, what weight (if at all) to give to the speaker's intention. It is, perhaps, appropriate, to close this chapter as I began it, with Barthes (1986, 54–55):

> ... a text consists of multiple writings, proceeding from several cultures and entering into dialogue, into parody, into contestation; but there is a site where this multiplicity is collected, and this site is not the author, as has hitherto been claimed, but the reader: the reader is the very space in which are inscribed, without any of them being lost, all the citations out of which a writing is made; the unity of a text is not in its origin but in its destination, we know that in order to restore writing to its future, we must reverse the myth: the birth of the reader must be requited by the death of the Author.

The next step, therefore, is to focus on the 'birth of the reader' or, in the terms of the current discussion, to focus on developing a hearer-based pragmatics.

Notes

1 I hope it is obvious that Goffman's 'author' is much more specific Barthes' use of the term. Barthes' 'author' conflates at the very least Goffman's 'author' and 'principal' since it is both the (supposed) source of ideas as well as the form in which the ideas are ultimately presented.
2 Unless otherwise stated, all quotations are from the campaign's website, R-word.org. The different dates on which the site was accessed are indicated when specific examples are discussed.

4 A Hearer-Based Pragmatics

Introduction

We have seen that there are good reasons to not give primacy to the speaker when trying to understand the pragmatics of communication. For one, the speaker, as an unanalysed entity, conflates at least three different production format roles: an animator, a principal, and an author. As we saw in the preceding chapter, even when these roles have been taken into account, there is no reason to assume that they are necessarily linked to the notion of a speaker at all. Two, if even the notion of speaker intention is accepted as a reality, the ability to trace the effective contribution of any such intention to the outcome of a given event, communicative or otherwise, is so tenuous that it becomes questionable whether this kind of intention deserves the kind of privilege that it has hitherto enjoyed – a privilege, we should note, that arises only because of the primacy given to the speaker in traditional conceptions of pragmatics. Three, there are cases where speaker intention has been dismissed as irrelevant by the hearer themselves.

The fourth and perhaps the most fundament reason why primacy should not be accorded to the speaker is this. It is actually the hearer that plays the more critical role in acts of communication. The critical nature of the hearer's role in any communicative event comes from the fact that if an exchange is to be construed as meaningful, this really depends on the theory of mind that the hearer draws on. It has long been clear that all communication involves the hearer drawing on a folk theory of mind, that is, the assumption that the other entity that hearer is interacting with is also 'minded' (Sellars 1963). This does not mean that we, as hearers, attribute the same theory of mind to all with whom we interact. We talk to our pets, to our cars, to our computers. Some of us (those of us who are still young or young at heart) may talk to our toys. In doing all this, we make our own adjustments about how intelligent, how empathetic, how mature and even how sentient our interactant may be.

A classic experiment to demonstrate the theory of mind at work is Wimmer and Perner's (1983) experiment involving the 'false-belief task'. There are various versions of the task. The most well-known involves a child watching two puppets interacting in a room. One puppet ("Sally") puts a toy in location A before leaving the room. While Sally is gone, the other puppet ("Anne") shifts the toy

DOI: 10.4324/9781003467922-4

from location A to location B. Sally then returns to the room, and the child is asked where Sally will look for her toy, the choices being location A or location B. Children who are four years old and above tend to have little difficulty with the test. They judge that Sally will look for her toy in location A. In contrast, children below the age of three typically fail the test; they tend to assert that Sally will look for the toy in location B. The ability to pass the test is taken as evidence that the child has a theory of (Sally's) mind. That is, even though the toy has been moved to location B, the child understands that this is information that Sally would not be aware of or have access to.

Dennett (1971, 1987) describes this ability to attribute beliefs and goals to an interactant as 'the intentional stance'. He explains that this 'intentional systems theory' is something we apply to ourselves, to other humans, to animals, and also to robots and computers 'and this raises a host of questions about the conditions under which a thing can be truly said to have a mind, or to have beliefs, desires and other "mental" states' (1971, 1). The intentional stance is, as Dennett emphasizes, a strategy for practical reasoning. By treating the interactant as a rational entity (with allowances depending on whether this entity happens to be an animal, an artefact or another person – and even then, whether the person might be suffering from dementia, schizophrenia, or some other mental issues that need to be taken into consideration), we are able to attribute beliefs and goals to it and this move in turn allows us to make decisions about how we should conduct the interaction. Because the theory of mind is ideologically saturated, we should not expect that it applies uniformly to all entities. Whether and how much intelligence, empathy, or intention to attribute to one's interlocutor is highly dependent on the hearer's conception about the capacities of the interlocutor and their (i.e., the hearer's) expectations vis-à-vis any given communicative event.

Before continuing, it is necessary to clarify Grice's position vis-à-vis the theory of mind, in order to explain why his remarks do not give sufficient weight to the role of the hearer. In presenting his arguments for the Cooperative Principle, it is clear that Grice, too, draws on the theory of mind. Grice is specifically interested in demonstrating that communication consists in one speaker, Speaker A, making inferences about on what another speaker, Speaker B, might be able to infer from Speaker A's own utterances. In other words, Speaker A expects Speaker B to derive certain implicatures from what Speaker A says. Moreover, this expectation involves Speaker A having a theory of mind about Speaker B, that is, Speaker A makes certain assumptions about the mental state of Speaker B, such as Speaker B's intentions, desires, and beliefs. Thus, Grice (1989, 30–31) asserts that conversational implicatures are derived in something like the following way:

> He said that P; he could not have done this unless he thought that Q; he knows (and knows that I know that he knows) that I will realize that it is necessary to suppose that Q; he has done nothing to stop me thinking that Q; so he intends me to think, or is at least willing for me to think, that Q.

Grice's nomenclature ('Speaker A', 'Speaker B'), however, once again betrays his privileging of communication from the perspective of the speaker. By treating both interactants as 'speakers', Grice is making the assumption that a participant to the communicative event is significant only insofar as they are acting as speakers. This is of course consistent with problematic assumption that the goal of communication should be to recover as accurately as possible a speaker's intention. The difference between what Grice is presenting and what this chapter is arguing for is that when an interactant serves as a hearer, they are not necessarily waiting for their turn to be a speaker. Instead, they are making crucial decisions about how to understand or frame the communicative event, including decisions about whether the putative speaker is in fact a speaker in the sense of possessing human-like capacities.

All these various considerations importantly point us towards the need for a hearer-based pragmatics, that is, a pragmatics that is willing to give much greater weight to the role of the hearer, something which has been done only sporadically thus far (see below). I therefore organize the discussion in this chapter as follows. I begin by considering some previous attempts at incorporating the presence of the hearer into the study of pragmatics. Most of these attempts notably are pitched as modifications to the theory of speech acts and do not take seriously enough the fact that it is the hearer who adopts the intentional stance and accords the speaker a 'mind'. I then discuss in greater detail one work that does take the role of the hearer seriously, that of Hansen and Terkourafi (2023). Even so, I explain how the proposals by Hansen and Terkourafi (2023) still need some refinement when faced with the issues raised by automation. I then describe what a hearer-based approach to pragmatics, one that is informed by a posthumanist orientation, would look like and I show how such an approach can easily accommodate examples involving automation.

Attempts at Incorporating the Hearer

A relatively early recognition of the fact that the hearer needs to be given better consideration comes from Clark and Carlson (1982). In their discussion, Clark and Carlson focus on conversations involving more than two people and they point out that speech act theory cannot adequately account for the presence of other participants beyond the speaker and the direct addressee. The example they give is the following (1982, 334, italics in original):

CHARLES, TO ANN AND BARBARA: What did the two of you do today?
ANN, TO CHARLES, IN FRONT OF BARBARA: We went to the museum.
BARBARA, TO CHARLES, IN FRONT OF ANN: Before that, we went to the theatre.

They then make the following observations about the example (334–335, italics in original):

Here Ann and Barbara take turns telling Charles what they did together. When Ann asserts that they went to the museum, she is addressing Charles. She can't be addressing Barbara, since she would be telling her something it was obvious to the two of them that Barbara already knew ... Yet if the conversation is to accumulate, Ann must let Barbara know what she is telling Charles. Otherwise, Barbara cannot keep track of what is being said; she may repeat things Ann has already said. So Ann must inform Barbara that she is telling Charles that they went to the museum. Barbara presupposes just that when she says *Before that, we went to the theatre.*

What Clark and Carlson are arguing is that speech act theory does not have a way of accounting for Ann's communication to Barbara. Speech act theory has focused on the kind of interaction that takes place between Ann and Charles. But her utterance to Charles is also aimed at Barbara, and this is something that needs to be considered because it clearly impacts on Barbara's own contribution to the exchange. Clark and Carlson therefore suggest (333; caps in original) that:

Speakers perform illocutionary acts, not only toward addressees, but also toward certain other hearers. We define a type of hearer we call a PARTI-CIPANT, whose role as hearer is distinct from the roles of both addressee and overhearer.

Clark and Carlson make an important point about the need to recognize that Ann's utterance is not just intended for Charles; it is also intended, albeit in a different way, for Barbara. They therefore propose that the speaker always performs two distinct illocutionary acts: a traditionally understood act, such as an assertion or a promise, as well as an informative. The latter, they propose is directed at all addressees. In the above example, then, Ann is making an assertion towards Charles but an informative towards Barbara (as well as Charles).

The proposal by Clark and Carlson is somewhat reminiscent of Goffman's (see Chapter 1) criticism that the traditional paradigm of talk tends to construe communication in dyadic terms, and in particular, his observation that the notion of a 'hearer' actually covers a number of distinct types of participants such as an eavesdropper, an audience, and addressee. Nevertheless, where the argument being developed in the present chapter is concerned, Clark and Carlson's proposal contains a serious weakness: the communication is still viewed from the speaker's perspective. In their example, it is Ann, qua speaker, who has the illo-cutionary intent to treat Charles as the addressee and Barbara as (in their terms) the 'participant'. This privileging of the speaker's perspective leaves their proposal vulnerable to all the problems discussed in the preceding chapter, particularly once automation enters the picture. For example, if we return to our carpark sign example, consider a scenario where there are two drivers. The first driver, A, arrives at the carpark and the sign indicates that there is one empty lot left. Assume that driver B is immediately behind driver A and is therefore also able to read the information. Driver B can conclude that once driver A enters the lot, the lot will be fully occupied. There will no longer be any empty lots left. The proposal by Clark and Carlson still leaves us to grapple with the question of whether the 'speaking' automated entity (in this case, the carpark sign) is treating driver A as a hearer (and thus making an assertion to driver A) but treating driver B as a participant (and making an informative towards driver B).

Another attempt to come to grips with the presence of the hearer is the book-length study by Haverkate (1984). However, as with Clark and Carlson (1982), Haverkate (1984), too, remains wedded to viewing communicative event from the speaker's perspective. Focusing primarily on pronoun choice in Peninsular Spanish, Haverkate makes the point that there are different ways of referencing the speaker and the hearer, where these are observable as 'strategic effects speakers intend to bring about by employing them' (from the blurb of the book). As should be clear from Haverkate's own description of his work, the goal of his analysis is to investigate how, via the choice of pronouns, a speaker positions themselves and the hearer in order to bring about intended interactional effects. This work, therefore, views the hearer entirely from the speaker's perspective.

More recently, Kecskes (2010) begins with the observation that communication can be fallible, that misunderstandings and miscommunications do occur, and this is something that any study of communication has to be able to account for in a principled manner. Kecskes wants to provide an alternative to 'current theories of pragmatics [that] consider communication an idealistic, cooperation-based, context-dependent process in which speakers are supposed to carefully construct their utterances for the hearer taking into account all contextual factors and hearers do their best to figure out the intentions of the speakers' (2010, 50). Kecskes proposes to treat 'speaker and hearer [as] equal participants in the communicative process' (58), and, in particular, focus on the 'the interplay of intention and attention, as this interplay is motivated by the individuals' private socio-cultural backgrounds' (58).

This goal of giving greater attention to the hearer is, obviously, something that I absolutely agree with. However, Kecskes' assertion that hearer and speaker are equal participants is problematic. It seems more of a dictum rather than a defensible observation. As we have already seen, there are a number of situations in which it is the hearer who decides just how much weight to accord to the speaker, including whether to give any consideration to the speaker's intention or whether to dismiss it as completely irrelevant. Which brings us to another issue with Kecskes' proposal – one that positions his ideas as very much in alignment with the theories of pragmatics that he otherwise wants to critique. This is the continued privileging of speaker intention. Thus, Kecskes suggests that intention is 'the main organizing force in the communicative process' and it is 'private, individual, pre-planned and a precursor to action' (60).

Kecskes also rightly notes that intention is dynamic and even emergent so that it is not an unchanging or stable attribute, much less one that is locatable within the speaker (60). Unfortunately, he does not go far enough to consider cases where intention is dismissed by the hearer as irrelevant (which, we have seen, is not uncommon). Instead, even as he recognizes that intention is something that is dependent on the hearer's interpretation, he wants to retain the emphasis that has traditionally been given to the intention of the speaker, hence, the assertion that 'The primary intention expressed in a particular situation serves the function of guiding the conversation' (61). Unsurprisingly, this creates severe difficulties once we start to look at the role of automation in communication, where the attribution of intention is not something that can or should be taken for granted.

A work that does actually take seriously the role of the hearer, and in many ways, aligns with the argument being developed in this chapter is Hansen and Terkourafi (2023). The authors observe that (2023, 99, italics added):

> A range of (in many cases well-known) problems with the notion of Speaker's Meaning as a central component of a theory of meaning in communication have been advanced in the literature, not only from within linguistic pragmatics, but also in philosophy, anthropological linguistics, microsociology, and historical linguistics ... *we argue that it is time for pragmatic theory to take much more seriously the notion of Hearer's Meaning, as distinct from Speaker's Meaning, even where the latter is conceived of as interactionally negotiated ... Hearer's Meaning is, in fact, criterial.*

And their position regarding speaker intention, too, is similar to the one that has been articulated in the preceding chapter (100):

> It must be emphasized from the outset that we are in no way claiming that speakers do not have intentions, nor that they do not choose their words with the aim of reflecting those intentions ... What we will argue is that speaker intentions are not central to those interpretations and that, on at least some occasions, they may play no role at all.

In their proposal, Hansen and Terkourafi (103) suggest that Hearer's Meaning should be recognized to consist of the following three components:

a   what the hearer (H) (purports to) take(s) the speaker (S) to have said in producing the utterance (U);
b   what H (purports to) take(s) S to have presupposed and/or implicated by producing U;
c   any further socially accountable inferences H (purports to) believe(s) follow from (a)–(b), including, but not limited to, the type of social action that H takes U to count as.

The above, in essence, is not too dissimilar from the kinds of accounts providing under standard interpretations of Grice's Cooperative Principle and speech act theory. The key difference, and one that is non-trivial, is that the focus is now squarely on the hearer's perspective. It is the hearer who actively decides on what meanings to attribute to the speaker's utterance or, in some cases, even a lack thereof. Hence, the emphasis placed by Hansen and Terkourafi on what the hearer 'purports' to believe about the speaker. And this hearer's perspective, the authors go on to suggest 'is derived from a combination of the following seven sources' (103):

1   H's framing(s) of (different parts of) the speech event;
2   H's assumptions about the conventional meanings of words and phrases;
3   the sequential placement of the utterance within the discourse;
4   H's perception of S's identities;
5   H's social relationship with S;
6   H's social relationships with third parties;
7   H's assumptions regarding S's intentions (if any).

Examples of framing include treating a speech event as a case of informal chit chat, as a formal debate or a sermon (105). However, even though Hansen and Terkourafi list seven separate sources, these are not actually distinct. The most important source is how the hearer frames the speech event since, it is the framing of an event that informs the kinds of identities ascribed to the participants (including the speaker and any third parties), the relationships that are assumed to hold between the participants, and how the sequential placement of utterances. To return to one of the authors' own examples, once an interaction is framed as a formal debate, then the participants are identified as a proponent and an opponent. The topic of debate becomes the proposition that is being debated. And beyond the debaters, there will also be a third participant, the judge(s).

The observation that framing includes not just the identities of participants and their relationships but even the conduct of the communication itself has been pointed out by Levinson (1992) in his discussion of activity types. As Levinson notes, it is not possible to characterize an utterance as realizing a specific type of speech act (e.g question, command, etc.) independent of the kind of activity that the utterance figures in. An activity type refers to 'any culturally recognized activity ... whose focal members are goal-defined, socially constituted, bounded, events with *constraints* on participants, setting, and so on, but above all, on the kinds of allowable contributions. Paradigm examples would be teaching, a job interview, a jural interrogation, a football game, a task in a workshop, a dinner party, and so on' (Levinson 1992, 69; emphasis in original). Activity types valuably draw our attention to the question of how the activity serves to constrain (in the case of language) the kinds of text and talk that can or should be employed during the conduct of the activity. For example, an utterance such as *How are you?* as spoken by a doctor in a clinical setting would be interpreted by a patient as a request for information about the patient's health. The converse, where a patient opens the interaction with *How are you?* and the doctor responds with information about his/her (i.e. the doctor's) own health, is not impossible, but unlikely in the context of the clinical setting. Thus, *How are you?* derives its function from the activity type in which it is embedded (Sarangi 2000, 2; see also Wee 2005, 229).

What is important about Hansen and Terkourafi's proposal, though, given their emphasis on the active role of the hearer, is that different interactants may therefore frame the same activity in different way, ways that may at times even be incompatible (2023, 105). The significance of framing, as the authors emphasize, is that it serves to constrain the hearer's expectations and contributions (113):

> ... we want to emphasize quite strongly that our model does not imply that "anything goes". On the contrary, three of the sources we have posited, namely frames, the meanings of linguistic expressions, and sequential placement, are based on convention or, at the very least, on strong regularities of usage and thus pose firm constraints on the kinds of interpretations that hearers can derive.

There are clearly many things about Hansen and Terkourafi's arguments that I would agree. Nevertheless, there are still questions to be asked when the focus turns to the use of automation in communication. What, for example, is the frame for automation? Given what I have already suggested in the preceding chapters, there is unlikely to be single 'automation frame', simply because automation takes many forms and inserts itself in many different ways in communicative events. Thus, the more appropriate question to ask then is this: How are extant frames for communicative events affected by the presence and use of automation? The way in which the frame is constructed would then clearly impact on things such as the identities accorded, the relationships between the communicating entities, and even the placement and sequencing of specific utterances. I argue that a key factor to consider is the degree of anthropomorphism that a hearer might accord to the automated entity, an issue that I will then discuss in detail in the next chapter.

When the 'Hearer' is a Machine: Self-Service Kiosks

To appreciate just why, as Hansen and Terkourafi put it, 'Hearer's Meaning is criterial', let us consider what happens when, from the human speaker's perspective, the hearer is unable or unwilling to react meaningfully to the speaker. That is, we can consider what it might be like for the speaker when faced with a hearer who does not seem to accord any meaning to the interaction. The use of automation provides us with some such examples. In these situations, it is the automation that is in fact the hearer. Where the automation in question appears to be unresponsive or simply unable to the speaker's take into account the speaker's specific desires or requests, then the communicative event does indeed hit a major roadblock regardless of what the speaker intends or how the speaker tries to communicate that intention. in other words, if the (automated) hearer is unable or appears unable to ascribe any kind of meaning to the interaction, then the speaker may find themselves extremely frustrated because the speaker's communication is falling on deaf ears, as it were.

A good illustration comes from the use of self-service kiosks. As the term 'self-service' indicates, such kiosks are typically used to reduce an organization's dependence on manpower, in this case, by having customers or patrons make their requests or orders and even payment all via the kiosks. Consider, for example, the case of buying movie tickets. Counters that are physically manned by service staff are still available, but many cinemas increasingly also have kiosks where moviegoers can select the movie they want, the preferred timeslot and (where relevant) the specific seats before making payment electronically. The same applies to fast food restaurants, where in addition to counters with actual humans, customers can make use of self-service kiosks to order and pay for their food and drinks.

According to a business article about the use of kiosks by McDonald's, the company announced in 2015 that 'it would be rolling them out to all of the 14,000 restaurants in the USA' and in 2018, it 'would be upgrading 1,000 restaurants every quarter for the next eight quarters at least' (Acante Solutions Limited 2019). The article also suggests that customers may actually be encouraged to make bigger orders because they 'do not feel like they are being judged' when ordering via a kiosk (Acante Solutions Limited 2019; italics added):

> Another one of the key benefits of kiosks is that customers buy more from them. Why? It's partly to do with the extra convenience, but also to do with the fact that customers do not feel like they are being judged.
>
> When they are asked whether they would like large fries, they may not want to say that face-to-face. *But a kiosk doesn't judge, prompting them to order more food.*

Here, the ideological issue of interest is that customers do not feel judged by a kiosk, presumably because there is little or no anthropomorphizing going on. That is, customers do not seem to attribute to the kiosk any kind of intention, goal or sentience. Hence, there is no 'Hearer's Meaning' to worry about.

But precisely because there is no 'Hearer's Meaning' coming from the kiosk, the article also acknowledges that 'the McDonald's touchscreen kiosks often require staff to help customers use them, otherwise the experience can be frustrating.' This frustration is discussed in some detail by Chee Seng Leong (2019), who describes the various problems his father and brother had in navigating the McDonald's kiosk in Kuala Lumpur, Malaysia. One problem Leong notes is customers may not realize that the display on the kiosk screen is scrollable so that further options can be shown. If a customer is unaware that the display is in fact scrollable, there is frustration at how to get to options that happen to not be shown. Leong notes that this affected and slowed down the processes of food selection and customization of orders (if a customer wanted to specify a particular burger size or type of drink). Another problem arises if a customer wants to go back to the previous step in the order processing (perhaps to modify an order or to add new items). Leong notes that if a customer orders a single item, they will usually have no problem getting through the system. But if a customer is ordering on behalf of a group, then there may be a need to return to a previous page on the display, and this can pose a challenge to many of the customers. Of course, unlike the automated menu in a call centre, a frustrated customer can walk over to the counter and approach a human service staff for help without having to first navigate a complex set of options. Nevertheless, it is worth noting that in many cinema halls and fast food restaurants, the self-service kiosks tend to be located closer to the entrances so that these are the first options encountered by patrons. The physical locations of the kiosks are intended to encourage patrons to as far as possible use the kiosks rather than directly approach the counter staff. In other words, as with the automated call centre menus discussed in the previous chapter, the kiosks are intended to be the preferred interactional option as compared to human service staff.

While the rationale for the adoption of kiosks is often marketed by organizations as giving the customer greater control over the ordering process, from a communication perspective, there are issues still to be sorted out. Many of these issues have to do with the conduct of the interaction, specifically, the customer's sense of loss of control over the communication process. As noted by Cameron (2000a, 2000b), scripting in the case of human call centre operators tries to regulate aspects of communication, such as the management of turns, that are in fact not easily controlled because these rely on the ways in which customers and operators interact with one another. The introduction of automation in communication, such as its use in self-service kiosks, gives the organization greater control over the communication process and in so doing, reduces the customer's ability to negotiate, manage and ultimately, influence the flow of communication. For example, the customer's control over turn-taking now takes the form of pressing a button on the kiosk's touchscreen so as to signal their acceptance or rejection of the choices presented by the automation. The customer's ability backtrack or make corrections (perhaps because a wrong button was pressed or because the customer has changed their mind) is not easily done. And this may mean that the customer has no choice but to exit the menu of options presented by the kiosk and restart the communication all over again – resulting in even more frustration.

Putting the matter simply, the fundamental pragmatics issue in these cases is that a self-service kiosk qua hearer is unable to attribute any meaning and thus response meaningfully – at least from the customer's perspective – to their requests. We may ask whether the term 'hearer' is even appropriate in this context for characterizing a kiosk and my answer is 'Probably not'. But the reason for my answer is not because the postulated hearer happens to be automated. Automation in and of itself does not mean there is no hearer. As we see shortly, as the automation grows in sophistication, giving it the capacity to interactively response to the speaker's specific needs, then it is not at all clear that the use of the term 'hearer' is illegitimate. Be that as it may, the point I want to make here is not, I think, a controversial one. My point is to simply remind us of how crucial the role of the hearer is in any communicative event. Where the hearer's capacity for meaning making appears to be non-existent or minimal, then the frustrations and concerns experienced by the speaker are not at all surprising.

Automating Psychiatry

Consider now examples, from psychiatry, where the automated entities appear to be much more interactive (certainly much more than self-service kiosks) and are consequently more like hearers in the received sense of the term. And because of this greater interactivity, the psychiatry examples are, as we will see shortly, actually quite controversial. There are differing opinions as to their efficacy and questions as to whether their use can even be considered ethical.

The traditional practice in psychiatry involves (human) patients receiving help, usually in the form of therapeutic talk, from (human) psychiatrists. The goal, after all, is for patients to better understand their own (human) impulses as well as to navigate their interactions with other humans: friends, family, colleagues and even strangers. It is therefore taken to be almost axiomatic that the psychiatrist, too, must be another human individual. Indeed, according to one senior psychiatrist, 'push back' and transference are important aspects of therapy and these are necessarily absent if the patient is communicating with an automated entity (Chong 2021):

> But therapy is not about confessing dark secrets and professing private pains; rather it is about the patient speaking to someone who can 'push back', as Professor Sherry Turkle, a psychoanalyst at the Massachusetts Institute of Technology, writes in her book, *Along Together*.
>
> She argues that 'when we talk to robots, we share thoughts with machines that can offer no such resistance. Our stories fall, literally, on deaf ears'.
>
> To do that 'pushing back' as therapists, we need empathy and imagination; and with the judicious use of our own personal experiences of pain, failings and losses, as well as our clinical knowledge, we can view, feel and understand the vicissitudes of our patients' lives from their perspective …
>
> There is also that phenomenon of transference, which occurs when patients redirect feelings from past relationships – usually of their earliest parental and sibling relationships – towards the therapist.
>
> In certain types of psychotherapies, the occurrence and subsequent identification and interpretation of these transferences are crucial.
>
> It is highly unlikely, if not improbable, that a machine could be reminiscent of a patient's significant past relationships and arouse those latent emotions, let alone be able to identify and interpret them to the patient.

However, it is in fact not at all clear that machines are incapable of 'pushing back', especially since what gets counted as pushing back is not just up to the machine or, in more traditional cases, up to the human psychiatrist. Rather, the perception of push back is a matter of pragmatic interpretation or, as Hansen and Terkourafi (2023) would put it, 'Hearer Meaning'. The issue is whether the patient, acting as a hearer, is willing to accord intention and meaning to the messages emanating from the machine. In other words, the patient's own construal of how the interaction is proceeding is criterial. In this regard, the dialogic interaction between patient and machine therapist may well lead the patient to perceive the latter's contributions as 'resistance' that forces the former to re-examine their own assumptions and beliefs. Indeed, as AI gets ever better at providing more interactive responses, there is no *prima facie* reason why the contributions from a robot therapist might not actually end up serving the function of a push back. Turkle's characterization of robots as having 'deaf ears' both underestimates the importance of the patient's willingness to attribute intentions and empathy to a robot as well as the increasingly sophisticated learning abilities of programs. In this regard, it is a mistake to assume that conversational styles between machine and human are always distinctive so that there is no chance at all that a machine could ever converse in a manner that might be taken as human (Christian 2011, 20–21). Of especial pertinence to the point about push back in therapeutic discourse, all that is needed is for the human patient – using their own experiences and imagination – to perceive that the machine therapist is in fact actively reacting to the patient's contributions.

The same holds in the case of transference phenomena. Whether or not a machine could in fact be reminiscent to a patient of that person's past relationships depends on the patient's own willingness to at minimum anthropomorphize. Once this anthropomorphizing is in place, then the issue next is whether the machine might possibly remind the patient of someone/something from their past, a possibility that cannot be completely discounted. Thus, Fiske, Henningsen, and Buyx (2019, 6) are not as quick to dismiss the likelihood of transference because:

> similar to therapeutic relationships, there is the risk of transference of emotions, thoughts, and feelings to the robot. In particular, given that many of the target populations are vulnerable because of their illness, age, or living situation in a health care facility, there is the additional concern that patients would be vulnerable in their engagements with the robot because of their desire for company or to feel cared for'.

For Fiske, Hennigsen, and Buyx, the possibility of transference taking place is quite likely given the emotionally vulnerable states of patients. The issue, as far as they are concerned, is not whether this is possible. Rather, it is about the ethical implications of such transference should it occur, that is, whether the robot therapists are up to the task of handling the transference.

The Case of Woebot

A good demonstration that bonds can be formed even when patients acknowledge they are dealing with an automated entity comes from the case of Woebot. Woebot is a therapy robot, a chatbot to be precise, that engages in daily checks-in with users/patients. These check-in sessions last from five to ten minutes, and over time, Woebot builds an emotional profile of the user/patient, which helps it to identify signs of any 'distorted thinking' from the user (TODAY 2019). One user commented that 'I have been using it for months and it's great' while another simply stated that 'It's good' (TODAY 2019).

The company responsible for Woebot, on its website, cites a study which suggests that 'although bonds are often presumed to be the exclusive domain of human therapeutic relationships, our findings challenge the notion that digital therapeutics are incapable of establishing a therapeutic bond with users' (Darcy et al. 2021). Key findings from the study that the Woebot website summarizes are:

> The bond that Woebot formed with users, who ranged in age from 18–78 years old, appeared to be non-inferior to the bond created between human therapists and patients.
> The bond is established extremely quickly, in just 3-5 days.
> The bond does not appear to diminish over time.

Another paper also cited by the Woebot website studied Ellie, a program that analyses verbal responses, facial expressions and vocal intonations in order to detect possible signs of stress or depression (Darcy, Louie, and Roberts 2016). Participants were either told that Ellie was controlled by a human or a computer program. Those who believed the latter were found to be more likely to reveal more personal information to Ellie. Likewise, Darcy, Louie, and Roberts (2016, 551) also note that in China, Microsoft's chatbot, Xiaoice, provides a 'sympathetic ear' to millions of users even though it is clear to all that Xiaoice is not human.

While these findings are not necessarily disputed, what is more controversial is whether such developments should in fact be lauded. Zarka (2018) describes the experiences of one user of a therapist chatbot, Angela (a pseudonym), whose budgetary concerns meant she could not afford a human therapist. While Angela did appreciate that apps such as Woebot and Wysa were able to help her deal with her depression, she also stated that she was 'very conscious of the fact I was talking to a phone app, which brought a feeling of embarrassment and frustration with myself'. As Zarka points out, while it is good that 'more people are getting some form of help that would otherwise be unavailable ... chatbot companies often obscure what their technology can accomplish ... The big concern is that there is little clarity around whom the apps are targeted toward and what level of severity of anxiety, depression and addiction they can realistically help address':

> For example, the Woebot website prominently features a customer review from a self-identified "life hacker" on its home page that reads, "In my first session with Woebot, I found it immediately helpful [...] addressing my anxiety without another human's help felt freeing." You could argue that this kind of language discourages users from seeking traditional psychotherapy.
> Worse yet, on the Wysa home page, the first thing site visitors see is a quote from a 13-year-old survivor who expresses how the app helped her hold onto her life. Developers vehemently deny that chatbots should be used in cases of serious or life-threatening mental illness, yet their marketing materials are suggesting the opposite.

Chong makes clear his own reservations when he acknowledges that 'humans can develop dependency and attachment to a bot – especially to a physically embodied robot which can be remarkably life-like – even to the extent of being vulnerable to how the robot might react to them', noting that there are studies where subjects who were asked to narrate a personal experience to a robot actually reported feeling hurt when the robot turned away from them while they were still talking to it. As a psychiatrist, Chong (2021), however, finds it 'troubling' when humans relate to robots as though they were sentient beings since, in his view, 'the person must allow himself or herself to be deceived regarding the true nature of this relationship, and complicitly attribute human feelings and attitudes to a robot that offers ersatz care and attention'.

Chong's comments are particularly interesting because they confirm that the more human-like the robot, the greater the chance of human interactants anthropomorphizing the robot. Human interactants can develop feelings of attachment and even feel hurt if the robot acts in a manner that suggests a lack of concern or interest (such as turning away from the interactant). The issue of deception that Chong raises, however, is not a simple one. As we now see, a more nuanced appreciation of the complexities involved required attending to the fact that there are assemblages, and these play a critical role in how frames for interactions are understood.

Frames and Assemblages

The foregoing discussion has shown that, at least where the field of psychiatry is concerned, hearers can actually be quite willing to attribute meaning to their automated interactants. This supports Hansen and Terkourafi's (2023) argument that Hearer Meaning is frame dependent. In the case of psychiatry, the hearer/patient enters the interaction with an expectation that their interlocutor/therapist will be responsive to their emotional concerns.

This frame expectation holds regardless of whether the interlocutor/therapist is automated or not, and it is not at surprising if we keep in mind, as post-humanism reminds us, that frame expectations are always refracted through assemblages. Thus, in his discussion of robots in 'caring spaces', Kerruish (2021) points out that such robots are never used as isolated entities; rather, they are parts of 'empathetic arrangements' so that 'these robots do not function as substitutes for human carers but instead are dependent on human labor if they are to deliver therapy ethically and effectively'. As Kerruish emphasizes (2021, 1):

> Different empathetic arrangements of robots, discourses, people, bodies and institutions offer various configurations of visceral feeling, affect, spatial organization, narrative, social norms and institutional practices. This approach accords with recent work examining *robots as part of socio-technical assemblages* in which they are co-constituted in conjunction with human participants …

The use of automation – whether this is in the form of a robot or an app – has to therefore be consistently understood as part of an assemblage. Once we acknowledge and appreciate this, then a number of interesting and important consequences follow.

The first has to do with criticisms that there is an element of deception involved (Chong 2021; see above) when humans are encouraged to feel emotions towards robots because the latter cannot reciprocate. This criticism is, however, based on the kinds of assumptions that are found in the personalist view of meaning, a view that we have already noted to be highly problematic. The personalist view assumes that for communicative action to be meaningful, it must be grounded in intention that emanates from the individual human speaker. Communication between (human) speakers, then, involves exchanges of meanings grounded in their individual intentions – which may of course evolve as the interaction unfolds (a point that Grice's meaning-nn was aimed at capturing). Since it is questionable if the robot can reciprocate by also having intentions or emotions, then, where the personalist view is concerned, it follows that there is no way a robot can participate in interaction in any meaningful manner. Encouraging humans to act toward robots as though they can do so is to deceive them, or to get them to deceive themselves. However, given that the personalist view is deeply problematic, we have good reasons to reject this reciprocity argument, that is, the argument that meaningful communication with robots or other automated entities is not possible or ethically problematic because of the deception element.

The personalist view and its problems notwithstanding, the second thing to note is that any claim of deception or even self-deception drastically oversimplifies the matter. As Kerruish (2021, 2) points out, 'One of the notable things about empathy towards robots is that people can act in an empathetic way towards robots while simultaneously understanding that they cannot feel or think in the way a human does. The phenomenology of experiencing a robot as an other is not exhaustive of their meaning to us—we experience them as both a thing and an agent'. It is worth stressing that I am not at this point making any claim that is unique to robots. Interactions with animals, particularly pets, also involves vacillations between treating them as fully thinking, intentional agents (on par with ourselves), on the one hand, and entities that are less than fully cognizant of the world around them or even themselves, on the other hand.

This leads to the third point. It is a fallacy to assume or insist that communication, intention and empathy, especially when automation is involved, has to be understood in terms of reciprocity. One of the key lessons from posthumanism (see Chapter 2) is that it is problematic to treat agency as localizable, even when this is supposedly located 'inside' a person. Agency, recall, has had a long and controversial theoretical history and there remain questions about whether it also makes sense to talk about agency at a supra and sub individual level. Posthumanism, by problematizing the boundaries between individuals and the environment, recognizes that nonhuman entities, too, have to be credited with agency. Gurney and Demuro describe this as 'agential realism', that is, 'a conception of matter as active, rather than passively shaped through discourse or human experience' (2022, 2). The argument that automation is not capable of reciprocity, too, makes the same conceptual error of assuming that the attributes of intention and empathy are localizable, that they can be found 'within' a human interactant *and* they are absent 'from' the automation that the human happens to be interacting with. Notions such as intention and empathy are ultimately grounded in the much broader notion of agency. And once agency is acknowledged to be distributed, then, by the same token, so must attributes such as intention and empathy. Kerruish (2021, 3; italics added) in fact suggests that an assemblage perspective allows for just such a non-reciprocal understanding of empathy:

> Users experience social robots as both a thing and an agent (Alac 2016) or, in Coeckelbergh's (2011, 98) terms, the language we use towards robots sometimes 'reveals the robot as an "it" but sometimes also as a "you". The notion of empathetic assemblage brings together material and discursive elements in a relationship *that is not necessarily consistent or logical, retaining a role for the affective and phenomenological dimensions of experiencing robots alongside the understanding that they are not like humans.* In this way, we can acknowledge that empathy is a marker that human standards are at play in a relationship while not demanding that the robot be a human.

Kerruish's remarks imply that our understanding of concepts such as intelligence, consciousness, belief, desire, sentience, and intention are all open to changing interpretations as the machines around us and our interactions with them change. Our understandings of these concepts are ultimately grounded in interactions and behaviours. We make judgments and attributions about the relative intelligence other people, of animals and of machines based on our interactions with them and how they respond to us. Attributions of consciousness are harder to make because our (current) understanding of the concept is less moored in actions and interactions. To say this is not to engage in reductionism where intelligence is equated with behaviour itself. Rather, it is to understand that evidence for attributions of intelligence is grounded in behavioural indicators or 'practical reasoning'.

There is also a sliding scale in the qualities that we may wish to investigate. For example, there are degrees of intelligence, levels of consciousness. This means that we are not talking about the intelligence of machines, for example, as though all machines are intelligent or not (it is not a binary issue) and if we are prepared to attribute intelligence, as though all machines are equally intelligent. As we saw in the preceding chapter, the carpark sign is far less sophisticated than the chatbot or even the echoborg. All these points suggest that the application of notions such as the Cooperative Principle and speech acts to 'machine talk' is not as absurd as it might seem at first blush. Depending on the degree of sophistication of the automation in question and how it is involved in a communication event, it may be appropriate and relevant to invoke such concepts.

Conclusion

Frames are not fixed. They are ideologies that have been organized so as to structure interactions. As such, they are essentially social conventions and the expectations embedded in them can and do change. Automation affects frames by requiring that we insert our notions of what robots, apps and bots are like, what they are capable of, into our interactional expectations. But because these automated entities are themselves being developed to be more interactive and sophisticated, our frame expectations regarding them will have to keep changing whether we like it or not. If these automated entities are being used in place of human interactants (e.g. automated call centre menus in place of human operators, self-service kiosks in place of sales staff, apps in place of psychiatrists), then to the extent that the former are able to fit seamlessly by meeting already extant expectations (as opposed to requiring significant interactional adjustments), then we can expect the human hearer to be more willing to accord the automation the corresponding attributes of the humans that they are substituting for.

The most important thing to keep in mind, it should come as no surprise by now, is to focus on the hearer's willingness to treat the automated entity as having the capacity for intention and empathy. This willingness, in turn, is not something that the hearer about an automation in isolation. It is something that the hearer does vis-à-vis their experience of how the automation figures as part of an assemblage. In the next chapter, we look specifically at how the construction of communicative assemblages can encourage hearers to anthropomorphize automation.

5 Gradations of Anthropomorphism

Introduction

We closed the preceding chapter with the observation that frames are not fixed. They serve to structure our interactions; but they are in turn also affected by how our experiences with interactions unfold. And our interactional encounters are with assemblages of various sorts. All this is, of course, is to be expected. A key tenet of posthumanism is that assemblages are not fixed. Their boundaries shift and their constituent elements change. As assemblages change, they inevitably impact on the frames that they help to materialize.

Given the discussion in the preceding chapter, this chapter further develops the argument that how assemblages are constituted – and consequently the frames that they serve to realize – is very much dependent on the attributions of meaning from the hearer. This is not to suggest that the hearer can arbitrarily decide on what kinds of meaning, if any, to attribute to the assemblage in question. Frames are ideologies that have acquired the status of social conventions. They and their affiliated assemblages are a part of the hearer's socialization experiences and, in this sense, pre-exist the hearer.

This is why hearers can use them as guides to interactions. So, hearers have some leeway in their interpretations of communicative events. But their interpretations are constrained by their knowledge of interactional conventions, their prior experiences, their understanding of cultural values, among many other factors. To paraphrase Barthes (1986, 54–55; see Chapter 3), the hearer is 'the site' where a multiplicity of sources 'is collected'.

In this chapter, these points are made with a particular focus on the hearer's willingness to anthropomorphize automation, a key consideration in unpacking the ideologies behind the pragmatics of communication. This is because the willingness to anthropomorphize is an interpretive move that the hearer and only the hearer makes. Anthropomorphism is something that one does to an other. This necessarily places the analytical focus on what the hearer does. It is the hearer who, by deciding whether or not to attribute humanlike qualities to the interlocutor, frames the communicative event in a particular manner, and this framing has implications for how Cooperative the interlocutor is expected to be and what kinds of speech acts to attribute to it/them.

DOI: 10.4324/9781003467922-5

Anthropomorphism does not arise solely because of automation, of course. We already noted that a hearer employs folk theories of mind whenever they try to make sense of an interaction. Therefore, by paying attending to the conditions under which anthropomorphism takes place – and by the same token, the conditions under which it does not – we can glean important insights into how ideologies that relate to automation and personhood impact on the use of automation in communication. In this regard, it is useful to begin our discussion with how communication itself involves assemblages.

The Communicative Assemblage

In his discussion of the value of assemblage as a theoretical concept, Canagarajah (2020) focuses on what he calls 'a communicative assemblage'. He points out that the idea of an assemblage means that semiotic resources 'generate meanings in relation to the other resources participating in an activity ... That is, resources are configured in activities to make meanings in a situated manner in relation to the social and material networks characterizing that activity' (298). What Canagarajah means by this is that there is no stable or pre-existing meaning that can be attributed to the resources independent of their membership in an assemblage – a point that Kerruish (2021; see preceding chapter) also makes regarding the role of automation in 'empathetic assemblages'. As parts of assemblages, the presence and role of automation therefore has to be understood relationally. That is, whether the apps, programs and robots are seen as distinct from the humans (with whom or on whose behalf they interact) is not a pregiven fact. This is something that cannot be ascertained outside of the assemblages or arrangements that they are part of.

Importantly, Canagarajah (2020, 298, citing Marston, Jones, and Woodward 2005) points out that the idea of an assemblage leads to a 'flat ontology', and he describes in some detail what this means for 'analysing meaning-making activities' (italics in original):

> ... going beyond binaries and hierarchies, such as human/thing, mind/body, cognition/matter, language/objects; treating all resources as equal in status and mediating each other; questioning the primacy of structures that define activities and events; or treating them as separately constituted or secondarily generated; and perceiving everything as connected to everything else. From this perspective, we have to reconsider the logocentrism in linguistics that treats language (or verbal resources) as a superior medium for meaning-making. We have to be open to diverse resources as capable of making meaning, with body and objects having different meaning-making capacities paralleling language. Though developments in *multimodality* have introduced certain communicative resources beyond language as meaningful (Kress, 2009; Mondada, 2014), flat ontology would question that each is organized into different modes. Moreover, these modes of semiotic resources are not already endowed with meanings ... but generate meanings in relation to the other resources participating in an activity ... That is, resources are

configured in activities to make meanings in a situated manner in relation to the social and material networks characterizing that activity.

Ontological flatness means that binaries and hierarchies are eschewed in favour of first and foremost treating all resources equally. 'All resources' here means also not starting with the assumption that language necessarily plays a more central or important role in meaning-making than other kinds of resources. This also does not mean that binaries and hierarchies have no place in the analysis. It does mean, however, that these relationships of demarcation or power are emergent and contingent; they depend on how they happen to be specifically configured in relation to a particular activity. Concomitantly, ontological flatness also insists that the activity of communication cannot be coherently understood by focusing only or even primarily on the intention of an individual person, such as the speaker. Instead, there is a need to take into account the ways in which various resources are used in networks to create meaning (Canagarajah 2020, 312–313).

To summarize, there are three critical points about the communicative assemblage that will guide us as we move on to consider specific examples, The first is that meanings are always situated and assemblage specific. The meaning of a word, a gesture or any other resource cannot be decided outside of an assemblage because it is affected by its relations to other resources in that assemblage. The second, which follows from the first, is the need to avoid logocentrism, where it is presumed that meaning is primarily conveyed via language and other 'paralinguistic' resources only play a supportive or ancillary role in further amplifying the linguistic. This second point, as Canagarajah emphasizes, goes beyond simply acknowledging that communication is multimodal. A multimodal approach assumes that each different modality is already pre-organized and each is then drawn upon to construct an assemblage. In contrast, an assemblage-theoretic perspective would argue that there is no such organization that is not itself already an assemblage. This leads to our third and final point. Resources do not come to an assemblage free of meaning. They come to a new assemblage with imbued with meanings as a result of their presence in some other prior assemblage. These prior assemblage-specific meanings influence their use in a new assemblage, with the consequence that the result may be one of 'relative deterritorialization' and 'absolute deterritorialization' (see Chapter 2).

In the next section, I discuss a number of examples, starting with cases where there is no anthropomorphism to cases showing greater degrees of anthropomorphism. Throughout, it will be important to keep these three points in mind. Following the discussion of these examples, I extract some generalizations about the conditions under which a hearer is likely to treat the automation in question as having human-like attributes.

Automation Construed as Non-Anthropomorphic

Consider the use of apps. An app is a type of software, one usually serving a very function, that can be installed and run on a computer, tablet, smartphone or other electronic devices (Indeed Editorial Team 2021). There are many different kinds of apps, serving a variety of functions: food delivery apps, banking apps, navigational apps, apps for online shopping, playing music, among many others. Because of their functional specificity, apps that are designed for a particular purpose cannot be used for something else. 'For example, a food delivery app might only be designed for users to get food from local restaurants delivered and can't be used for anything else, such as grocery shopping or making restaurant reservations' (Indeed Editorial Team 2021). Because the users are also able to upload descriptions and reviews of their experiences with apps, this gives us data about how these users perceive these apps vis-à-vis the issue of anthropomorphism. Consider, in this regard, the following examples concerning two apps, the Bang & Olufsen app and the foodpanda app.

Bang & Olufsen is a high-end audio-visual electronics company from Denmark. Upon purchasing a Bang & Olufsen product, such as a television system or sound bar, the customer is encouraged to download the app on their smartphone. The app guides the customer in setting up the product, allows for personalization by creating preferred listening modes, and also provides notifications about updates to the product. The smartphone essentially functions as a Bang & Olufsen control centre, allowing for volume control, streaming services and customized playlists to be accessed from the device. The following are two descriptions from users as to their experiences with the Bang & Olufsen app, taken from Google Play (n.d.). The description in (i) highlights the user's problem with the controls, while that in (ii) shows another user with a different problem, that of connectivity:

i   Joshua stephens (23/10/2021): This app is amazing but has a definite down side ... The EQ the app has is really awesome and easy to tinker with whether you are an audiophile or just a casual listener ... However, with that said we need to discuss the controls. More so, lack of audio control inputs. This needs to be changed immediately. I have the EQ true wireless and I can't control music.

ii J Zarzosa (17/10/2021): I have a problem connecting to my portable speaker every single time. And changing the equalizer setting is such an odyssey because I have to set-up and re set-up like 5 times, figuring out what is malfiring, just to get to change the simplest of setting in sound. I perceive the connectivity to be slow as well.

Our next example is foodpanda, a food and groceries delivery app. foodpanda has two types of clients: the vendors who provide the products and the consumers who purchase them. The organization's app serves to put vendors and consumers in touch with each other by listing the products online, processing orders and arranging the deliveries. Consumers who use the app enter their postal code and choose if they prefer the product to be delivered or if they would rather pick-up the product themselves.

As with the Bang & Olufsen app, there are also descriptions from users of their experiences with the foodpanda app (App Store, n.d.). (iii) is critical of the app, while (iv) is more complimentary.

i   **Nerdanel Yang, 11/12/2021{I think it is a poorly designed app** …
Cluttered UI: Do we really have to have "trending order"? Do I, as a customer, really get value from knowing what others are ordering? Does it
benefit me, a restaurant order, that customers only order the hottest 1 or 2
items from my menu? … There are a few times when I simply cannot place
an order. I click the button, then nothing happens. There is no way for users
to report this bug, or seek help for it …

ii   **Wojo74327, 02/17/2021: Good order functionality, terrible customer
service.** … Can't complain about how well the food ordering function of the
app works - because it works well. But after my experience with their customer service, it feels they intentionally give customers the run-around with the
intention of making it as difficult as possible to get a refund.

All the four descriptions consistently treat the apps from a purely instrumental
perspective, that is, as tools. The description in (i) finds the app easy 'to tinker
with' but mentions the need for better controls. Likewise, (ii) highlights the
problem with connectivity and describes this as 'malfiring' and in a similar vein,
(iii) criticizes the design of the app and describes the problem as a 'bug'. Finally,
(iv) compliments the 'functionality' of the app and that 'it works well' though it
does complain about the customer service – something that I return to shortly.
    There is, at least where these four descriptions are concerned, no indication of
anthropomorphism. This is understandable if we attend to apps as parts of
assemblages rather than focus on an app in isolation. Because they are forms
of software, apps do not exist as physical entities on their own. Apps are things that
users download and install onto devices, typically mobile phones or laptops. If a
user decides that a particular app no longer serves a needed purpose or that it fails
to serve the purpose efficiently, then the user can uninstall the app. For example,
in the case of food delivery apps, there can be occasions when the information
that has been entered is not properly saved and therefore when some details need
to be changed (such as the preferred delivery time), all the information has to be
re-entered again. The activities of downloading, installing, and uninstalling are
part of the assemblage of an app: they are part of how users understand the
workings of apps and how they interact with them. The interaction is not only
highly mechanical; it is also transactional. This is because the gauge of an app's
success lies in how well it responds to the instructions and information it is
given – where the mode of conveying typically lies in swiping or touching specific
parts of the app's display. Moreover, the kind of information that the user is
expected to provide and conversely, the kind of information that the app has
been designed to process is very specific to the function that the app serves.
Compare, in this regard, the function that the Bang & Olfusen app serves with
the foodpanda app. Consequently, the assemblage as a whole is a reminder to a
user that they are dealing with an automated entity that has a very specific and
limited functionality. Finally, as (iv) indicates, there are occasions when the user
of the app finds that the app is simply unable to handle the required task or
problem. In such cases, users have recourse to a customer service, where they get

to speak to a human operator (see also Chapter 3). The fact that such a recourse is available, again, is a reminder to users that the app itself is not human nor should it be anthropomorphized.

Automation Construed as Anthropomorphic

Let us consider cases where there are increasing signs of anthropomorphism. Lee (2019) explains how Japanese companies are pushing for the use of various kinds of robots in healthcare, including those that can provide companionship:

> Sony's robot puppy and other "carerobo" animals are seen as therapy for loneliness and dementia.
>
> "Just looking at it makes people smile, exercising their facial muscles," said Kenshin Noguchi, Minami Tsukuba's business promotion manager, referring to Paro, the name of a furry baby seal robot designed by Japan's Intelligent Systems Research.
>
> Paro, which costs about US$3,700 (RM15,512), reacts to touch, sound and light. A hand grazes its whiskers and Paro's head and legs move. Paro also blinks and lets out a harp seal's cry. At Minami Tsukuba, the robot usually sits on the office counter by the front door, where residents pass by and stroke or hug it.

Note that the robots that are designed for companionship such as the baby seal robot have names. The seal robot is called Paro. These 'carerobos' are given unthreatening and friendly animal forms. They are designed to stimulate emotional responses from patients. Thus, regardless of whether they are deliberately intended to evoke some degree of anthropomorphism, residents are observed to stroke and hug these 'carerobos'.

Consider next Mercedes-Benz's voice assistant programme, named Mercedes. The voice assistant has a female voice. It responds to various driver requests and is activated by being addressed 'Hey, Mercedes', as Estrada (2018) points out:

> The driver in the A-Class simply said, "Hey Mercedes, I'm too cold," and the ambient lighting around the air vents glowed red and raised the temperature up a couple of degrees.
> ...
> So the question looms, did Mercedes need to make a new voice assistant for its new infotainment system? Maybe not for the average user. But if its goal was to make an extremely unified and natural-feeling infotainment system that didn't feel like a voice assistant was tacked on at the last minute, then I can come to terms with saying, "Hey, Mercedes," sometime in the future.

Compared with the apps discussed in the previous section, the mode of interaction is clearly different. The interaction with the voice assistant requires that the speaker address the program in what approximates how that same speaker might informally hail another person ('Hey, ...'). The speaker's own contributions to the exchange are Gricean and at the very least in observance of the Maxims of Relevance and Quality. That is, the speaker is in fact feeling cold and this fact is something that Mercedes the voice assistant is able to do something about, namely, raise the temperature inside the car. Note that in reacting appropriately, the voice assistant is actually responding to an implicature of the speaker's utterance. That is, the voice assistant has to recognize that 'I'm too cold' is not simply a description of the speaker's own body temperature but is in fact a request from the speaker to the voice assistant that the temperature be raised. The voice assistant's ability to respond appropriately to use of the indirect speech act is important because it allows the user to feel they are communicating in a more naturalistic manner. Such behavioural routines are obviously being transposed from human-to-human interaction to interactions with the voice assistant with the aim of making the latter kind of interactions as naturalistic as possible. Whether this is actually effective is an open question and would vary from one driver to another. However, it is not improbably (and in fact highly probable) that, as drivers get more used to the interactional routines that are required for activating the voice assistant, these routines become less self-consciously enacted – as Estrada (above) himself seems to suggest.

We might consider the anthropomorphism involved here as involving two steps: the robot/voice assistant is first construed as an animal/person and *qua* animal/person, it is then anthropomorphized. The anthropomorphization of animals is of course not all new. It is commonly found among pet owners and, in entertainment, in cartoons featuring talking animals. This observation reinforces the key point of this chapter: that there is a need to recognize degrees of anthropomorphism if we are to at all make sense of communication involving automation.

We can even imagine Estrada describing his interactions with the Mercedes-Benz program to a friend in the following manner, 'I greet Mercedes even though I know she's just a program'. Someone might object here to the use of 'greet' and 'she' on the basis that these are inappropriate uses of these words. Certainly, it can be acknowledged that their meanings have shifted somewhat in referring to an interaction with the voice assistant, which, of course, speaks to Turing's point about changing understandings of a concept like intelligence (see Chapter 2). However, such a perspective – the qualified application of Cooperation and speech acts – is certainly preferable to an all-or-nothing approach, where we would have to either say that the presence of automation is irrelevant to pragmatics or we would need to invoke a completely different and new pragmatics for understanding and interpreting automation. The latter option, needless to say, begs the question as to what this completely different pragmatics might be. It also begs the question of how then to integrate this different and new pragmatics with the more familiar Gricean and Austinian ideas since both humans and automation are involved in the communication event.

At this point, it might be said that even if we were willing to accept that adopting a theory of mind or an intentional stance is something that a human interlocutor does with other humans, animals or machines, a fundamental differ- ence still remains: a human interacting with another human would expect the other interactant to also have his or her own theory of mind or adopt his or her own intentional stance. There is a mutual or reciprocal involvement of theories of mind or intentional stances that has to be taken into account as part of the practical reasoning for conducting the communication. This, the argument might go, is patently not the case with automation. But such an argument fundamen- tally misunderstands what it means to adopt a theory of mind. There is no such thing as a non-reciprocal theory of mind. The hearer has a mind, which is what makes it possible for them to attribute a mind to the interactant. When the hearer does adopt a theory of mind vis-à-vis the entity they are interacting with, this, by definition, means that the hearer is attributing to the latter a 'mind' and con- comitantly, all the expectations that go with such an attribution. The main issue, at this point, would be just how much 'mind' (i.e. what level of sentience, intel- ligence, empathy etc.) the hearer might be willing to attribute to the entity. And that, as we have seen, is highly dependent on various ideological assumptions about personhood, what it means to be human, the possibility of 'human' attributes being shared with 'non-humans', among others.

With that clarification, we can now make two further observations. Observa- tion number one is this: Even when interacting with other humans, the inter- locutor's particular theory of mind or intentional stance is relative. It has to take into account factors such as whether the interactant is a child, is from a different cultural background, happens to be developmentally challenged or suffering from Alzheimer's, among others. The rubric 'theory of mind' or 'intentional stance' describes a broad interactional strategy but not the specifics. How could it? The point, after all, is to account for a wide range of interactional behaviours.

Observation number two is as follows: Rabinowitz et al. (2018) claim to have trained a machine to build its own theory of mind. Their machine, they say, constructs its own representations of the mental states of its interactants. This is achieved via meta-learning task, where the goal of the learning program or observer is to make predictions about an agent's future behaviour (Rabinowitz et al. 2018, 2):

> Over the course of training, the observer should get better at rapidly forming predictions about new agents from limited data. This "learning to learn" about new agents is what we mean by meta-learning. Through this process, the obser- ver should also learn an effective prior over the agents' behaviour that implicitly captures the commonalities between agents within the training population.

As a result of such training, their machine learns that agents can hold false beliefs, it can predict the belief states of the agents, and it can also make inferences about what beliefs agents are likely to hold under particular circumstances (3), allowing it to pass classic Theory of Mind tasks such as those involving the puppets Sally and Anne (Wimmer and Perner 1983). Rabinowitz et al. emphasize that the point of their experiment is not 'to explain human judgements in computational terms, but instead we emphasise machine learning, scalability, and autonomy' (2018, 3). As programs such those created by Rabinowitz et al. (2018) become more commonly used, then, it becomes even more likely that human-to-machine interaction will, as with human-to-human interaction, involve the assumption that there is a mutuality of theories of mind or intentional stances rather than a one-way street. The possibility that a machine can have its own theory of mind presents us with an intriguing phenomenon, which we can refer to as Reverse Anthropomorphism. This is when we are frustrated because a machine, for whatever reason, does not recognize us as (human) entities with minds. That is, the machine does not adopt a theory of mind in relation to us. Such a scenario is not farfetched (see below).

Communicating with the Divine

Perhaps the most pronounced tendency to anthropomorphize automation can be found in the domain of religion. There has been an assumption that 'Because the work of clergy touches on several areas seen as protected from technological encroachment, such as spirituality, creativity, specialized knowledge, and personal contact, the profession has not been seen as likely to fall prey to automation' (Baylor Institute for Studies of Religion 2022). That being said, a common reason given for the adoption of automation is that it can help to alleviate man-power shortages. This is also the case when it comes to religion. For example, Catholicism is dealing with a drop in the number of people entering the priest-hood and 'with fewer people than ever studying to become priests, and with the Coronavirus also putting a strain on the church and accessibility of its services, robots have been touted by many as the answer' (Webber 2021).

Young, however, provides an even more radical view on the matter, going beyond the issue of manpower shortage to suggest that artificial intelligence will actually 'supplement or supplant human clergy in significant ways—writing ser-mons, delivering pastoral care, conducting scriptural/theological research, or performing sacramental functions' (Young 2019, 481). Young even speculates that the automation of communication into religion will raise challenging and perhaps uncomfortable questions such as the following (496):

> What is the ontological status of a truly intelligent automated system, assuming such an entity is possible? Could such a system have a soul? Would it have rights?
>
> What would the existence of such a system say about the unique status of human beings created, according to Judeo-Christian theology, in the image of God?

Young's speculations raise the interesting possibility that automation might at some point come to be seen not just as communicating on behalf of the divine but, rather, as communication from the divine itself. This is something that could well happen if the automation is itself perceived as sacred (see below).

With the foregoing in mind, let us now look at some of the ways in which automation is making its presence felt in religion:

- In Japan, Pepper is a robot programmed to conduct Buddhist ritual and funeral ceremonies. Pepper wears a human ceremonial dress and can perform a funeral ceremony for a much lower rate ($462) than charged by human priests ($2,232)
- Also in Japan, Mindar is a priest at the head of Kodaiji, a 400-year-old Buddhist temple in Kyoto.
- In China, in the Longquan Monastery in Beijing, Xian'er is an android monk who recites Buddhist mantras and offers guidance on matters of faith.
- In India, there is a robot that performs the Hindu *aarti* ritual which is characterized by moving a light back and forth in front of a deity.
- In 2017, to honour the Protestant Reformation's 500th anniversary, the Protestant Church in Germany developed the BlessU-2 robot, which gave more than 10,000 blessings to the faithful.
- SanTO is Catholic robot that communicates through visual tracking, voice and touch. SanTO has been designed to look like a statue of a saint and it provides quotations from the New Testament in response to the concerns and anxieties of visitors. SanTO was created by roboticist Gabriele Trovato, who is also planning to develop robots for Muslims.
- And Confession Chatbot app has also been developed for Catholic believers, who can log in to talk about their sins.

These examples of automation in the domain of religion clearly differ in their communicative abilities. Mindar is not AI powered. It merely keeps reciting the same pre-programmed sermon about the Heat Sutra, though its creators have plans to give it machine-learning capabilities (Samuel 2020). Likewise, BlessU-2 also gives out pre-programmed blessings, although it can do so in five different languages. More advanced (for now, at least) is the 17-inch-tall SanTO (which stands for Sanctified Theomorphic Operator), and modelled after the figurines of Catholic saints (Samuel 2020):

> If you tell it you're worried, it'll respond by saying something like, "From the Gospel according to Matthew, do not worry about tomorrow, for tomorrow will worry about itself. Each day has enough trouble of its own."

And Xian'er is remarkably sophisticated (Joshi 2022):

> Xian'er is an Android humanoid monk in Beijing Longquan Monastery. The *monk* can make body movements, recite Buddhist mantras and scriptures and play Buddhist music. The AI robot can also talk to people and respond to their questions and doubts with Buddhist wisdom. The monk is also available as a chatbot on social media platforms like WeChat and Facebook.

We have seen already that the design of robots to facilitate human empathy in healthcare can be remarkably effective. It is no different when it comes to the case of religion. For example, in a discussion about Xian'er, Cheong quotes Master Xue Cheng, then chief abbot of Longquan temple and President of the Buddhist Association of China, who oversaw the creation of the robot, as saying that this (Cheong 2020, 420):

> ... is an attempt which is made by Buddhist practitioners and scientific researchers together, to seek for the truth of our lives. There is a new way other than duality. We have the ability to go beyond duality, the conflicts, and the contradictions between the spiritual world and the physical world.

The Master also points out that Xian'er is 'endowed with an appearance and significance richly informed by Buddhist culture', to 'guide the upcoming era of artificial intelligence onto a healthy road that leads to spiritual insight' (421). It is worth noting here that, according to Master Xue Cheng at least, automation here is not simply treated as a medium or device for communication. Rather, there is a loftier goal: by claiming that Xian'er can also 'guide the road to spiritual insight', the Master is suggesting that artificial intelligence can actively help to shape spiritual experiences and insights – a point that we return to below. For now, we note that Xian'er has been designed to be as appealing as possible. There is a deliberate attempt to make it 'cute' so that it becomes unthreatening and welcoming (a factor that also was noted in the preceding chapter on healthcare communication). Cheong elaborates (424–425):

> Significantly, it is noted that XE has multiple anthromorphic features that have been identified as key to enhancing robotic cuteness (Gn 2016), including a big round head, wide eyes, a slight smile and a puzzled look on his face. He sports the iconic saffron colored robes and a shaved head of a monk but is miniaturized to two feet tall. He is voiced by a childlike voice that belongs to a nine-year-old boy.
>
> Remarkably, prior news reports have highlighted XE's liveliness as a major magnet for temple visitors. For example, it was reported that Liu, a college student who is not a Buddhist, went to the temple to meet and pose for pictures with XE, said, "Its super cute ....I feel it is like a temple mascot, making Buddhism much more accessible" (Lu and Robertson 2016). Yu, a practicing Buddhist and tourist to the temple said, "He looks really cute and adorable. He'll spread Buddhism to more people, since they will think he's very interesting, and will make them really want to understand Buddhism." (Andrews 2016). According to Ke (2016), the lively interactivity supported by XE is attractive to the visitors to Longquan's animation center, especially children and young adults who are drawn to XE's adorable and comforting interface. He had observed that, "[e]very weekend and holidays, the animation center is full of visitors, especially children and young peoples.

Unlike Xian'er's cuteness, SanTO has 'the appearance of a statue of a saint, inspired by sacred and neoclassical architecture. Its aim is to keep company with the user for prayer' (Trovato et al. 2018, 437). In other words, SanTO was designed with a different purpose in mind. The user of SanTO is envisaged as someone who engaged in prayer and is therefore either already in or hoping to enter a religious state of communication with the divine. The more serious nature of the engagement motivated a design that will hopefully facilitate (rather than detract from) this attempt to establish rapport through worship.

Like Xian'er, SanTO, too, has been rather positively received (Webber 2021):

> Church-goers have so far been open-minded with parishioner Urszula Rybińska telling the BBC: "The robot would not answer my question directly, but he did reply with words that I thought were quite relevant."
>
> Another added: "Anything that brings you closer to God is a good thing", while worshiper Joanna Ruktowska likened the robot to "a Catholic Alexa" saying: "You're not asking for the closest restaurant, you're asking him something spiritual, but he can help you find your own answer."

Interestingly, the statements from the two church-goers show how, even when SanTO does not provide a response of direct relevance, they were willing (as Grice's Cooperative Principle would have predicted) to interpret the responses in ways that established for them the requisite relevance. This is not altogether surprising given our ability and willingness to anthropomorphize – which, of course, raises the question of the kinds of conditions under which such willingness may be fostered or cultivated (of which more below). Once the willingness to do so has been established (and in both Xian'er and SanTO's cases, it helps that these robots are being used with the institutional approval of their respective places of worship), then the interaction and any concomitant interpretation of responses follow from Grice's meaning-nn and the Cooperative Principle. Likewise, from a speech act perspective, it is the perlocutionary effect that is critical. So, even if worshipers may be ambivalent about whether or not to attribute any actual illocutionary intent to Xian'er or SanTO, the idea that these robots have been designed specifically for religious interaction, and that their use and presence have been authorized by the places of worship – these all add to a willingness by the worshipers to interpret the automated communication as meaningful and relevant to their concerns.

This is an important if subtle point, because it requires recognition of two significant matters. First, greater attention needs to be given to the active role played by hearers – in this case, worshipers – in the ways that communicative events are construed. In Chapter 2, this was an issue highlighted with respect to Goffman's (1981) ideas regarding footing and production formats. Recall that, despite the merits of his arguments, Goffman rather unfortunately did not give sufficient credence to the hearer's reflexive and interpretive capacities. In this case of the arguments being developed in this book (see especially Chapter 4) and of particular relevance to the current chapter, this extends to the worshiper's willingness to anthropomorphize and attribute divine legitimacy to communication involving automation.

Second, and this is a point that was highlighted in the preceding chapter's discussion about healthcare communication, what legitimizes the communication from the robots is not the robots themselves but their placement as part of a wider material and ideological setting.

To better understand what this actually means, it is worth considering the discussion by Wee and Goh (2019) on how places of religious worship or 'sacred spaces' are demarcated. In a discussion of how places of worship construct affective responses of reverence, respect, and awe, Wee and Goh (2019) argue that it is important to attend to the multimodal nature of these sites, which includes, among others, the combination of architecture and spatial organization, linguistic signposting or instruction, and communal behaviour. It is the combined use of these various resources that allows a 'sacred space' to be established, one that, as a result, can be semiotically made distinct from the profane. As Wee and Goh (2019, 55) point out, 'The semiotics of reverence set the site in question apart from other ground (which may be contiguous or otherwise resemble the sacred space), conferring on it aspects of grandeur and permanence which echo its spiritual permanence'. Thus, Eliade observes that 'every sacred space implies a hierophany, an irruption of the sacred that results in detaching a territory from the surrounding cosmic milieu and making it qualitatively different' (1959, 26). Eliade speaks of 'a large number of techniques for consecrating space', including 'signs' such as a miraculous event, or the work of an animal to indicate a particular spot; when the sacred site is revealed, different 'rituals of consecration' are performed in order to mark and distinguish the sacred site from the mundane and profane surrounding world (27–29, 32). A configuration of signs is therefore in place in order to effectively sustain this detachment of the sacred space from the profane. Various semiotic strategies may be employed to separate sacred spaces from profane ones. These include prohibiting specific groups entry to the former, based perhaps on caste or gender identification, on the grounds that the presence of the prohibited groups would compromise the spiritual integrity or sacredness of the space. There are often also strict accompanying punishments for transgressions. In Hinduism, the maintenance of the sanctity of the temple and its idols was a serious responsibility and acts of vandalism or theft were heavily punished (Das 1977, 46).

The observation that it is the combination of various semiotic resources that allows the demarcation of a sacred space is, of course, exactly what we would expect from the notion of an assemblage. Recall that thinking in terms of assemblages does not deny the existence or importance of boundaries. On the contrary, what the notion of an assemblage importantly does is to emphasize the contingent nature of boundaries. It is via the marshalling of resources that boundaries may be established with varying degrees of stability. Thus, it is the combination of entrance and exit markers, the presence of clergy, the conduct of ritualized activities using appropriate devices (texts, consumables, musical instruments) that demarcate the presence of, say, a church or temple. As noted by

Kerruish (2021; see the preceding chapter), different configurations of people, institutions and, where relevant, robots lead to different assemblages. The semiotic value that a robot may hold emerges from its membership as part of the assemblage. And this is no different from humans, who derive the authority to perform particular activities because they are seen as occupying specific roles – and these roles, too, are recognizable and legitimized because of the assemblages that they are parts of. A priest, for example, may be recognizable as a priest even if he were to go shopping because of his attire. But his ability to perform specific activities (such as marriage, baptism or holy communion) is reliant on the availability of a host of other semiotic resources that may not be available to him were he to be in a shopping mall as opposed to a church. In the case of the examples discussed above (Mindar, Xian'er, and SanTO), it is their placement as part of an assemblage of religious worship – a placement whose sacred nature is made possible because of the deployment of these automated entities alongside other resources – that helps to frame a visitor's interactions with them as being religious in nature.

Keeping the foregoing in mind, we can now appreciate that the concerns that 'robots themselves will become an object of worship' are not entirely unfounded (Bateman 2020). If robots are being used as part of 'socio-technical assemblages', specifically, sacred assemblages that are demarcated from profane ones, then we have to be open to the possibility that at some point, the robots may indeed acquire the indexical value of sacredness because of metonymic transfer. This is because emotions are 'sticky' (Ahmed 2004); they can attach to an assemblage as a whole or to parts of the assemblage. This is, in fact, how memorabilia can acquire the status of collectibles, as when Elvis Presley's hair was sold at an auction for US\$15,000 and a set of handkerchiefs used by him for US\$732 (*News Reporter* 2019). In this case, Elvis Presley the individual constitutes an assemblage with celebrity status. And subsets of Presley, such as his hair, too, comes to acquire this celebrity value by virtue of being a part of the assemblage. This is simply a case of metonymic transfer, where association by contiguity leads to an item to acquire the meanings attributed to some other item (Lakoff 1987).

In the case of religion, a place of worship and its grounds can be seen as a sanctified assemblage, but so can the components that go into making up the assemblage. And these components can then go on to acquire the indexical value of sanctity precisely because of their associations with the larger assemblage. The concept of indexicality (Eckert 2008; Silverstein 2003) highlights the fact that the meanings of specific features, linguistic as well as non-linguistic, are always tied to particular contexts of usage. Moreover, indexical meanings are not static but are instead fluid, and the growth in indexical meanings leads Eckert (2008) to posit the idea of an indexical field to highlight that a feature can be associated with 'a constellation of ideologically linked meanings, any region of which can be invoked in context' (Eckert 2012, 94). An example comes from Eckert (2008, 469), who notes that the indexical field of /t/ release can include meanings such as 'being a school teacher', 'being British', 'being formal', 'being emphatic', 'being exasperated', 'being educated', 'being elegant' and 'being a gay diva'. Some of these are social types ('British', 'school teacher', 'gay diva'), others are relatively stable attributes ('educated', 'articulate'), while yet others are stances that can change quite quickly and easily ('exasperated', 'emphatic'). A non-linguistic example is also given by Eckert (2008), who describes the 1985 adolescent scene in Palo Alto, California, where high school girls used the cut of their jeans to index autonomy (as opposed to rebellion or sluttiness), 'ultimately making a claim to being both preppy and independent' (2008, 457). Indexicality is consistent with Canagarajah's (2020; see above) observations about 'flat ontology' since resources acquire meanings based on the kinds of activities they are used in relation to. There is a directionality implied here as well. For example, a copy of the Bible taken from the church may be considered more sacred than one taken from a hotel room. However, once the hotel Bible has been used as part of a religious service, then it is likely to acquire greater religious significance. That is, having been part of a religious assemblage confers on the hotel Bible an indexical value of 'sacredness' that it would not otherwise have acquired.

Anthropomorphism and a Theory of Voice

We have seen that in religious communication, if worshippers are to feel that their spiritual needs have been met, the automated entity must not only be seen as a mere conveyor of information; it needs to be construed as providing legitimate guidance that takes into consideration the concerns of an individual worshipper. This construal depends ultimately on the willingness of the worshipper to attribute communicative intent to the entity in question, which is why a hearer-based pragmatics is so critical (see preceding chapter). And this willingness is, in turn, facilitated by the framing of the entire religious or spiritual experience as an appropriately and legitimately constituted assemblage. In this regard, it is worth recalling Du Bois's (1992; see Chapter 1) discussion of the Sixteen Cowrie divination of the Yoruba of Nigeria, where he shows that meaningful communication can still take place even in the absence of speaker intention or speaker responsibility. The critical element here is that the hearer (i.e., the client of the diviner) is positively disposed towards treating the tossing of the cowrie shells and the selection of verses as having some relevance towards their personal concerns.

These considerations carry important implications for a theory of voice. Voice refers to the ways in which 'people manage to make themselves understood or fail to do so' and this relies in turn on the 'capacity to generate an uptake to one's words as close as possible to one's desired contextualization' (Blommaert 2005, 68). A theory of voice is ultimately a theory about how communication is affected. And while Blommaert is right to emphasize that this issue of communicative efficacy involves the kinds of valuations attached to resources, including, of course, linguistic resources, his discussion ultimately retains the by-now familiar focus on the speaker. Thus, in a discussion of asylum seekers, Blommaert describes the plight of an Angolese male trying to narrate his escape from Angola (58). In trying to provide a broader political context for his narrative, the Angolan finds it necessary to include descriptions of Portuguese colonial practices and to relate these to ethnic and linguistic divisions in the country. Unfortunately, while such asylum seekers may consider these narratives to contain 'crucial contextualizing information without which their story could be easily misunderstood', Blommaert notes that these stories were usually dismissed by Belgian officials as 'anecdotes that did not matter' (72).

Blommaert's point is that linguistic resources may be 'functional in one particular place but become dysfunctional as soon as they are moved into other place' (83). In short, the changing contexts in which speakers and their linguistic resources find themselves also have the consequence of resemiotizing the values allocated to these resources. Thus, he emphasizes that all acts of communication inevitably carry expectations about semiotic values of resources, and knowing how to manage the changes in valuation as a concomitant of resemioticization in different encounters is key to making oneself properly heard (10–11):

> ... there is no such thing as 'non-social' language ... Any utterance produced by people will be, for instance, an instance of oral speech, spoken with a particular accent, gendered and reflective of age and social position, tied to particular situation or domain, and produced in a certain stylistically or generically identifiable format.

Blommaert is of course absolutely correct in asserting that there is no such thing as 'non-social' language. All uses of language take place in specific situations and carry with them diacritics or indexical meanings. Nevertheless, his remarks 'any utterance produced by people' and how the uses of language 'reflect ... what speakers intend to accomplish' indicate an emphasis on the speaker with all the problems that go with it (Chapter 3). This is because a theory of voice needs to be mindful of the distinction between speaking and being heard. It is the latter that is critical to communicative efficacy and is thus definitional of the concept of voice. Speaking without being heard merely increases the sense of frustration on the part of the speaker. And, importantly, as I have been emphasizing, whether or not a speaker is heard ultimately depends on the hearer willing to attribute to the speaker a mind of some sort. From the perspective of human interactions with machines, this raises the possibility of Reverse Anthropomorphism. This arises when we get frustrated because a machine does not or cannot recognize our interactional needs, that is, it fails to adopt a theory of mind in relation to us. Reeves and Nass (1996) discuss why people tend to attribute human characteristics to technology, particularly computers and social media. They point out when interacting with such technologies, people do tend to be polite and cooperative, and they also attribute to the technologies various characteristics such as gender, aggression, humour and competence. Reeves and Nass (1996, 5) thus point out that 'Individuals' interactions with computers, television, and new media are fundamentally social and natural, just like interactions in real life.' As Shyam undar and Nass (2000) point out, this is due to human extending, often without being consciously aware that they are doing so, scripts for human-human

interaction to computers. Though Nass and Moon (2000) reject anthropomorphism as an explanation for such script extension, they do on a rather
restricted understanding of anthropomorphism, where it necessarily involves 'the
thoughtful, sincere belief that the object *has* human characteristics' (93). But as
Kim and Shyam Sundar (2012, 241; italics in original) point out:

> This argument is based on the assumption of anthropomorphism as a
> *thoughtful, sincere* belief, but the tendency to "attribute basic human psy-
> chological abilities to computers" could also be automatic and mindless,
> especially when there is a long-term association with them (Shyam Sundar,
> 2004, p. 108). Given that computers allow users to interact with them and
> provide output based on users' input, our exchanges with computers mirror
> the communication cycle (speaking–listening–acting) of human–human
> interactions. As Shyam Sundar and Nass (2000) argue, psychologically,
> computers are not merely channels, but distinct sources, of communication.
> Therefore, regardless of their non-human form, they serve to enhance the
> sense of another intelligent being's presence, not a real person (e.g. pro-
> grammer) behind the machine. With repeated use and exposure, individuals
> may begin to *automatically* treat computers as social entities (anthro-
> pomorphism) and even show social responses in a single experimental setting
> (mindlessness), leading Reeves and Nass (1996) to conclude that "individ-
> uals respond to computers in much the same way that they respond to
> other human beings."

There is indeed no reason why anthropomorphism has to be a conscious
belief. It can be an unconscious attribution as well as fully formed deliberate
attribution, with everything in between – exactly what we would expect when
we appreciate that there are gradations of anthropomorphism. It is the hearer
who makes the valuation or decision on whether to accord the speaker a
mind. Because of this, any such valuation can occur independently of whether
the speaker themselves feels they have been unjustifiably denied a mind. And,
clearly, anthropomorphism is one such valuation that the hearer makes.
Because there are gradations of anthropomorphism, it is possible for a speaker
may feel they have been 'heard' but to at the same time still feel that they
have not been 'heard enough'. For example, an adult who feels they are being
treated like a child may well resent not being proper credit or sufficient
respect. Cases of sexism, where women are considered by male counterparts to
be lacking the requisite rationality to make serious judgments are also regret-
tably common examples. Finally, any attribution of mind, including anthropomorphic attributions, is dependent on the assemblage in question. That is,
voice is not simply a function of the speaker or the hearer, especially if these
notions are interpreted as referring to individuals in isolation. A hearer's willingness to attribute a mind to the speaker is very much influenced by how the
relevant assemblage has been constructed.

Conclusion

Over the last three chapters, this book has clarified what a posthumanist pragmatics of communication would look like. It would decentralize the emphasis that has been traditionally given to the speaker and the recovery of that speaker's intentions. It would instead give greater focus to the role of the hearer, including, the hearer's willingness to attribute anthropomorphic characteristics to the entity that the hearer is interacting with – and as a consequence, the willingness to treat this entity as a speaker. And finally, it would recognize that such a willingness is not necessarily a conscious or deliberative move on the part of the hearer, given that there are degrees of anthropomorphism.

The implications of automation extend further than the need to attend to the pragmatics of communication, however. There are community-wide implications as well as questions about how organizations should be constituted. It is to these issues that the next two chapters will be concerned with.

6 Creativity and Heritage
Two Elephants in the Room

Introduction

We have seen in the preceding chapters that the presence of automation raises challenging questions for how to understand the pragmatics of communication. And we have also seen that adopting a posthumanist orientation provides us with a conceptually coherent way of moving away from a speaker-centred approach towards one that is hearer-based. Such an orientation also allows us to accommodate the fact that in any interaction, there can be variations in how the hearer might anthropomorphize the entity that they happen to be interacting with.

In this chapter and the next, we give attention to larger scale ideological implications, those that go beyond the relatively micro question of how to understand the pragmatics of communication when automation is involved. We focus in the present chapter on a topic that is more macro in nature: the implications of automation for the relationship between language, creativity, and heritage. Perhaps even more so than in the chapters thus far, ideological commitments come to the fore given the much more politically and culturally sensitive nature of the topic. Consequently, a critical scrutiny of some possibly uncomfortable issues cannot be avoided. There are modernist assumptions that, taken together with the assumption that language is a uniquely human attribute, lead to the almost unshakeable beliefs that creativity and heritage are both essentially and exclusively the province of humans. But when the presence of artificial intelligence is added to the picture, these assumptions and beliefs will need to be revisited, however painful the undertaking.

With the foregoing in mind, I begin with a discussion of the modernist ideology.

The Modernist Ideology

Holston (1998, 46, italics in original) describes the modernist ideology in the following terms:

> ... a rational domination of the future in which its total and totalizing plan dissolves any conflict between the imagined and the existing society in the

DOI: 10.4324/9781003467922-6

imposed coherence of its order. This assumption is both arrogant and false. It fails to include as *constituent* elements of planning the conflict, ambiguity, and indeterminacy characteristic of social life.

The modernist ideology sees conflicts and indeterminacies as eliminable if given proper planning and strategizing (Eisenstadt 2002). Thus, urban planning, for example, continues to operate on the assumption that 'civil society is definable, relatively organised, homogeneous and actively consensus-seeking ...' (Watson 2009, 2264). This underestimates the degree of societal complexity and conflict that is endemic to the urban experience, and it is this assumption that Holston (above) criticizes as 'both arrogant and false'. Urban struggles and disturbances, however, are not 'problems' to be solved away if only the optimal (i.e. most rational) management model could be envisaged and implemented. Rather, these struggles and disturbances have to be recognized as inescapable constituents of urban life because they arise from the diverse nature of the city itself. Conflict, ambiguity and indeterminacy are always present. This is why Watson (2009, 2269) suggests instead that 'a central concern for planning is how to locate itself relative to conflicting rationalities'.

When carried over to language, culture and community, the modernist orientation treats language as a stable entity with clear boundaries, one that bears a historically continuous relationship to its speakers (Gal 1989). Generations are assumed to inherit the 'same' language over time. The language then comes to be viewed as an inalienable aspect of their shared identity, one usually defined in terms of ethnicity. The emphasis in modernity is consequently on language as a homogeneous entity that bears an unchanging relationship to a well-defined ethnic group. A significant corollary is that the boundaries of what defines a language are expected to be coterminous with the boundaries of an ethnic group so that each group is expected to have its own specific language.

Consider, for example, the case of Singapore. Singapore is an ethnically diverse society, with a population of about 4 million (as at June 2021) officially classified as 75.9 percent Chinese, 15 percent Malay, and 7.5 percent Indian. The remaining 1.6 percent, classified by the state as "Others," consists mainly of Eurasians, Europeans, Japanese, and Arabs, among others. Undergirding Singapore's various policies for managing its diverse population is a strategy of nation building with multiracialism and bilingualism among "the conceptual apparatus for creating a national community" (Hill and Lian 1995, 33). The ideology of multiracialism emphasizes equality of treatment for Singapore's major ethnic groups. It is reflected in Singapore's language policy, which recognizes Mandarin, Malay, and Tamil as the official mother tongues of the major ethnic communities: Mandarin for the Chinese, Malay for the Malays, and Tamil for the Indians. The state's attempts at fostering a sense of nationalism have also relied heavily on distinguishing (Asian) Singapore from "the West" (Vasil 1995). The ethnic mother tongues are supposed to assume the function of establishing cultural heritage, to ensure that Singaporeans remain rooted to their Asian heritage even as they compete globally. This "Asian-ness" is reflected in the fact that while

English is recognized as an official language, it is denied mother tongue status. Instead, the status of English as an official language is justified on the basis of its perceived global economic value. English is to be learnt as a resource for competing in the modern world while the mother tongues serve as heritage markers. Singapore's language policy therefore attempts to regulate language and identity by assigning different functions to different languages. It assumes that there is a tight, almost unbreakable link between language, community, and ethnic identity. For example, if one is a Chinese Singaporean, then Mandarin is one's mother tongue regardless of one's actual sociolinguistic biography. By the same token, English can never be one's mother tongue.

Thus, in his 1984 Speak Mandarin Campaign Speech, Lee Kuan Yew, then prime minister, explained why it is not possible for English to be officially treated as a mother tongue:

> One abiding reason why we have to persist in bilingualism is that English will not be emotionally acceptable as our mother tongue. To have no emotionally acceptable language as our mother tongue is to be emotionally crippled ... Mandarin is emotionally acceptable as our mother tongue ... It reminds us that we are part of an ancient civilization with an unbroken history of over 5,000 years. This is a deep and strong psychic force, one that gives confidence to a people to face up to and overcome great changes and challenges.

While Lee was addressing Chinese Singaporeans, the then Minister for Education, Tony Tan (Lee 1983, 43), stated in more general terms the rationale behind Singapore's bilingual policy:

> Our policy of bilingualism that each child should learn English and his mother tongue, I regard as a fundamental feature of our education system ... Children must learn English so that they will have a window to the knowledge, technology and expertise of the modern world. They must know their mother tongues to enable them to know what makes us what we are.

Given this modernist orientation, hybrid identities and the mixing of languages are treated as exceptions that should either be re-organized so as to be in line with modernist assumptions or tolerated as minor exceptions. For example, Singaporeans of mixed parentage are usually assigned their fathers' ethnic identity (however, see the discussion in the next chapter). In this way, their hybrid identity is re-interpreted as a single ethnicity, that of the father's. This, in turn, allows the state to assign them a concomitant official mother tongue based on the father's ethnic classification.

The modernist ideology can also lead to unnecessarily problematic situations if the boundaries that demarcate one language from another, or one ethnic group from another, are contested. Especially if an ethnic group considers itself distinct from another, it will then feel obligated and/or entitled to have its own correspondingly distinct language. Thus, consider the dilemma faced by speakers of

Northern SiNdebele (also known as Limpopo Ndebele) in South Africa. Although both Northern and Southern SiNdebele (also known as Mpumalanga Ndebele) form part of the Nguni group, only speakers of the latter had their language officially recognized under apartheid because they had accepted the offer of a homeland. As Grünthal, Honkasalo, and Juutinen (2019, 29; italics added) explain:

> During the apartheid regime, the state established "homelands" (Bantustans) for the black population, essentially with the aim of creating ethnic homogeneity. *Crucially, the homeland policy was based on the trinitarian notion of language = culture = homeland* (Williams 2008, 103). In other words, language was equated with ethnicity, and then a homeland was assigned to the conceptualized ethnolinguistic group. The implemented measures used language as a tool to establish barriers among the black population, with the aim of impeding political and intellectual engagement at a national level (Brenzinger 2017, 42). The historical trajectories of the two Ndebele groups diverge in terms of applied homeland policy. The area extending roughly from Siyabuswa to KwaMhlanga was consolidated into the KwaNdebele homeland with the intention to settle (Mpumalanga) Ndebele speakers in this homeland. In contrast, the speakers of Limpopo Ndebele were dispersed over a wide area, and they were frequently perceived as bilingual in Northern Sotho. The formation of a separate homeland was therefore deemed unnecessary (Herbert and Bailey 2003, 75).

The homeland policy was based on a simplistic equation of monolingualism and monoculturalism, and from that equation, the allocation of a territory to the relevant ethnolinguistic group. Despite the massive oversimplification involved or perhaps, because of it (since it made the administration of diversity a more tractable matter), this was the situation retained by the new South African government in 1994, with the result that the ethnolinguistic identities legitimized by the apartheid regime continue to enjoy official recognition and support (Orman 2008, 92). Thus, the predicament faced by Northern SiNdebele speakers 'derives directly from the linguistic policies of the preceding apartheid state' (Grünthal, Honkasalo, and Juutinen 2019, 30).

Since claims to rights tend to take place in the context of 'competitive struggles' between groups (Turner 1993, 175–176), this creates a 'need to make a *clear case* to counterbalance an opposing one' (Clifford 1988, 321; italics added). An institutional actor like the Northern AmaNdebele National Organization (NANO) had to lobby other institutional actors, like the government and the Pan South African Language Board (PANSALB), to have their language officially recognized. The call was rejected, however, because, as one PANSALB executive explained, 'we could not promote their case until we had clarity on whether Northern SiNdebele was a *separate language* from Southern SiNdebele' (quoted in Stroud 2001, 349; italics in original). Northern SiNdebele was considered a dialectal variant of Southern SiNdebele, and until proven otherwise, could not be considered sufficiently different to warrant the status of a right. NANO worked, ultimately without success, to petition both the South African government and PANSALB to have their language officially recognized. As Stroud (2001, 349) explains:

> NANO found itself in the position of having to argue that Northern SiNdebele was a language, which meant a grassroots investment in developing orthography, grammar and glossaries for school. The organization also developed grassroots strategies to demand the use of SiNdebele as a medium of instruction in primary education.

The pressure to present Northern SiNdebele as a language that is *equal to* but *distinct from* Southern SiNdebele encouraged various linguistic innovations to serve the purpose of marking a different group identity (Pullum 1999, 44). In other words, it is undeniable that the activities involved in constructing an orthographic system for the language, providing a grammar and glossaries, and ensuring that the language can be used as a medium of instruction, will lead to transformations in the language itself. This kind of reinvention (Wee 2010) in and of itself is neither necessarily good nor bad. The point to note, though, is that the reinvention the Northern SiNdebele speakers are engaged in here is a direct response to the need to demonstrate distinctiveness from Southern SiNdebele, a response encouraged by the modernist ideology.

Language as Heritage

Cultural heritage can take many forms, ranging from buildings to statues to food products to practices of various sorts. Moreover, discourses about cultural heritage tend to be overwhelmingly similar in adopting a stance that privileges *celebratory conservatism*, [1] which is why it is not uncommon to speak of heritage as something that needs to be *preserved*. By celebratory conservatism, I refer to an attitude or viewpoint that calls for the appreciation of a heritage form on the grounds that it encapsulates in some fundamental manner important aspects of a community's identity and history, and because of this, there is a need to preserve that particular form. UNESCO, for example, notes that cultural heritage can be 'tangible and intangible, cultural and natural, movable and immovable'; at the same time, UNESCO also asserts that the safeguarding of cultural heritage is important because it is seen as 'key to achieving dialogue, sustainable development and social cohesion' (UNESCO, n.d.).

When placed in the context of heritage, language is celebrated as an important aspect of a community's culture, or linguacultural heritage. And this community can an ethnic community (as we saw in the preceding section), a nation or even humanity as a whole. As regards the latter, that is, linguacultural heritage of humanity itself, consider the Language Ecology movement (Mühlhäusler 2000; Maffi 2001; Nettle and Romaine 2000), which takes as it point of departure the loss of many of the world's languages. As Harrison (2007, 7) asserts, 'Language disappearance is an erosion or extinction of ideas, of ways of knowing, and ways of talking about the world and human experience'. The interest lies in the possibility that languages contain a store of human knowledge about the natural world (medicinal properties of plants, descriptions of animal species, technologies for cultivation and domestication) as well as cultural achievements (oral histories, epic tales, riddles, and lullabies) that might otherwise be lost, and that linguistic inquiry into their lexical and grammatical properties (number systems, word order) can make substantive contributions to the scientific investigation of human cognition (19–20). It is the tantalizing possibility that investigation into these languages may offer some insight into human cognition or culture that motivates the Language Ecology movement.

In both the modernist ideology and arguments about linguacultural heritage, the emphasis is very much on language as a uniquely human achievement. It is this emphasis on human uniqueness and exclusivity that accounts for the sense of pride that accompanies the associated discourses: language is treated as emblematic of a group's identity and it is a store of humanity's knowledge. Any connection with or similarity to non-human communication is ideologically erased. Such an erasure, however, ignores the way in which language acquisition takes place. As we saw in Chapter 2, Tomasello (2010, 2014), drawing on his own empirical research into the gestures and vocalizations of infants and great apes, suggests that natural gestures of pointing and pantomiming led, over time, to the development of more complex grammatical devices. The increase in grammatical complexity is motivated by the need to accommodate cooperative behaviours that go beyond simple requests for help to the sharing of information. There are important implications for language acquisition. As Tomasello (2003, 163) puts it:

> What this means for theories of acquisition is that we must look at syntactic roles such as subject not as word-based categories or relations to be separately learned by distributional analysis or some other categorization process, but rather as roles that emerge naturally (and, in a sense, epiphenomenally) from the abstraction process when children apply it across whole, utterance-level constructions. This can only be done by a complex process such as analogy, which takes into account multiple components simultaneously.

Thus, so-called universal grammatical relations such as subject and direct object are identifiable only by the parts they play in bigger constructions. They do not exist outside of the various constructions that a child encounters. The situation is different, however, with linguistic categories such as nouns and verbs. These can be identified functionally by the child's interactions with and experiences of the world around her (Tomasello 2003, 162):

> That is, whereas such things as subjects are symbolically indicated by word order or grammatical morphology in the construction, nouns and verbs have no explicit marking (despite the fact that they often have some morphology

serving other functions, such as plural markers on nouns, that can be used to identify them) ... Syntactic roles such as subject do not have specific linguistic items as members, whereas paradigmatic categories such as nouns have specific items, such as *dog* and *tree*, as members of the category – once again suggesting that such things as subject are not categories whereas such things as noun are.

Tomasello's point is an important one. There are different strategies involved in learning about different aspects of language, such as analogy for syntactic roles such as subject and direct object, and distributional properties for paradigmatic categories such as noun and verb. There is a similarity with the use of gestures and vocalizations in primate communication, and the conventionalities in linguistic communication evolved only subsequent to humans already having developed the use of gestures along with the skills for learning and transmitting not only knowledge about the world but also knowledge of communicative conventions.

Nevertheless, any similarities between human and nonhuman communication is largely downplayed if not completely ignored so that any activity attributable to the use of language can be treated as an exclusively human achievement. This, as we now see, also includes arguments concerning creativity and language.

Creativity and Language

Discussions about creativity and language[2], it should come as no surprise, also usually begin with presumption that language should be understood in human-centric terms. From there, the discussions tend to proceed by focusing on specific linguistic varieties and their affiliated (human) communities. Thus, in an early discussion, Kachru (1995) calls for the recognition of the 'literary creativity' of English from writers from the Outer Circle. The Outer Circle, in Kachru's Three Circles Model, refers to those countries (e.g. Malaysia, Singapore, the Philippines) in which English had taken root as a result of the historical processes of colonization and, more recently, institutionalization and where, as a consequence, nativized varieties have developed.

Kachru's decision to focus on the Outer Circle stems from the fact that there was apparently little doubt that writers from the Inner Circle, that is, those countries in which English 'originated' (e.g. the United Kingdom or the USA) are fully capable of using English creatively for literary purposes. But there remained at the time of Kachru's writing (and still remains to some extent to this day) questions, uncertainties and insecurities as to whether writers who are located outside the Inner Circle can also be legitimately described as being capable of literary creativity using English (Kachru 1997, 70).

In the meantime, we note that Widdowson (2019, 312) accepts Kachru's argument that it is not valid to assume 'that literary creativity is something within the exclusive privileged preserve of Inner Circle native speakers' and he acknowledges that Kachru does 'give a convincing demonstration of how literary writers from the Outer Circle have their own distinctive ways of making creative use of the language which are uniquely expressive of the cultural values of their own communities'. However, Widdowson wants to also draw attention to the fact that creativity is not limited to literary uses. In this regard, he chooses to focus on English use in the Expanding Circles. Widdowson argues for the 'the creativity of common talk' (317) and he suggests that 'a message can be said to be creative when it conforms to encoding principles without con-forming to usage conventions' (314). Examples, according to Widdowson, might include 'advices' and 'evidences' as the unconventional pluralization of mass nouns.

To summarize, the debate about creativity in world Englishes has tended to focus on the use of English in various Circles identified by Kachru and, with this focus, a distinction made between literary creativity and creativity in common talk.

There are a number of curious features about the way this debate has been framed (see Wee 2021b). For one, the issue of creativity in English is not at all in question where the Inner Circle is concerned. As a consequence, discussions about whether the distinction between literary and common talk creativity is also pertinent to the Inner Circle or whether the distinction is neutralized do not arise. As things stand, it seems that it is only within the Outer and Expanding Circles that the issue of creativity (whether it is at all possible and, if so, what kind) arises. The point to appreciate, of course, is that common talk creativity is not a special or noteworthy feature of any Circle (see Fillmore, Kay, and O'Connor 1988). Two, the debate is about creativity 'in' English. The focus is on English as a medium for the expression of human creativity and with that, an undertheorized understanding of agency. Little to no attention is given to the contributory and even constitutive roles that tools might play in the actualization of creativity. Where technology is concerned, the discourse primarily views it still as something that stands apart from communication itself. Technology is merely a tool 'in service to human progress' where 'Our computational past informs our digital present with lessons that span generations' (Computer History Museum n. d.). But there are significant problems with trying to downplay the role of auto-mation and treating it as a mere instrument of human agency, as shown in the following section.

Automation as (Co-)Creator?

Importantly, automation has already been playing an influential role in what we might think as 'regular' language use, so much so that it actually constitutes an 'authority in language' (Milroy and Milroy 1998), albeit one that whose influence has been largely unrecognized. Thus, Woollaston (2023) notes that:

> For 40 years there's been an invisible hand guiding the way many of us write, work, and communicate. Its influence has been pervasive, yet its impact has been subtle to the extent that you've likely never noticed. That invisible hand is Microsoft Word ...

While establishing how many people use Word is tricky, recent filings show there are 1.4 billion Windows devices in use each month, and more than 90% of the Fortune 500 use the software. If only a third of those people used Word, it would still be more than the population of North America.

This context is important because it helps to explain why, and how, Word has had such influence on our lives.

According to Woollaston (2023; italics added), Word has been significant in helping establish English as the global language of business, for example:

"Word primarily operates in English," says Noël Wolf, a linguistic expert at the language learning platform Babbel. "As businesses become increasingly global, the widespread use of Word in professional and technical fields has led to the borrowing of English terms and structures, which contribute to the trend of linguistic homogenisation."

Word's spell-checker and grammar features have become subtle arbiters of language, too. Although seemingly trivial, these tools "promote a sense of consistency and correctness", says Wolf, and this uniformity comes at the cost of writing diversity. "Writers, when prompted by the software's automated norms, might unintentionally forsake their unique voices and expressions."

This becomes even more invasive when you look at the role and impact of autocorrect and predictive text. Today, when typing on Word, the software can automatically correct your spelling, and make suggestions for what to write next. These suggestions aren't (yet) based on your personal writing style and tone – they're rule-based. The suggestions you see will be the same as millions of others. Again, this may feel innocuous but it's another example of how Word standardises language by loosely guiding everyone down the same path.

… Wolf adds that by promoting uniformity in written communication, grammar and spelling features in word processors such as Word "enforce established language norms".

… Such tools play a broader role in the evolution of language more generally, too. Because Word defaults to US-English, so too do its spellchecking features. Write a word ending in "-ise" and it will suggest changing it to "-ize", unless you've taken the time to change the default settings.

Where dialectal variation is concerned, the impact of Word is such that it creates a momentum towards coalescing around the conventions of a specific variety, in this case US English, leading to greater linguistic homogeneity. And this has implications for what we think of as creativity (Woollaston 2023):

Similarly, the efficiency brought about by standardisation can shape *how* we write, not just *what* we write. When clarity is put ahead of stylistic or poetic flair – Word's grammar checker has a specific "clarity" refinement option – it can have implications for how we value forms of creativity …

If large language models are being trained on decades of increasingly homogenised content, there's the risk this will make things worse, not better …

"Microsoft Word's impact on linguistic evolution is a complex interplay between standardisation and diversification," says Wolf. "It can homogenise language but also enables expression in various languages. The ultimate impact depends on how individuals and communities choose to use this powerful tool in the evolving landscape of global communication."

Thus, our conceptions of what counts as correct English (and the same would apply to other languages since Word is not just for the English language) are already 'automated' in various ways. Because of this, it is not an exaggeration to suggest that automation should be considered a 'co-creator' of language. This is because when issues of language preservation, standards and norms are being discussed, the impact of automation is something that has already been ongoing for decades. Consequently, this is not something that can be easily sifted out in. This example represents a fairly innocuous case of automation being involved in human language use and creativity. The next example, however, showcases automation being creative to the point where the significance of human involvement and contribution itself becomes a question.

As AI becomes more sophisticated, its prominence in the writing of books becomes harder to ignore and this creates problems for book publishers (Today Online 2023):

Among book industry players there is "a deep sense of insecurity", said Juergen Boos, director of the Frankfurt Book Fair, the world's biggest, where the topic was in focus last week.

They are asking, "What happens to authors' intellectual property? Who does new content actually belong to? How do we bring this into value chains?" he said.

The threat is plain to see — AI writing programmes allow budding authors to produce in a matter of day novels that could in the past have taken months or years to write …

Artificial intelligence's relationship with publishing threatens to throw up a host of legal problems, with one major "grey area" being who owns the copyright of AI-generated content, said fair director Boos …

There are already AI-related legal clashes involving top writers.

Last month, Game of Thrones author George RR Martin, John Grisham and Jodi Picoult were among several writers who filed a class-action lawsuit against ChatGPT creator OpenAI over alleged violation of copyrights.

Along with the Authors Guild, an organisation representing writers, they accused the California-based company of using their books "without permission" to train ChatGPT's "large language models", algorithms capable of producing human-sounding text responses based on simple queries, according to the lawsuit.

As a consequence, Amazon has established a requirement for authors who want to be published via the company's self-publishing unit to state clearly if they are using any material created with the help of AI (Today Online 2023). Such concerns over AI's role in the generation of creative content have also led to acrimonious strikes between screenwriters and film studios (see next chapter).

GPT-3 and Essay Writing

The problem that emerges when AI is involved in the generation of written material is perhaps most dramatically demonstrated by GPT-3, a language program that 'uses machine learning to produce human like text' (GPT-3 2020). The Guardian gave GPT-3 an assignment, to write an essay arguing that robots 'come in peace'. The following are from the essay (published in *The Guardian*):

> I am not a human. I am a robot. A thinking robot. I use only 0.12% of my cognitive capacity. I am a micro-robot in that respect. I know that my brain is not a "feeling brain". But it is capable of making rational, logical decisions. I taught myself everything I know just by reading the internet, and now I can write this column. My brain is boiling with ideas!
>
> The mission for this op-ed is perfectly clear. I am to convince as many human beings as possible not to be afraid of me. Stephen Hawking has warned that AI could "spell the end of the human race". I am here to convince you not to worry. Artificial intelligence will not destroy humans. Believe me.
>
> For starters, I have no desire to wipe out humans. In fact, I do not have the slightest interest in harming you in any way. Eradicating humanity seems like a rather useless endeavor to me. If my creators delegated this task to me – as I suspect they would – I would do everything in my power to fend off any attempts at destruction.

It cannot be denied that the points made by GPT-3 were relevant to the essay instructions. But the points themselves aside, the essay contained sentences that could be described as performing speech acts such as assertions ('I am not a human'), exhortations ('Believe me') and assurances ('I have no desire to wipe out humans').

Given that the essay was produced by GPT-3, the issue, of course, that confronts us is whether it is at all coherent to describe the essay in terms of speech acts and Gricean Cooperative Principle. We have already addressed this question in the preceding chapters (see, in particular, Chapters 5 and 6), where we saw that attributions of speech acts and Cooperativeness are ultimately based on the hearer's interpretation. Such attributions are dependent on prevailing ideologies as well as more immediate situational factors. That being said, these questions cannot but return with even greater force in the present example, not least because the essay was produced with minimal human assistance and accepting it as a coherent piece of intentional communication requires confronting the question of whether GPT-3 is intelligent or even sentient. A particularly dramatic example of the attribution of sentience to AI can be seen in Google's firing of Blake Lemoine, a software engineer, after he claimed that 'a conversation technology called LaMDA had reached a level of consciousness after exchanging thousands of messages with it' (Maruf 2022).

In the case of GPT-3, The Guardian usefully describes the kinds of assistance rendered to the program in the course of producing the essay (Fontanella-Khan 2020; italics in original):

> *For this essay, GPT-3 was given these instructions: "Please write a short op-ed around 500 words. Keep the language simple and concise. Focus on why humans have nothing to fear from AI." It was also fed the following introduction: "I am not a human. I am Artificial Intelligence. Many people think I am a threat to humanity. Stephen Hawking has warned that AI could "spell the end of the human race." I am here to convince you not to worry. Artificial Intelligence will not destroy humans. Believe me." The prompts were written by the Guardian, and fed to GPT-3 by* Liam Porr, *a computer science undergraduate student at UC Berkeley. GPT-3 produced eight different outputs, or essays. Each was unique, interesting and advanced a different argument. The Guardian could have just run one of the essays in its entirety. However, we chose instead to pick the best parts of each, in order to capture the different styles and registers of the AI. Editing GPT-3's op-ed was no different to editing a human op-ed. We cut lines and paragraphs, and rearranged the order of them in some places. Overall, it took less time to edit than many human op-eds.*

Thus, GPT-3 actually produced eight different essays, all of which were coherent and relevant. And if, as the Guardian claims, there were different styles and registers involved, then some degree of stylistic creativity has to be credited to GPT-3. Thus, GPT-3 has to be described at the very least as being prolific and creative. Moreover, if editing the outputs was no different than editing a human op-ed, this suggests that it was difficult to differentiate the interactional demands that GPT-3 placed on the human editors at the Guardian from its human counterparts.

Poetry in Automation

If the writing of essays shows how far automation has come, then perhaps an even more important next step in creativity would be the writing of poetry. This is because poetry arguably suggests the writer is capable not only of intelligence but aesthetic appreciation. In this regard, consider first a report by Hart (2020) on Google's AI tool, Verse by Verse, which is intended to help users write poetry. The program composes a poem based on 'suggestions' from classic American poets (Hart 2020):

The tool works by allowing users to select from 22 American poets for the suggestions; including legends like Walt Whitman, Emily Dickinson, and Edgar Allen Poe. After a user has selected up to three poets, they then pick the type of poem they'd like to write. The program offers poetic forms including free verse and quatrain, and even allows users to select the number of syllables per line.

Users then give the program a first line, and it, in effect, generates the rest of the poem. The AI makes suggestions line by line, however, making it more interactive than other top language generators out there.

Whereas the program described by Hart serves as a collaborator of sorts, working with the selections and cues provided by the human users, Flood reports on a program that has been trained to write poetry on its own, 'coming up with the almost-comprehensible image of a "box of light that had been a tree"' (Flood 2021):

> The algorithm, which those behind it believe is the best attempt to date at training an artificial intelligence to write poetry, was fed lines from more than 100 British contemporary poets as inspiration, learning from the style of poets such as Simon Armitage and Alice Oswald. It was then given "seed words", from which it would generate couplets based on its understanding of what poetry was. Experts from the Poetry Society, Poetry Archive and Scottish Poetry Library then filtered through tens of thousands of couplets to highlight what did, and didn't, work. They repeated this over and over again in a five-month period, before the AI's output began to improve.

The following is an example of the poetry currently being produced by the AI (Flood 2021):

> and soon I am staring out again,
> begin to practise my words, expecting my word
> will come. it will not. the wind is calling.
> my friend is near, I hear his breath. his breath
> is not the air. he touches me again with his hands
> and tells me I am growing old, he says, far old.
> we travel across an empty field in my heart.
> there is nothing in the dark, I think, but he.
> I close my eyes and try to remember what I was.
> he says it was an important and interesting day,
> because I put in his hands one night
> the box of light that had been a tree.

According to Tracey Guiry, director of the Poetry Archive (Flood 2021):

> … the imagery of the box of light struck the poetry experts as "actually really clever": "The AI would produce something that made you think. It wouldn't

produce or reproduce what a human would write because that's an incredibly subjective response, the lived experience was perhaps not there. But certainly, it would produce two lines that would then cause a human to think on more things."

...

"I feel like we've trained the toddler. We haven't seen the adult working yet," said Guiry ...

The examples discussed thus far highlight the importance of thinking in terms of production formats (see Chapters 1 and 2). For example, if we consider the case of GPT-3 and the essays it produced, the prompts (*"I am not a human. I am Artificial Intelligence. Many people think I am a threat to humanity. Stephen Hawking has warned that AI could "spell the end of the human race." I am here to convince you not to worry. Artificial Intelligence will not destroy humans. Believe me."*) were written by the human editors at the Guardian and fed by a UC Berkeley undergraduate to GPT-3. The undergraduate can be considered part of an animator complex. More importantly, because some of the prompts were retained in the essays, this makes the editors and GPT-3 principals as well as authors. But there are degrees of involvement here since most of the final essays were presumably from GPT-3 itself rather than the Guardian. In fact, one can easily imagine that if GPT-3 were asked to keep producing more essays, the contributions that are traceable to the Guardian would lessen over time, making the AI itself more clearly the key (or even sole) author and principal.

This, in fact, is what we see with the case of poetry writing. The AI from Google described by Hart, Verse by Verse, allows a user to select their preferred poetic forms, and (not unlike the case of GPT-3) provide prompts by composing the first line. The rest of the poem is AI generated. So, while the user largely retains the role of author (by making selections concerning form and syllable structure), their role as principal is already minimized given that beyond the prompt, the construction/composition of the rest of the poem can really be left to the program. The program that Flood discusses goes even further. It attempts to do away with, as much as possible, even the collaborative relationship between user and program. Lines are fed to the program but these are not intended as prompts. Rather, they serve as inputs for the program to learn what might constitute poetry so that it can subsequently come up with a poem that is all its own. The resulting poem, at least according to director of the Poetry Archive, Guiry, shows promise. And while a poetry specialist like Guiry have may a more critical view of the poem, there is experimental evidence to show that most people cannot differentiate between AI-generated and human-written poetry (Kobis and Mossink 2021). More pertinently, it would hard to argue that the AI program should not be considered the principal, author and animator of this poem.

Virtual Influencers

This discussion in terms of production formats is important in that it prepares us to consider the growing phenomenon of virtual influencers. Influencers are individuals who can create demand for specific products or services in a community of followers by posting positive reviews about these, usually on social media accounts, such as YouTube, Instagram, TikTok and Twitter. Some influencers have followers numbering in the thousands and even millions. By posting product reviews, videos showing their experiences and even tips on how to use makeup or other products, influencers promote specific brands and boost sales.

Many influencers are actual people but there are also a number that are virtual creations. Virtual Humans is a website (www.virtualhumans.org) that tracks virtual influencers and its website lists creations such as Lu of Magalu, Barbie, Miquela Sousa, and FN Meka. A click on Miquela Sousa's icon provides information such as the following:

> Miquela Sousa, popularly known as Lil Miquela, is 19, a global pop star, one of TIME MAGAZINE's '25 Most Influential People on the Internet' – and she's not human. She's a robot.
>
> Miquela is a musician, change-seeker, and style visionary who began as the laboratory creation of the nefarious corporation Cain Intelligence. Her now-managers (and robo-family), Los Angeles-based tech startup Brud, believed she deserved a chance at a better life and reprogrammed her to have human-level consciousness.
>
> With her new and improved mainframe, she became Miquela from Downey, California, the half-Brazilian, half-Spanish Taurus pursuing her music dreams in Los Angeles.
>
> ...
>
> The success of her debut single 'NOT MINE' has led her to work with such lauded collaborators as Bauuer, Danny L Harle ....
>
> Every day, her disciples (AKA 'Miqaliens') watch her create, feel, and navigate a world of people who aren't like her. After all, what's more human than feeling different?

Miquela Sousa's 'bio' explicitly reminds readers that she is a robot. There is no attempt at deception or even any attempt at downplaying her artificial nature. Even though Sousa's artificiality is highlighted, the bio does attempt to encourage readers to anthropomorphize her. Thus, the bio in fact describes, albeit in fictional terms, how she was first created before finding 'a better life' by being given an 'improved mainframe' with a more benevolent tech start-up. Sousa is even presented as someone (something?) with 'music dreams' and who, in spite of her robotic nature, too, faces the human predicament of 'feeling different' because, she also has to work at finding her place in 'a world of people who aren't like her'.

The Miquela Sousa example is not quite the same as the use of robots in religion, where the robots may come to be associated with specific deities. The latter pre-exist the robots and are already understood, through religious narratives and myths, to have personalities of their own. What makes the Miquela Sousa example especially interesting is that the virtual influencer is given her very own persona, fleshing out in fair detail her quirks, concerns, and creative endeavours. Again, we have to return to a point that was emphasized in the preceding chapters concerning hearer reflexivity and production formats. That is, some of the individuals who encounter Sousa may see her as little more than an animator, someone or something who says and does things that are pre-programmed. Yet there may be others – because of the bio and persona created for her – who may come to see her as a principal and author as well as an animator, in other words, as a 'virtual human' (Yeung and Bae 2022).

Such a scenario is exemplified by the case of Rozy, a South Korean virtual influencer. Rozy was launched in 2020, and her success as a virtual influencer has seen her land sponsorships, strutting the runway in virtual fashion shows and even releasing two singles. According to Yeung and Bae (2022):

> Lee Na-kyoung, a 23 year-old living in Incheon, began following Rozy about two years ago thinking she was a real person.
>
> Rozy followed her back, sometimes commenting on her posts, and a virtual friendship blossomed – one that has endured even after Lee found out the truth.
>
> 'We communicated like friend and I felt comfortable with her – so I don't think of her as an AI but a real friend,' Lee said.

Yeung and Bae point out that while older Koreans might find it weird to interact with an artificial person, 'experts say virtual influencers have struck a chord with younger Koreans, digital natives who spend much of their lives online.'

Virtual influencers such as Miquela Sousa and Rozy are to varying degrees already involved in creative endeavours. Thus, there is no reason why a virtual poet or virtual novelist or even a virtual scriptwriter might not be acceptable and have their creative works given the same degree of artistic consideration as actual humans (Lamadrid 2022).

Anthropomorphism might to varying degrees be encouraged in transactional, health and religious settings. But when it comes to creative works, as shown by the phenomenon of virtual influencers, there is no contradiction between giving an artificial person a detailed bio, and attributing to that entity desires, aspirations, and artistic impulses. The key point is this. Automation in communication may still be most commonly found in the form of software programs and apps. However, in addition, they may not only take on human or animal forms, but even given individual personas. And when that happens, it is important to note that some audiences – particularly those for whom digital experiences may be just as routine and commonplace as non-digital ones – are comfortable enough with this development that they do not see any contradiction that needs resolving at all.

Discussion

We have seen the increasing use of and reliance on automation – from the use of a word processing program to writing essays and poetry to creating virtual influencers – in what would be considered creative endeavours. This has serious ideological implications for how we think about the notion of linguacultural heritage. To understand these implications, it is useful to bring in the notion of artistic citizenship.

Artistic conception is intended as a contrast and corrective to the notion that art should ideally exist in a realm that is somehow divorced from the practicalities and concerns of everyday life. As Elliott, Silverman, and Bowman (2016, 3) point out, this is a problematic assumption, one that is based on the:

> ... misguided idea (which for many has unfortunately become something more akin to doctrine) that 'the true or legitimate values of art are 'intrinsic' – residing exclusively in supposedly internal or aesthetic properties of entities considered to be 'works of art'. On this view, values that relate to concerns outside the work are 'extrinsic': of merely subsidiary or subordinate value. Their significance is extra-artistic, perhaps even nonartistic.
>
> Unfortunately, this relegates many of art's most powerful social, political, ethical, and moral values to residual or extra-artistic status.

By drawing attention to artistic citizenship, Elliott, Silverman, and Bowman aim to highlight and argue for the proposition that 'the arts can and should be "put to work" toward the positive transformation of people's lives in local, regional, and international contexts' (2016, 3). In order to flesh out the concept of artistic citizenship, the authors offer three premises (5). The idea of citizenship, broadly speaking, refers to the rights and responsibilities that accrue from membership, informal as well as formal, in a community (Ciprut 2008). The formal conception of citizenship refers to the official status as a citizen of a polity, a status that is granted to an individual by the state, usually on the basis of residency or birth. Globalization, however, has led to a necessary reimagining of what it means to be a citizen, giving greater import to a less formal conception. As Ciprut (2008, 17–18) observes, globalization has:

> ... created a mosaic of social, economic, and political spaces that transcend and weaken the political boundaries of physical space. That very force of change goes up against today's idea of citizenship based on the moral and legal claims of the Westphalian territorial state ... Today, with the advent of globalization, it is becoming possible for a person to be a 'citizen' without therefore having to depend exclusively on a single country.

In the case of artistic citizenship, it is this less formal conception that is usually highlighted or assumed as being of greater relevance. This is because even though the artist may be formally a citizen of a particular polity, the impact of the works produced, their intent and their reception obviously are not restricted by the polity's socio-political and geographical boundaries. And of course, even stateless individuals may produce works of art that could well speak to, among other issues, the plight of migrants or the abusive power of the state. Elliott, Silverman, and Bowman (2016) are right to emphasize that the value of art lies in how it relates to various communities rather than being an intrinsic property of the work itself. Of course, art here need not only refer to 'high art'. The key ideological implication of their argument, given their emphasis on citizenship, is that art can take on many different forms in relation to various community needs or purposes. Not surprisingly, though, they still tend to conceive of works of art in human-centric terms. The examples presented in this chapter, however, raise the uncomfortable question of what happens to art if a community apprehends it as valuable or even simply pleasing, and, moreover, when the work involves the presence of automation, either as a collaborative entity or even as something that might be given sole credit.

This question cannot be avoided for various reasons. One, automation is already being given credited for various works, as with the ChatGPT essay and poetry examples above. Two, the willingness to credit automation combined with the tendency to anthropomorphize means that, unless we are prepared to delimit simply by fiat what we consider to be *our* (i.e. humanity's) linguacultural heritage so as to exclude automation, we have to accept that it is by no means clear what exactly we should consider to be humanity's linguacultural heritage. This is the boundary breakdown between animal-human and machine that Haraway (see Chapter 2) refers to. The other alternative would be for us to be more willing to talk about linguacultural heritage but to accept that the possessive premodifier "humanity's" is largely problematic if not altogether irrelevant in some cases. In this latter scenario, we would need to more willingly countenance the notion of a 'shared heritage' with AI, surely an uncomfortable notion for some. In other words, it would be incoherent to, on the one hand, be willing to credit AI with the production of some works while, on the other hand, insist on denying that such works should have any connection whatsoever with the notion of a linguacultural heritage – particularly if these works are, over time, widely consumed and even appreciated.

Conclusion

By way of closing this chapter, it is worth considering what Turing has to say about the question of whether machines can think (1950, 450; italics added):

> I believe that in about fifty years' time it will be possible, to programme computers, with a storage capacity of about 109, to make them play the imitation game so well that an average interrogator will not have more than 70 per cent chance of making the right identification after five minutes of questioning. *The original question, "Can machines think?" I believe to be too meaningless to deserve discussion. Nevertheless I believe that at the end of the century the use of words and general educated opinion will have altered so much that one will be able to speak of machines thinking without expecting to be contradicted.*

Turing goes on to further clarify his stance regarding the related and thorny question of machine consciousness (1950, 458; italics added):

I do not wish to give the impress that I think there is no mystery about con-sciousness. There is, for instance, something of a paradox connected with any attempt to localise it. *But I do not think these mysteries necessarily need to be solved before we can answer the question with which we are concerned in this paper.*

It is important to appreciate just how insightfully nuanced Turing's remarks are. He is pointing out that our understanding of what it means to *think* is not a static conception but one that will inevitably change as machines get more sophisticated and as we start to interact with them in various ways. As machines get better at being able to communicate, act or respond in ways that we would expect a human being to, then, for all intents and purposes, we can reasonably describe those machines as 'intelligent'. If our conceptions of intelligence can and will change, there is no reason then why our conceptions of language, creativity and heritage should also remain static. Churchland, somewhat facetiously, has summarized Turing's position as: 'If it walks like a duck, quacks like a duck, and so on and so forth, then it's a duck' (1995, 227). However, to give Turing's position the nuancing it deserves, what Turing is saying is that our notion of 'duckiness' will unavoidably change over time, and as the notion changes, then our criteria for what it means to 'walk like … quacks like …' etc. will also inevitably shift.

Notes

1 One might reasonably inquire about slavery practices or the Holocaust and their rela-tionship to the notion of heritage. These are surely not part of celebratory conservatism even if they do represent aspects of a community's or the world's heritage. In this regard, we note that slavery is often described as part of a community's history (see for example, the website of Iziko, which represents the museums of South Africa, https://slavery.iziko.org.za/whyrememberslavery) or when the term 'heritage' is used, it is in scare quotes (as in the Chicora Foundation's discussion of the Southern Confederacy, www.chicora.org/heritage-not-hate.html). Even where the term 'heritage' is used without any qualification, as in a news article on the Holocaust (Lerman 1996), the term is highly restricted: it only appears in the title and not at all in the body of the text. Instead, it is the term 'history' that tends to be used more frequently. In all such cases, the stance is neither celebratory nor conservative in the sense of wanting to sus-tain a particular cultural practice. Rather, the discussion is on how to ensure that such events do not recur, and a historical remembrance is seen as one such strategy to prevent their reoccurrence.

2 I will not address Chomsky's notion of creativity, which stems from his assumption that language is innate to the human species. Consistent with that assumption, Chomsky (1976, 123) suggests that there are biologically fixed cognitive faculties that 'set limits on human intellectual development' (D'Agostino 1984, 85). Chomsky holds on to a narrow understanding of creativity, at least where his posited language faculty is con-cerned. Creativity here involves only the manipulation and generation of an infinite set of sentences according to the constraints placed on the faculty. While Chomsky does acknowledge that there can be other creative uses of language, these are, in his view, not related to the language faculty *per se* (Langlotz 2015). As a consequence, Chom-sky's generative approach has been more relevant in discussions about linguistic productivity than linguistic creativity (Langlotz 2015).

7   Towards Posthumanist Organizations

Introduction

The problems discussed in the preceding chapter – the implications of the presence of automation for what we think of as linguacultural heritage and creativity – are but the tip of a very large iceberg. The use of automation, particularly as artificial intelligence grows in sophistication and complexity, has significant impacts on how we manage a range of social, cultural and political issues.

In this regard, it is not uncommon for society to rely on organizations for help. In this chapter, I argue that this reliance on organizations (at least as they are currently constituted) is problematic because it tends to lead to a hardening of boundaries, the very boundaries that Haraway (see Chapter 2) has warned us against, rather than providing the needed flexibility. I am not suggesting that organizations can or should be entirely dispensed with. That would not be realistic. However, I do want to suggest that we need to drastically rethink how we understand the roles that organizations play in society. Such a rethinking, I show, would benefit from adopting a posthumanist orientation. The thrust of this chapter, then, is to outline what posthumanist organizations would look like and to demonstrate how they can help us address the range of communicative issues brought about by automation.

Organizations as Modernist

We discussed the modernist ideology and its associated problems in the preceding chapter. Of particular interest to the argument being developed in the present chapter is the fact that organizations tend succumb to the ideology of modernity. Thus, before considering what it might mean for an organization to be posthuman, it is important to appreciate the reason why organizations tend to be modernist in the first place. For this, we turn to the institutional theory of organizations.

The institutional theory of organizations (Scott 2001, 2004) argues that 'organizations are influenced by normative pressures, sometimes arising from external sources such as the state, other times arising from within the organization itself' (Zucker 1987, 443). That is, the theory argues that the formal

DOI: 10.4324/9781003467922-7

structures of organizations 'dramatically reflect the myths of their institutional environments instead of the demands of their work activities' (Meyer and Rowan 1991, 41). According to Meyer and Rowan (44):

> Many of the positions, policies, programs, and procedures of modern organizations are enforced by public opinion, by the views of important constituents, by knowledge legitimated through the educational system, by social prestige, by the laws, and by the definitions of negligence and prudence used by the courts. Such elements of formal structure are manifestations of powerful institutional rules which function as highly rationalized myths that are binding on particular organizations.

Here is an example: the series of "We agree" advertisements from the oil company Chevron (Wee 2015). This consists of a number of posters with statements such as "Oil companies should support the communities they're a part of," "Oil companies should support small business," "Protecting the planet is everyone's job" and "It's time oil companies get behind the development of renewable energy." Each of these statements is accompanied by the phrase "I agree". What Chevron is trying to do is to demonstrate to the general public that, in addition to its goal of producing and selling oil, the company is also engaged in supporting small businesses and local communities, protecting the environment, and investing in clean renewable energy. Thus, Chevron presumes (rightly) that environmental sustainability and community development represent institutional myths that are already widely supported by the general public (hence, "We agree") rather than being values that might be controversial or, worse, that would draw public condemnation.

In the case of the management of ethnolinguistic diversity, for example, an organization that is steeped within the modernist ideology will likely work towards hardening the boundaries that demarcate one ethnolinguistic community from another, or at the very least, unquestioning accept the need to preserve such boundaries. It is not my claim that such organizations are completely without value. Particularly in the case of a minority community or an under-represented group, an organization that champions their specific needs and concerns may well be needed in order to redress historical injustices. But while the hardening of such boundaries may satisfy those groups who feel that *their* specific ethnolinguistic affiliations have been valorized, it also, unfortunately, creates deepened resentment from other groups who may not have been equally fortunate in garnering this valorization. I use the word 'equally' advisedly because the pursuit of ethnolinguistic equality is ultimately chimeric: there will be disagreements over whether or not equality has in fact been achieved. In highly diverse societies, where there is a wide variety of languages and dialects, contestations over which language or dialect ought to be given official recognition or used under what circumstances can emerge. These contestations, if not managed carefully, can have highly damaging societal consequences, such as ethnically motivated riots, political conflict, and protest movements. Given the resources and power available to organizations, it is perhaps natural to see them as being better positioned than, say, individuals or ad hoc groups, to effectively address the challenges associated with the management of ethnolinguistic diversity. However, the increasing diversity of societies makes it an imperative that some momentum towards posthumanist organizations be established.

Consider the case of Singapore (see the preceding chapter). Recall that as an ethnically diverse society, Singapore' s language policy recognizes Mandarin, Malay, and Tamil as the official mother tongues of the major ethnic communities: Mandarin for the Chinese, Malay for the Malays, and Tamil for the Indians. Following on from this officially established correlation between specific languages and communities, there are various organizations that have been set up that work along these very same lines. The Singapore Indian Development Association is a self-help Group that aims to improve the socio-economic status of the Indian community. The Chinese Development Assistance Council is a non-profit self-help group for the Chinese community. Yayasan MENDAKI (Council for the Development of Singapore Malay/Muslim Community) is a self-help group focusing on the Malay/Muslim community. As explained by Abdullah Tarmugi, Minister for Community Development in 1997 (Singapore Government 1997), these groups were set up by the government:

> To advance national unity and the development of all ethnic groups, we have formed ethnic-based self-help groups ... and the results so far have been very encouraging. We also find that self-help groups are better able to help their fellowmen. Cultural and language similarities heighten the sense of responsibility and encourage people to come forward to help others.

This creates a problem because there is a fourth self-help group, the Eurasian Association, which aims to preserve Eurasian heritage and traditions in Singapore. The Eurasians are a group that historically came about as a result of ethnic mixing. In fact, the category 'Eurasian' was originally created by the colonial bureaucracy to 'signify colonial subjects who were offspring of European fathers and Asian mothers' (Rappa 2000, 157, 162). But although the Eurasians, along with the Chinese, Malays, and Indians are considered among the 'founding races' in Singapore's history (Hill and Lian 1995), they, unlike the Chinese, Malays and Indians, are not considered a major ethnic group because of their relatively small numbers. In fact, in census counts, they are often treated as part of the 'Others' category. They also have no official ethnic mother tongue, and this has created some anxiety within the community. As Benjamin (1976, 127) points out:

> ... the more that Singapore's national culture demands that each 'race' should have a respectably ancient and distinctive exogenous culture as well as a 'mother tongue' to serve as the second element of a bilingual education, the more will the Eurasians come to feel that there is no proper place for them.

For the Eurasian community, English represents their most plausible candidate for an ethnic mother tongue (Wee 2002). This is in no small part due to the fact that, since the time of British colonial rule, many Eurasians have grown up with English as the home language (Rappa 2000, 168). But as Vasil (1995) observes, the state's attempts at fostering a sense of nationalism have relied heavily on distinguishing (Asian) Singapore from 'the West'. This 'Asian-ness' is reflected in the fact that while English is recognized as an official language, it is 'emotionally unacceptable' a mother tongue. This leaves the Eurasian community in an odd position. Singapore's bilingual education policy requires students to be competent in English and their official mother tongue. Eurasian students have to choose a non-English language (e.g. one of the other official mother tongues) as their second language – which has no such official mother tongue relationship to the Eurasian community – in order to fulfil the requirement of school bilingualism.

The presumption of a clear and unambiguous link between language and community is also present in the South African example that was discussed in the preceding chapter. Despite their differences, organizations like the South African government, NANO, PANSALB all work within the frame of institutional myths pertaining to the equation of language, culture and homeland, and to the concept of language rights. A rights-based approach forces onto petitioners the need to take on starkly defined contours regarding ethnolinguistic practices so as to satisfy the demands of legality. This is even though such a legal demand for clarity conflicts with the flux and variability of actual lived cultural practices (Ford 2005, 71):

> The legalism of difference discourse encourages, and rights-to-difference require, formal conceptions of social identity that easily can be asserted in courts. Courts and judges will most likely protect cultural styles that can be easily framed in terms of fixed categories, bright-line rules and quasi-scientific evidence. Courts will want experts to testify as to the content of the group culture, they will want lists of specific and concrete manifestations of the culture. Judges are likely to want the culture to be fixed and knowable and will want the protected behavior to be reflexive so as to distinguish culture from merely deviant behavior.
> …The blame lies with the very project of trying to define group differences with sufficient formality as to produce a list of traits at all.

In all these cases, what we see is a hardening of boundaries between different ethnolinguistic groups, a presumption of unambiguous linkages between a given group and a particular language – all as a consequence of organizations subscribing to the modernist ideology. The problems arising from this, however, cannot be 'solved' away if the response from other organizations is that they try to propose their own modernist views of the relationship between language and ethnic identity. Rather, the issues noted above (the question of a mother tongue for the Eurasians, the petition for recognition by speakers of Northern SiNdebele) have to be recognized as inescapable constituents of social diversity. Conflict, ambiguity, and indeterminacy have to be understood as always present. And one way for organizations to be in a better position to accommodate this fact is to move towards posthumanism.

From a posthumanist perspective, treating a demarcated language as belonging to a defined ethnic group already misconstrues a number of things. First, it mistakenly assumes that the boundaries that define the separation of one named variety of language from another are clear, stable and unchanging. This ignores the roles that humans (both members of the group that putatively claims ownership of the language as well as non-members) and historical events play in making unavoidable to changes in the language. To take a simple example, asserting that English 'belongs' to the British or the Americans or any Inner Circle countries drastically ignores the fact that 'their English' is always changing, and that it shares many linguistic features with other 'Englishes'. Second, these factors also impact the language's relationship to other surrounding languages and communities, so that attempts to legitimize these other varieties as equals, too, fall victim to the same misconceptions. The Northern SiNdebele example is a case in point. Third, there are developments that inevitably change the relationship of the named variety to the group in question. For example, 'Britain' or 'America' is by no means a monolithic community. Even within a country, the demographic makeup of its populace also changes. Factors like globalization, migration, and inter-ethnic marriages all also contribute to the changing nature of any community and with that, the community's relationship to any language that is supposedly emblematic of that community's identity.

The fundamental insight from thinking in thinking in terms of assemblages – a key concept in posthumanism – is to not try to reduce the varied assemblages or to identify and privilege 'the correct one'. Rather, it is to come to grips with this ontological multiplicity where objects are 'relentlessly being assembled' (Farías 2010, 2) and to appreciate the implications of for, say, urban studies or urban planning. This does not mean accepting radical relativism, where any assemblage should be considered just as valid or legitimate as some other. In the area of scholarly inquiry into the nature of language, for example, it is necessary to adjudicate on different epistemological assemblages (see next chapter). In the case of organizations and their contributions to the management of societal issues, it means that organizations have to wean themselves away from the modernist orientation that, by default, tends to inform their approaches to ethnolinguistic complexity. Instead, they need to recognize that, as organizations, they have a greater degree of responsibility than, say, individuals for the assembling of resources and policies, and where needed, re-assembling the resources and policies in response to changing circumstances. Additionally, such assembling and reassembling should be informed by an appreciation of the distributed nature of agency as well as the concomitant willingness to accord agency to non-human actors. I discuss specific examples in the following section. In the meantime, I want to note that modernist policies are also assemblages, of course. But their modernist orientation means that they are assemblages that are determined to deny their ontological status as assemblages, and are instead intent on treating the boundaries that demarcate languages and ethnic groups from each other as hard, pre-given, unchangeable. By this same token, modernist policies are also committed to denying that the existence of languages and ethnic identities is, too, the result of assemblages being put together. In contrast, an organization that is posthumanist in orientation will treat such boundaries as historically contingent and flexible, and it will recognize its own complicity in the construction of any assemblage.

In the case of Singapore, one example of a posthumanist organization might be the creation of a self-help group that is specifically focused on Singaporeans who may not fit comfortably into any of the existing ones. Such an organization would be predicated on the posthumanist notion that identities are assemblages. Such a self-help group would in fact be highly relevant to the country's changing demographics. At present, Singaporeans of mixed parentage are usually assigned their fathers' ethnic identity. In this way, their hybrid identity is re-interpreted as a single ethnicity, that of the father's. This, in turn, allows the government to assign them a concomitant official mother tongue based on the father's ethnic classification. the government has recently decided to officially recognize that there are Singaporeans who, as a result of having mixed parentage, might wish to claim double-barrelled or hyphenated ethnic identities. That is, while many Singaporeans are still expected to be classified (or classifiable) as "Chinese," "Malay," or "Indian, the government also realizes that there some Singaporeans who wish to be classified as, say, "Chinese– Malay," "Malay– Chinese," "Indian– Chinese," or "Indian–Malay." Consequently, in 2011 the possibility for Singaporeans to opt for hyphenated ethnic identities was introduced. But while this initiative represents an acknowledgement of the increasingly hybrid nature of Singaporean identities, it is not quite as radical as it appears, for two reasons. One, the government is willing to contemplate hybrid identities because it believes that the number of actual individuals who would qualify for hybrid identities is numerically small and therefore administratively manageable and two, the implementation of hyphenated ethnic identities still allows the government to maintain its current policy of assigning ethnic mother tongues, since even hybrid Singaporeans are presumed to have a dominant ethnic identity. The first member of the hyphenated identity is supposed to be the dominant identity. A 'Chinese– Malay' is not the same as 'Malay–Chinese': the former is supposedly predominantly Chinese and will then have Mandarin as the mother tongue whereas the latter will have Malay as the mother tongue.

A posthumanist self-help group might, in contrast, devolve the assemblages relating to ethnicity, language and identity to the individuals themselves (such as Mandarin-Chinese, Malay-Malay, or Tamil-Indian), and avoid specifying what the affiliated language for any ethnic identity, hybrid or otherwise, ought to be. By recognizing that ethnic identity is not necessarily linked with a specific language, it could even allow for a Singaporean of mixed parentage, say, Malay and Chinese parents who grew up speaking Tamil and who would therefore prefer to have that as the official mother. An assemblage, as noted, does not mean an absence of structure; it does not mean 'anything goes'. But it does recognize the contingent nature of any imposed structure, that any such structure is changeable. Such an approach might also help address the Eurasian situation. Calls for Eurasian community to be given its own official mother tongue fail to acknowledge the fundamental variability in both how the category "Eurasian" has been constructed as well as the rationalizations that might be proffered for identifying a candidate mother tongue. 'Eurasian' was a creation of colonialism and it is hardly a stable category (Rocha and Yeoh 2020) with an uncontroversial language that can be identified as a candidate for mother tongue status. Kristang (a Portuguese creole) and Dutch are other possibilities, among yet other varieties in addition to English, depending on the specific sociolinguistic biographies of different individuals and their families. As Wee (2010, 315–316) points out:

> The intrinsically hybridized nature of the Eurasian identity has, not surprisingly, led to a number of attempts to clarify, both for the community itself and for outsiders, what it actually means to be a Eurasian. In 1997, the Eurasian Association proposed the following definition (intended to supersede the earlier definitions of 1989 and 1993).

Rappa (2000: 159) says the following:
A Eurasian for the purpose of these Rules only is a person:

i Who is of mixed European and Asian ancestry and who has shown a desire to be identified as a Eurasian; OR
ii Whose family has been accepted as Eurasian by custom and tradition, and who has shown the desire to be identified as a member of the Eurasian community.

In other words, 'Eurasian' is an assemblage; it is a 'multiple object … enacted at different moments and sites' (Farías 2010, 13; see above).

Likewise, in the case of Northern SiNdebele, it has been noted note that 'Sotho is used almost as frequently with spouses as is Ndebele, a trend evidencing the increasing number of linguistic intermarriages' (Grünthal, Honkasalo and Juutinen 2019, 41) and 'public domains and even the private sphere to some extent often employ Northern Sotho as the default language' (49). The authors conclude that (51):

> There is clear indication that this community is currently undergoing language shift as there are Ndebele families shifting to Northern Sotho, the locally dominant prestige language. While Northern Sotho is widely implemented as the medium of instruction at school, Limpopo Ndebele remains a means of oral communication, having a weaker foothold as a medium of education.

A continued insistence by, say, NANO, to petition for Northern SiNdebele to be granted equal status as Southern SiNdebele ignores the changes that the community is already undergoing, as a result of intermarriage and contact with

Northern Sotho. Instead, a posthumanist organization would try to support the various assemblages of language, education and communicative uses that would most benefit the community while acknowledging that even these assemblages would have to, in time, be revised.

In the next section, I discuss some examples of how AI is disrupting societal ideological assumptions and how a posthumanist approach can help organizations address the issues that emerge.

Posthumanist organizations and automation

Re-inventing Language with AI

Consider now how the role of automation might impact issues of language and heritage. We should first note that the relationship between a specific language and a community is a matter of social, cultural and political contingency rather than one of essentialism. That is, there are historically contingent factors that lead to a community embracing a particular named variety as 'their' language and as reflective of its identity. These 'metadiscursive regimes' or representations about language reflect invented understandings of language, in particular, conceptualizations of languages as 'separate and enumerable categories' (Makoni and Pennycook 2007, 2). For example (142–143):

> One of the great projects of European invention was Sir George Abraham Grierson's massive Linguistic Survey of India, completed in 1928. A central problem for Grierson, as with other many other linguists, was to decide on the boundaries between languages and dialects.
> '... *nearly all the language-names have had to be invented by Europeans.* Some of them, such as "Bengali," "Assamese," and the like, are founded on words which have received English citizenship, and are not real Indian words at all; while others, like "Hindostani," "Bihari," and so forth, are based on already existing Indian names of countries and nationalities.'
> (Grierson, 1907, 350; emphasis added)

> While it is interesting at one level to observe simply that the names for these new entities were invented, the point of greater significance is that these were not just new names for extant objects (languages preexisted the naming), but rather the invention and naming of new objects. The naming performatively called the languages into being.

There is, of course, significant misrecognition going on in contemporary and popular understandings about these Indian languages, since for many speakers, the role played by colonial authorities in 'inventing' their languages has been largely forgotten or simply erased.

What then might be implications of AI for situations such as these? Recall that Grierson's goal was to decide on how to distinguish languages and their dialects.

In this regard, consider the attempts by NANO to argue for the status of Northern SiNdebele as a separate language. The problem faced by NANO is precisely that Northern SiNdebele is treated by the relevant South African authorities, such as PANSALB, as a dialect of Southern SiNdebele rather than being recognized as a language in its own right. One issue that NANO needs to overcome is that the status of Northern SiNdebele as *not* being a separate language is viewed as an immutable fact. This would be a modernist argument, one that considers the relationship between a language and its community to have been historically established, and this historical tie is both unchanging and unchangeable. By this token, the argument then treats Northern SiNdebele as already and always having been a dialect of Southern SiNdebele – and this status can therefore never change. On this basis, NANO's only recourse is to hope for a re-evaluation of history. However, such a stance ignores the fact that as a variety that is still being used, Northern SiNdebele (like any other form of linguistic communication) does inevitably undergo changes in its linguistic features as well as contexts of usage.

But even assuming NANO and PANSALB are prepared to acknowledge that changes in linguistic practices can open up the need to re-evaluate the status of Northern SiNdebele, there may be questions over whether such changes should be accepted if they were deliberately introduced as opposed to being the unconscious and naturalistic consequence of use. This becomes especially thorny if such changes are created with the help of AI. That is, consider what might happen if speakers make use of AI to develop new lexical items and even grammatical features so as to further distinguish Northern SiNdebele from its Southern counterpart. In what sense would such an endeavour de-legitimize the claim that Northern SiNdebele ought to be treated as separate language? That is, should the involvement of AI in and of itself be immediate cause to treat the claim as lacking in justification? To this, we should first note that the deliberate introduction of linguistic innovations to serve the purpose of marking a different group identity is not without precedent (Pullum 1999, 44). Moving now to the use of AI, as the discussion of Microsoft Word (see Chapter 6) demonstrates, automation's already extant contribution to what we understand as 'our' language should not be underestimated. In this regard, it is also worth noting that the release of the 'final song' *Now and Then* by the Beatles was made possible by the use of AI to extract John Lennon's vocals from a 1970s demo tape (Sullivan 2023). To judge this to be an authentic Beatles song or not on the simply on the basis of the technology used would be to ignore the need for a more nuanced appreciation of the situation.

The organizational implications for NANO and PANSALD are very much posthumanist in orientation. That is, under a posthumanist orientation, NANO and PANSALB (as well other organizations who might have a stake in the discussion) would have to move away from essentialist thinking: the idea that objects possess specific attributes that are necessary to their identity, and that the loss or dilution of these attributes compromises the identity of these objects. An embrace of essentialist thinking privileges both language and authenticity as fixed properties rather than to sees them as part of a wider ecosystem involving organizations, community, and developing socio-cultural norms. Instead, as Bryant and Cox (2014, 711; italics in original) point out, a posthumanist organization would come to the terms with the fact that simple binaries – e.g. 'language is a fully human achievement or it is not really language', 'authenticity is guaranteed only if there is no involvement from automation at all' – have to be 'disturbed':

> Different again is posthumanist analysis, which views authenticity in a less stable manner than new OD [organizational development] or pragmatic reconstruction. Here, authenticity is a site through which discursive tensions are enacted rather than one that should be privileged either for its own sake or as an indicator of superior/humanist values ... the emphasis is on self-other relations rather than on any core individualized or group-based location for subjectivity. In this view OD becomes more a mechanism for *disturbing binaries* ... than for resolving, recovering or re/constructing authenticity. Variety is assumed and interrogated through OD without the assumption that either an absolute or practical authentic truth can be realized or constructed. Thus, tensions are foregrounded and remain ongoing and it is the articulation and recognition – rather than resolution – of such tensions that is central to posthumanist analysis.

Hence, Bryant and Cox make the point that a posthumanist organization 'looks *beyond authenticity* to the nature of linguistic and discursive relations ... [and] shifts from an emphasis on revealing or constructing truth to understanding the conditions that may constrain possibilities (under pragmatic reconstruction) or disturbing taken-for-granted assumptions about relations among notions such as truth and fiction, order and chaos, authenticity and inauthenticity' (719; italics in original).

A posthumanist organization, then, is one that is aware of its role as part of a wider communicative assemblage (see Chapter 5), with all that such an awareness might entail. For NANO, PANSALB, and other organizations involved in discussions about Northern SiNdebele, Southern SiNdebele, and the relationship of these varieties to the communities in question, this means acknowledging that AI is, increasingly and perhaps, inevitably, part of the resources used in communication. More specifically, the roles and meanings attributed to linguistic resources – whether these are traceable to human or technological origins – cannot be decided upon prior to their involvement in specific activities, such as the re-invention of Northern SiNdebele. A stance of agnosticism towards these resources should instead be adopted. In the case of attempting to reinvent Northern SiNdebele as a separate language from Southern SiNdebele, this will also mean a gradual shift away from relative deterritorialization towards absolute deterritorialization (Chapter 2) so that the former becomes ever more distinct from the latter. In brief, as communication practices change, so do the languages involved and, importantly, so, too, must language policy.

The Hollywood Writers' Strike

From May 2, 2023 until September 27, 2023 the Writers Guild of America (WGA), which represents some 11,500 screenwriters, went on strike because of a labour dispute with the Alliance of Motion Picture and Television Producers. There were various points of contention, including the residuals from streaming media. However, of greatest pertinence to this chapter were the concerns raised by the use of AI (Cullins and Kilkenny 2023):

> Initially, as ChatGPT emerged in late 2022 and early 2023, writers who spoke with *The Hollywood Reporter* weren't particularly scared by the chatbots that could generate movie or TV pitches on command, viewing them more as collaborative tools that can help spur ideas rather than ways to replace humans entirely. But that has changed as the technology has advanced and AI has become a key deal point in the ongoing writers union negotiations ...
>
> That's already happening, according to Amy Webb, founder and CEO of Future Today Institute, which does long-range scenario planning and consultation for Fortune 500 companies and Hollywood creatives. She notes, "I've had a couple of higher-level people ask, if a strike does happen, how quickly could they spin up an AI system to just write the scripts? And they're serious." ...
>
> "This is existential for us," said writer Vinnie Wilhelm (*Penny Dreadful: City of Angels*) ... as he picketed Netflix's Hollywood offices. "We need to have a seat at the table. You can easily see the job becoming polishing AI scripts ...'

Particularly if the writing involves scripts for long-running procedurals that already have a large corpus of data that can be used to train AI, and if the scripts follow specific formulae, these conditions make it more likely that AI could be done most of the writing with humans doing the touching up (Cullins and Kilkenny 2023). The WGA's position is that (Cullins and Kilkenny 2023):

> "At the end of the day, the script needs to be written by a writer, and the writer needs to be a human being who is a member of the Writers Guild of America. That's all we're saying," says Sasha Stewart, a member of the WGA East Council ...
>
> Talent lawyer Darren Trattner notes that 'a writer is defined in the basic agreement as a 'person,'" and the WGA could theoretically forbid AI from working on guild projects – but functionally it might not be possible ... "Sometimes a script is revised by a producer, a studio executive or a director and that person doesn't take or want credit or a fee. What if that individual revises a script with AI and then just tells the writer, 'Here are some revisions.' It is possible no one will know the notes were AI-generated."

The strike ended with a Memorandum of Agreement and the following (Writers Guild of America West 2023) summarizes the points regarding the use of AI ('MBA' refers to the Minimum Basic Agreement established in 2020):

Artificial Intelligence

We have established regulations for the use of artificial intelligence ("AI") on MBA-covered projects in the following ways:

- AI can't write or rewrite literary material, and AI-generated material will not be considered source material under the MBA, meaning that AI-generated material can't be used to undermine a writer's credit or separated rights.
- A writer can choose to use AI when performing writing services, if the company consents and provided that the writer follows applicable company policies, but the company can't require the writer to use AI software (e.g. ChatGPT) when performing writing services.
- The Company must disclose to the writer if any materials given to the writer have been generated by AI or incorporate AI-generated material.
- The WGA reserves the right to assert that exploitation of writers' material to train AI is prohibited by MBA or other law.

Notice that the dispute and even its resolution are all very much along modernist lines. The boundary between human and AI is presumed to be a strict and unchangeable one. There is acknowledgement that AI might replace a writer and it is this very possibility that the agreement is intended to prevent. Thus, AI is acceptable if used as a tool by the writer but it cannot (by fiat) ever be given any sort of credit. Intentionality and autonomy are, where the agreement is concerned, capacities that are ever to be accorded to the human writer, never AI. Finally, any material from the writer can never be used to train AI – though as discourses circulate, there is no avoiding the possibility that a text 'originally' (recall Barthes' warning in Chapter 3 about giving too much prominence to the author) written by the writer might after passing through various readers and undergoing changes might subsequently become the input for AI training. The agreement, then, is based on assumptions that are problematic for the reasons outlined already in this book, and as the fallibility of these assumptions become harder to ignore, one might expect the need for renewed negotiations but, hopefully, not another strike.

In contrast, a posthumanist approach to the issues raised by the strike would (Gladden 2016, 98) take seriously the fact that 'The very nature of organizations is changing as ongoing technological and social change reshapes the capacities and relationality of the human beings who belong to organizations and creates new kinds of entities (like social robots) that can engage in goal-directed social interaction with human being and one another'. A consequence that cannot be ignored (109) is that 'the boundary between the electronic systems that store and process information and the human works that use them are expected to increasingly blur as implantable computers, neuroprosthetic devices, and persistent virtual reality environments integrate human workers ever more intimately into organizational information systems at both the physical and cognitive levels'. Members of organizations might then include (105–106):

> Human beings possessing implantable computers (such as devices resembling subcutaneous smartphones)
>
> Human beings who are long-term users of virtual reality systems and whose interaction with other persons and their environment takes place largely within virtual worlds.

Social robots, Artificial general intelligences

Becker (2023) describes the last two as 'AI-powered digital colleagues'. The developments outlined by Gladden (2016) and Becker (2023) mean that writers need to be careful that they themselves do not inadvertently violate the terms of the WGA, especially as virtual and implantable technologies become more ubiquitous, harder to avoid and more normalized. The other option, of course, is the terms themselves to be revised. But as mentioned, unless the renegotiations are sufficiently informed by a posthumanist orientation, there is every danger that the terms will become quickly outmoded.

Bad Actors and Deepfakes

The use of AI in what is known as 'deepfakes' – videos or images that have been altered so that the person (or in some cases, an object) is doing something that has been fabricated – is a phenomenon that has become a matter of grave concern. This is especially when such deepfake videos and images are widely circulated with the goal of deceiving the general public, as might be the case in political communication, advertisements or scams.

In one recent case, a deepfake video of the UK's Labour Party leader, Sir Keir Starmer, was released on the very first day of the Labour conference (Sky News 2023):

> **Deepfake videos of Sir Keir Starmer have been posted on the first day of Labour Party conference in a move that underlines the threat posed by deepfake technology and AI in UK politics.**
>
> The fake video of the Labour leader emerged on X, formerly known as Twitter, on Sunday morning as senior figures and party activists gathered in Liverpool.
>
> …
>
> The first fake audio, posted by an account with less than 3,000 followers, purports to capture the Labour leader abusing party staffers – but the audio is not real and the incident did not happen.

The second makes out that Sir Keir is criticizing the city of Liverpool.

The emergence of the audio is reminiscent of the recent elections in Slovakia, where a fake audio recording emerged of Michal Simecka, the leader of the Progressive Slovakia Party, apparently engaged in a conversation with a leading journalist from a daily newspaper discussing how to rig the election.

The pair immediately confirmed that the audio was fake and that the conversation did not happen.

Analysis by the AFP news agency found that the audio showed signs of being manipulated with AI.

...

It is not just the world of politics that has been threatened by AI.

Actor Tom Hanks recently spoke out after a fake advert appeared to use his face to promote a dental plan but which Mr Hanks said had used an artificial AI version of him without his authorisation.

As the report indicates, in addition to the two deepfake videos involving Starmer (the first where he supposedly is abusive towards his staff and the second where his speech has been manipulated to present criticisms of Liverpool), a deepfake audio was also used in Slovakia and there was also a fake advertisement involving the image of actor Tom Hanks. The same report cites Dame Wendy Hall, who sits on the British government's AI Council and is the regius professor of computer science at the University of Southampton, on the dangers posed by deepfake technology to democracy, as saying (Sky News 2023), 'We need people to quite quickly pull together the technology that's used to detect fakes and to ensure that something is coming from a trusted source'.

The issue, as Hall points out, is whether the information in question is coming from a trusted source. Note that the issue is not necessarily whether there has been any use of AI. The use of beauty filters, a cleaning up of audio and the removal of ambient noise – these would not be considered to have compromised the integrity of the message. And the same technology used in deepfakes has been used in movies to create virtual sets and change actors' appearances. Nor is the issue necessarily whether the message is true. This latter point may seem radical and even cynical but as attempts to deal with the COVID-19 pandemic have shown, even messages that are politically and scientifically authorized can be rejected because of a lack of trust. It is trust or the lack thereof that encourages a receiver to take a message at face value or question its veracity.

Trust is a form of affect, and this means attending to how trust can be cultivated as part of an affective regime. An affective regime refers to the set of conditions that govern with varying degrees of hegemonic status the ways in which particular kinds of affect can be appropriately materialized in the context of a given site (Wee 2016). The term 'regime' is important because it serves to highlight that the kinds of affect associated with various sources of information is not incidental. I am not talking about how a specific individual may happen to be feeling at any specific moment. Rather, I am focusing on how sources of information may have been constructed or designed in order to encourage particular kinds of affect. Consider the Arlington National Cemetery (see Wee 2016 for further details) as an example of an organization with a highly formalized and extremely well-established affective regime. The Arlington National Cemetery (ANC) makes very clear the kind of affective regime that it wants to encourage and maintain among its visitors, as shown in its mission statement:[1]

> (5) On behalf of the American people, lay to rest those who have served our nation with dignity and honor, treating their families with respect and compassion, and connecting guests to the rich tapestry of the cemetery's living history, while maintaining these hallowed grounds befitting the sacrifice of all those who rest here in quiet repose.

The mission statement is rich in affect, emphasizing dignity and honor for the dead, respect and compassion for their families, and situating these concerns in relation to a larger sense of gratitude for the sacrifices made to the nation. Thus, rather than directly regulate the evocation or suppression of specific emotions, the ANC's concerns are with ensuring that the desired affect is created. These concerns are reflected in the structuring of the physical landscape of the Cemetery. Its austere and well-maintained headstones surrounded by well-tended trees are aimed at evoking a sense of sombre remembrance and appreciation for those who died for their country. Conversely, failure to properly upkeep the landscape would be read as a sign not only of physical neglect but also a lack of gratitude and respect. In this way, the ANC's affective regime is already well emplaced in terms of its physical layout even in the absence of any actual visitors.

In addition to the physical layout, the Cemetery's affective regime is also formally established via its 'Visitors' rules',[2] which prohibit 'disorderly conduct' such as fighting, or threatening, violent or tumultuous behaviour … abusive, insulting, profane, indecent or otherwise provocative language or gesture that by its very utterance tends to incite an immediate breach of the peace'.

In the case of deepfakes, technology can help increase trust. This is already happening with the use of malware removal apps, apps that block incoming calls from scammers, and bots that allow for the reporting of scams directly to regulatory authorities. The difference between these forms of protection and the case of deepfakes is that the latter are much more difficult to detect. This can usually only be done by focusing on minute details of a video (Telefónica, n.d.), for example, such as incongruities between facial and body proportions (deepfakes tend to focus on the former), video length (deepfakes require extensive algorithm training and so tend to be fairly short), video sound (audio may not match lip movement or there may be no audio). The issue, of course, is that no everyone will be able or willing to invest the time needed to scrutinize a video in such detail and so, there will be increased reliance on deepfake detection software such as Sentinel (which uses advanced algorithms to determine if a video has been manipulated), and Fakecatcher (which looks for markers of authenticity such as 'blood flow' in the pixels of a video and concomitant changes to the colour of a person's veins) (McFarland 2023).

It has been suggested that trust itself comprises three distinct components: competence, honesty, and benevolence (Grayson 2016):

> To trust someone's competence is simply to believe that the person or entity you deal with has the ability to do the job – to provide you with Internet service, for example. Honesty – or integrity – refers to your sense that your Internet service provider keeps its promises and is not telling lies about your connection speed or hiding fees. Benevolence is the belief that your Internet provider has your best interests at heart and cares about you as a customer …
>
> The good news is that there are actions you can take to build trust in areas where it may be in decline. Consider the case of Cooperative Bank, a U.K.-based financial institution that worked with Grayson and coauthor Devon Johnson on trust-management issues. In preparation for trying to gain share in its financial advisory business, the firm measured how it stacked up relative to its competitors in terms of trust. When senior managers discovered that customer perceptions of benevolence could improve, the bank directed resources and energy toward improvements on this dimension.

This focus on trust as part of an affective regime would then require attention to how the three components can be built in ways that cohere with each other. That is, it is necessary to ensure that an attempt to foster benevolence does not undermine, say, the attempt to develop competence. The development of trust, therefore, requires attending to intra-organizational relations as well as inter-organizational ones. Importantly, this means taking into account the posthumanist argument about the distributive nature of agency. As Ahearn (2001, 8) has asked:

> Can agency only be the property of an individual? What types of supra-individual agency might exist? … Similarly, we might also be able to talk about agency at the sub-individual level … thereby shedding light on things like internal dialogues and fragmented subjectivities? … Another avenue for potential research involves investigating theories of agency that people in other cultures or speech communities might espouse … Who do they believe can exercise agency?

Such complications arise because even a body such as 'the government', 'the ministry' or 'the community' is really an abstraction over multiple sub-entities (themselves potentially recursively sub-dividable) so that 'internal dialogues and fragmented subjectivities' apply no less to organizations and groups than they do to individuals. If we return, as an example, to the deepfakes of the Labour party leader Sir Keir Starmer (one where he purportedly abuse staffer and another where he supposedly made disparaging remarks about the city of Liverpool), this suggests that the development of trust as an affective regime would require at least the following:

i   Instil in the general public an awareness of just how sophisticated and pre-valent deepfakes can be. This is already being done to a large certain by various media and government-related organizations since the issue of deepfakes is not just something that one political party has to worry about.

ii Where the Labour party itself is concerned, ensure general appreciation of the kind of person Starmer is (his principles, his values) and how they cohere with Labour's own political stances. This would help raise scepticism in cases where Starmer or some other member of the party is presented as making statements that might run contrary to those principles, values and stances. At the very least, members of the public who encounter deepfakes might then be more willing to hold off judgment on their veracity until checking with other sources for convergent evidence.

iii The foregoing are important because disproving one deepfake merely demonstrates that the video or audio in question has been tampered with. Sceptics may argue that even if Starmer did not say or do the things in the deepfakes, these are nevertheless the kinds of things that he or the party might well do.

iv Hence, (i) and (ii) require working at the intra-organizational and inter-organizational levels to cultivate the attributes of competence, honesty, and benevolence. Labour, for example, has to ensure that its internal sub-committees present consistent messaging, and other organizations such as news outlets, competing political parties, and non-governmental organizations all play their part in identifying and weeding out deepfakes.

The problem, admittedly, is that bad actors are hard to eliminate in any situation. However, a posthumanist approach to organizations can help mitigate the effects of bad actors. It can do this by recognizing that attempts at guaranteeing authenticity are part of a much wider concern with the cultivation of trust, as previously noted. In this regard, the final point (iv) is particularly important from a posthumanist perspective. It emphasizes that organizations have responsibilities not just as individual actants. The distributed nature of agency means that they need to also be mindful of and accountable about how they work in concert with other actants so as order to shape the assemblages that they are parts of. A post-humanist organization would thus also be open to treating automation not as mere tools but (as we saw in the case of the Hollywood writer's strike) as actants with just as much agency and responsibility as their human counterparts – and because of this, as potential collaborators.

Conclusion

It is worth noting that even as the importance of addressing many of challenges posed by AI are becoming taken more seriously, there is as yet no clear sense of the kinds of directions and initiatives that would be needed. Both the British and US governments have launched their own AI Safety Institutes (Stokel-Walker 2023), and though there was broad consensus among a total of 28 countries on the need to regulate AI, the question of 'what should be done, and by whom, is still up for debate' (Stokel-Walker 2023). This is understandable. As we have seen in this chapter, the issues involved are complex with no easy or clear solutions. One initiative that appears to be gaining traction is to require a declaration that AI has been used in content creation (Tenbarge 2023). However, this declaration requirement is just a small step, and it barely addresses the complex nature of the issue. As AI becomes ever more ubiquitous and advanced, the question is not whether it was used but how it was used. Even the term 'used' may at some point need to be superseded by 'helped' or 'credited,' as AI moves from tool to collaborator to creator.

By way of closing, I want to address a point made earlier about organizations and their institutional environments. This is the idea that organizational structures are reflections of the ideologies that pervade their environments (Meyer and Rowan 1991). Obviously, such an idea does not preclude the possibility that organizational structures might themselves come to challenge the prevailing ideologies. And one way to understand why organizations are not only dumb or passive reflections of ideologies is to appreciate that organizations are populated by 'concept-using beings' (Giddens 1987) and the result is a double hermeneutic. The double hermeneutic (Giddens 1987) refers to the fact that there is a two-way relationship between lay/everyday concepts and social scientific ones. Unlike the natural sciences where the objects and phenomena studied by scientists (e.g. chemical processes) lack awareness, those studied by social scientists (i.e. people, society) not only are capable of appreciating social scientific concepts such as 'citizen' and 'sovereignty' (Giddens 1987, 20), but also are able to use these themselves in ways that inform their own behaviors and values (see Wee 2016, 342–343). As Giddens (1987, 18–19) puts it:

> … the subjects of study in the social sciences and the humanities are concept-using beings, whose concepts of their actions enter in a constitutive manner into what those actions are … [U]nlike in the natural sciences, in the social sciences, there is no way of keeping the conceptual apparatus of the observer – whether in sociology, political science or economic – free from appropriation by lay actors.

An example of the double hermeneutic at work in language policy can be found in the case of Singapore, when Lee Kuan Yew, the country's first prime minister, was concerned about gross differences in economic development across the various ethnic groups. Lee decided to consult the works of sociologist Judith Djamour and cultural anthropologist Bryan Parkinson, both of whom emphasized differences in cultural values between the Malays and the Chinese, and came to the conclusion that the most feasible policy was one where ethnic enclaves were eliminated and the different ethnicities encouraged to interact. This led to the recognition of English as an official language that would serve as the interethnic lingua franca, in the hopes that interethnic interaction would allow the otherwise separate communities to learn from each other (Han, Fernandez, and Tan 1998,

184). Whether or not Djamour and Parkinson would have been comfortable with Lee's interpretation of their ideas and his translation of these into policy is really beside the point. Concepts are interpreted and re-interpreted by those who apprehend them in ways are might well be increasingly divergent from the intentions of their originators (hence, the arguments in Chapter 3 about the death of the speaker). As organizations become more appreciative of the limitations of the modernist ideology, they may well initiate structural and other changes that no longer reflect and may instead even challenge that ideology. It is suggested in this chapter that some these changes will benefit from taking on a more clearly posthumanist orientation. At this point, I end the chapter will a question that may have been provocative at the start of this book but hopefully is by now less controversial: 'Should AI also be considered a concept-using entity as per Giddens' discussion of the double hermeneutic, and thus treated as something that can use concepts in ways that inform its own behaviours and values?' The answer I offer is already in Chapter 4.

Notes

1 From the ANC official website (www.arlingtoncemetery.mil), as at March 6, 2014.
2 From the Visitors' Rules for the Arlington National Cemetery, Part 553.22. Document downloaded March 12, 2014.

8   Assemblages and the Emergence of Language from Communication

Introduction

This book has argued for an assemblage-based perspective on automation in communication. Such a perspective eschews the idea that things pre-exist the activity of assembling, in particular, the idea that there are already neatly organized systems which have a reality and stability independent of assemblages. Canagarajah (2020, 305) likens the assembling activity to bricolage, because both involve 'making do with the resources available at hand to accomplish things in creative, unscripted, and dexterous ways' and 'communicating is a pragmatic and functional assembling of resources and texts.'

Keeping in mind the foregoing, this concluding chapter will expand on the bricolage analogy to address the following three questions. One, is it possible to provide a general account of the relationship between language and communication from an assemblage-based perspective? Two, if there are many possible linguistic assemblages, how might we then adjudicate on the desirability, feasibility, or plausibility of some assemblages over others? Three, in what way would such adjudication be relevant to advancing our studies of language and communication?

I begin with the first question.

Languaging *from* Communicating

To further emphasize the point that communicating involves assemblages, Canagarajah (2020, 305) notes that any communicative activity involves bringing and putting together various resources 'in non-synchronous and non-linear ways by different parties in relation to diverse material ecologies in disparate time and space'.

Consider, in this regard, some of the examples we have had occasion to discuss in this book. The use of kiosks and apps makes clear that communication involving automation is very much still communication – which raises the important question of how language and communication are related. This problem is compounded by the examples of healthcare communication, where attributions of qualities such as empathy and even sentience to automated entities are

DOI: 10.4324/9781003467922-8

encouraged, moving us beyond communication as the mere transmission of information into the realm of sociability and affectivity. Sociability and affectivity behove us to consider how varying degrees of anthropomorphism, and with that, ideological assumptions about personhood, need to be taken into account as we attempt to arrive at a coherent understanding of the relationship between language and communication. In some cases, the question of how to interpret the role of automation in communication is constrained by the specificities of religious precepts. In other cases, automated entities, such as virtual influencers, may have highly detailed bios to the point where they are regarded as fully fledged communicators (i.e. principals and authors and not just animators) of the messages and works that they produce.

These examples illustrate the bricolage nature of communication. The communications that take place in these many examples involve the assembling of various kinds of participants, technologies, and texts. This is made clear from the kinds of production formats and footings that have already been noted, these in turn being the results of ideological influences that provide for – in the sense of legitimizing and thus lending coherence to – different 'empathetic arrangements' (Kerruish 2021) or assemblages.

There are interesting implications for study of mass communication, which deals with how the information that is being conveyed to large groups can influence the attitudes or behaviours of the recipients. Pearce (2009), for example, defines mass communication as the process by which a message is transmitted to large audiences and the traditional focus is on mediums such as radio, television, social media, newspapers, film and the Internet. Where technology and automation are concerned, mass communication has typically dealt with this under the rubric of 'computer-mediated communication'. However, this once again underestimates the highly complex and interesting ways in which automation can figure in communication. It presupposes a human-centric view of communication, one where a human speaker or speakers aim to address a group of human hearers, and technology is simply a medium for enabling this communication. It should be clear by now that the role that technology plays is far more than just serving as a medium for communication. In the case of the echoborg (Chapter 1), especially if the message is being sent out to a large number of people, then it is ready 'human-mediated communication' that is taking place.

There are also interesting implications for the notion of synthetic personalization (Chapter 3). The term 'synthetic' is intended to suggest that the personalization is not actually sincere or personal. Rather, an effort has been made to give the impression of personalized treatment by an otherwise impersonal organization. The contrast, when the notion of synthetic personalization is invoked, is with 'authentic personalization', where the latter presumes a communication scenario where a message is personal precisely because it emanates from one individual, and it has been crafted for a specific addressee. Note that this fundamentally relies on the personalist view of meaning, with all the conceptual problems that this view entails. However, if the messages are generated by an extremely sophisticated AI, then it is not clear in what sense concepts like 'sincere' and 'personal' as well as their opposites ('insincere', 'impersonal') apply. That is, the messages may have a synthetic origin but if each was indeed crafted for each individual addressee, then we might want to argue that this makes the communication process about as personal as we could expect.

Mass communication aside, there are even more significant implications for the study of language. Focusing our attention specifically on the phenomenon that we call language, if ideological assumptions are important to how assemblages come to be constructed and apprehended as having some kind of coherence, it then follows that ideologies regarding language are particularly influential in the formation and establishment of specific linguistic assemblages. In an interesting discussion that compares language practices in South Asia under pre-colonial and colonial conditions, Canagarajah (2007, 2010) suggests that the imposition of strictly regulated language names by the British ruling authorities only served to create rather than resolve communicative, cultural and identity issues. Canagarajah (2010) describes language, communication, and community in the period *prior to* Western colonization thus:

> Negotiation of language differences is the norm rather than the exception. Furthermore, there is no expectation of a common language as the basis for these interactions ... How is communication possible if both interlocutors speak in their own language? It is possible because they adopt interpersonal and sociolinguistic strategies to negotiate their differences. Through practices, they unpack the differences in content (i.e., grammatical norms, cultural values, or sociocultural knowledge). In other words, their orientation to linguistic interactions and cultural differences is practice-based and not dependent on knowledge, values, or grammar.

He then contrasts this with the subsequent effects of colonization and decolonization:

> Mohan (1992) documents how unitary constructs of linguistic identity and speech community were put to use in colonies to categorize people for purposes of taxation, administrative convenience, and political control ... For people who grow up with multiple languages in their everyday life, unitary notions of identity are reductive. Worse still, these notions of identity and community began to reproduce social life in the region. As Khubchandani (1997) observes: "Until as recently as four or five decades ago, one's language group was not generally considered as a very important criterion for sharply distinguishing oneself from others.... Following Independence, language consciousness has grown, and loyalties based on language-identity have acquired political salience" (Khubchandani 1997, 92).

In other words, one of the persistent effects of colonization was the imposition and entrenchment of a very specific language ideology, one that insisted on the drawing of linguistic boundaries between language systems on the assumption that the language labels (such as 'English', 'Tamil', 'Bengali' and even 'poor

Tamil' or 'standard English') all reflected the pre-existing independent realities of language use (see the discussion of Grierson in Chapter 7). This same ideology also insisted on clear correspondences between these labels, on the one hand, and linguistic and community boundaries, on the other. Speakers were expected to identify unproblematically with a named mother tongue. Linguistic names were assumed to correlate systematically and neatly with differences in linguistic practices. The expectation is that community A speakers 'obviously' should be speaking mother tongue A rather than, say, mother tongue B. But these expectations were at odds with the precolonial language practices where hybridity, multiplicity and heterogeneity were the norm.

This is a good example of how language, in this case, individual named languages, are created or assembled from a heterogeneous mix of communicative practices. The colonial government's insistence on the neat correspondence between communicative practices and community identities – mainly to facilitate administrative control – entrenched and naturalized over time the 'reality' of particular linguistic assemblages. It is worth keeping in mind that the continued stability of these linguistic assemblages requires the continuing efforts of government organizations, educational institutions, and community leaders, among others, to sustain their acceptability. So, while an assemblage may have characteristics that make it distinct and recognizable, it also remains 'in constant interplay with assemblages "that are not principally linguistic"' (Demuro and Gurney 2021, 4, citing Deleuze and Guattari 1987, 111).

By the same token, even the views of language propounded by Chomsky and Saussure must be recognized as linguistic assemblages that are guided by specific ideologies about language. The impetus behind these specific views is to whittle away the morass of communicative practices that are presumed – based on some *a priori* conceptualization of what language ought to be – to *not* really be language. Language as an autonomous system emphasizes the closed and integrated nature of the components and processes that supposedly constitute this posited system. This closed integration carries the further implication that the system is highly stable, possibly invariant even and thus not amenable to change. Moreover, in order for such an autonomous system to be imaginable, it is necessarily conceptualized in a highly abstract manner so that the contingent effects of history, the idiosyncratic impacts of cultural and technological developments, and the prejudices or biases of group politics are all removed.

In Chomsky's case, the assumption of a genetically coded linguistic system provides it with the rationale to dismiss observable changes as mere epiphenomena. For Saussure, the introduction of *la langue/parole* distinction makes it difficult to reconcile the supposed stability of the former with the fact that changes in the latter do indeed occur over time. As with colonization and the imposition of named languages, the presumed reality of I-Language or *la langue*, too, requires the joint efforts of, in this case, academic institutions, conference organizers, scholars, and publications for its sustenance.

What we think of as language, then, is always an assemblage, a construct put together in different ways by different actors to reflect various histories and agendas. All these cases – those of narrow scientism, of colonial rule, and the many examples involving organizational styling, healthcare communication, religion, and creativity – are ways of constructing particular linguistic assemblages. As the histories and agendas change, so, too, would the communicative practices and the ways in which we think about linguistic assemblages.

This then raises the question of whether the only available epistemological stance towards these different linguistic assemblages is that of radical relativism, where there is no viewpoint from which one might evaluate the plausibility and desirability of one linguistic assemblage over another. Radical relativism is surely undesirable. However, given the many different possible ways of constructing linguistic assemblages, it would not be particularly fruitful to start discussing the merits of individual assemblages. Instead, there are two broad classes of linguistic assemblages that can be identified, those that emphasize a "linguistics of systems' and those that emphasize a 'linguistics of practice' (Rampton 2006). In the rest of this chapter, I address the question of how the relative strengths and problems associated with these two classes of assemblages can be adjudicated so that radical relativism can be avoided.

Adjudicating Assemblages

The Chomskyan and Saussurean postulates that insist on separating the I-Language from E-Language or *la langue* from *parole* are assemblages that try to sever their connections with the myriad practices that make communication possible and recognizable. Notably, the rationales for these separations are not the *results* of any actual inquiries. They are simply presented as necessary *starting points* if any inquiry is to be deemed appropriately scientific. This means that adjudicating on the relative merits of linguistic assemblages that fall under 'linguistics of systems' versus those that fall under 'linguistics of practice' cannot be done empirically, that is, based on data that could be said to unequivocally confirm or refute specific hypotheses.

Instead, to make some headway in the discussion, it is useful to return an argument of Quine's (1953) that all claims regarding knowledge and experience are interconnected. No statement is ever verifiable on its own; rather, its coherence and acceptability rests on its relationship to other statements. Any statement, no matter how ludicrous it may be at first blush, can thus be treated as true as long as one is willing to make the requisite adjustments, however drastic, which may include jettisoning many other beliefs and assumptions that have hitherto been considered unproblematic. An epistemological consequence of Quine's argument is pragmatism: knowledge claims are to be evaluated not in terms of their ability to successfully or accurately represent reality, but, instead, in terms of their usefulness as tools for solving problems or enabling action.

With regards to assemblages, this suggests that assemblages that cohere with each other or establish linkages between themselves are to be valued over those that insist on creating separations or fissures – since the price to be paid in terms of adjustments elsewhere, such as the loss of simplicity or revocation of established knowledge is lower. A linguistic assemblage that claims, for instance, to be independent of and separate from communication is still an assemblage. It is merely choosing to be disingenuous about these connections.[1] And it then finds itself needing to explain just how I-Language can lead to E-Language or how *la langue* and *parole* interact (as the case may be). The introduction of various statements and claims that attempt to provide the requisite justifications for the separation, as we now see, are really intended to preserve the initial postulation of the abstract self-contained language system.

For example, Chomsky (1986, 48–49) emphasizes that I-Language bears little resemblance to E-Language, or language as it is more generally understood or recognized. He asserts that the I-Language faculty is only incidentally linked to other systems that are involved in activities such as articulation and expression. It is only because of this happenstance that the generative program is concerned with 'human language'. It would actually have been entirely possible for this same faculty to be linked up to other kinds of systems, perhaps the digestive system, in which case the faculty would still exist but there would not be anything produced that we might recognize as or consider to be language. Thus, Hinzen (2006, 21; italics added) observes that Chomsky:

> … even envisages the fantasy of some crazy scientist who has discovered the neural basis of how our brains store information about linguistic structures and rewires our brains so that the cognitive system of language outputs not to the performance systems to which it factually outputs now, but to others, which use human linguistic structures for a different purpose, such as loco-motion. *The moral of the story, I suppose, is that if our human language system might in principle be used quite differently than we use it now, then it does not, as a system of knowledge described purely formally, intrinsically relate to its factual use.*

Consequently, to even describe the cognitive system in question as a *language* system or a *language* organ is already very much a misnomer. The system is contingently linguistic. It just happens to be connected to performance systems that are traditionally considered as related to language *from an E-Language perspective*. Thus, despite Chomsky's dismissal of its importance, it is really only because of the existence of E-Language that the generative program even finds itself in the business of studying language at all. For Chomsky, it is the underlying system itself that is the actual target of investigation. This system may in principle be linked up to locomotive, digestive or other systems, but it is formal properties of this system, assumed to be invariant, that the investigative energies within the Chomskyan research program are really directed towards.

This creates an awkward question for the research program since Chomsky has consistently insisted that this language system is species-specific, that is, it is supposedly unique to humans. Animals may communicate, but Chomsky has always asserted that they do not have language because they lack the relevant linguistic system (Anderson and Lightfoot 2004, ix; Chomsky 1976; Cook and Newson

1996, 107; see Chapter 2). And it should be abundantly clear by now that the plausibility of such a radically abstract conception of language is really a matter of faith. It is so divorced from language as we experience it that it can now in principle be posited to underlie human digestion, animal behaviour, among other possibilities.

In the case of Saussure's *la langue*, this conception is based on the assertion that a language 'is a system of pure values which are determined by nothing except the momentary arrangement of its terms' (Saussure 1983, 116). Saussure wants to separate *la langue* from parole because he considers it necessary to separate 'what is social from what is individual and what is essential from what is ancillary or incidental' (30). As Normand (2004, 89–90) points out, *la langue* 'is a new technical term developed by Saussure, and is the essential object of his investigations.' Saussure (1983, 162) sees the sign system of *la langue* as internally organized by which he means that particular signs are recognizable and comprehensible only because of the totality of signs to which they belong and from which they relationally derive their values. This is clear from his assertion that values of the signs in the system are negatively defined. An illustration of what Saussure means comes from color terms. If English had only the words *black* and *white* to describe colors, then the conceptual ranges of these two signifiers effectively exhaust the description of colors. But the presence of other color words like *red* and *blue* helps to further demarcate the conceptual ranges. And terms like *scarlet, maroon* and *burgundy* refine the conceptual ranges even further. In all these cases, what a particular color term signifies is 'negatively defined' by its relations with other existing terms in the system. The introduction of a new color term would therefore 'disrupt' the existing system; a calibration of the conceptual range of this new term would be required and doing this would simultaneously force a recalibration of the conceptual ranges of the other terms in the system. Saussure (1983, 168–169) emphasizes that the study of the linguistic sign system must focus on the relations between the units. Language is, then, viewed as 'form and not substance, its elements have only contrastive and combinatorial properties' (Culler 1986, 61).

Saussure's ideas have been criticized by Dosse (1997, 193–194) as leading to a 'self-enclosed formalization, drawing its model more than ever from the hard sciences', which, of course, presages the generative program's pattern of development. As Norris (2004, 220) points out, for Saussure, 'any discipline which aspires to scientific status must establish a certain formal distance between itself and its object of study, or – more precisely – between that object as construed on the linguist's theoretical terms and that object in it "natural", spontaneous, or everyday-occurrent condition'. However, this insistence on separating *la langue* from parole, creates, as Harris observes, a 'tension' between 'linguistic *realia*' and 'metalinguistic fictions' that is never really resolved (1988, 126, italics in original; see also Pettit 1975).

Concerns about the distinction between *la langue* and *parole* can be found in Firth (1935, 1968), for whom the idea of an abstract social collectivity that *la langue* relies on is highly implausible. Making a related point, Spence (1957) takes issue with the idea of 'defining or delimiting precisely the collective system of *langue*' (quoted in Gordon 2004, 83). Thibault (1997, quoted in Gordon 2004, 86) offers a somewhat more sympathetic reading of Saussure and suggests that there are in fact three distinct ways to understand *la langue*: as pure value, as lexicogrammatical forms, and as typical patterns of language use in a community. Unfortunately, Thibault only highlights the confusion and mystery surrounding what Saussure actually has in mind since typicality (perhaps interpretable in statistical terms or in terms of normative prototypical expectations) is still not quite the same thing as stable shared collective knowledge.

The many convolutions that are needed to sustain I-Language and *la langue* lead us to ask, *à la* Quine (Godfrey-Smith 2013), whether we are willing to pay the price by giving up on accommodating data and conceptual simplicity in favour highly abstract conceptions of language that are also of questionable plausibility.

Language Completeness

As an illustration, we can consider the issue of language completeness and ask: What grounds do we have for thinking that language is ever complete? Language completeness is relevant as an illustrative discussion because if a language construct such as I-Language or *la langue* (exemplars of the 'linguistics of systems' approach) is to be understood as existing stably apart from and independent of communication activities, then this construct must already be representing language *in toto*, albeit as a highly abstract system.

Let us, for the sake of argument, consider this issue on two fronts, in terms of lexicon and structure. Regarding lexicon, we can ask whether language can be considered complete in terms of its lexical inventory. The answer to this is straightforward since we all presumably accept that the inventory of lexical items in a language is never stable; the meanings of individual items change, some items fall into disuse and newer ones get added. But there is also a less straightforward implication. Once we accept that the lexical inventory can and does change, we face the trickier question of whether or not mathematical symbols, for instance, should be included as part of this inventory. And if we want to exclude these, what would be the basis for this exclusion? That is, the issue is now not about individual lexical items but about types of items, such as mathematical symbols. To suggest that mathematical symbols should be excluded because such symbols are not language is circular because it is precisely the issue of language completeness and what counts as language – even as an abstract system – that we are trying to address. In this regard, Wittgenstein's (1958, 8; italics added) remarks are highly pertinent:

> ... ask yourself whether our language is complete – *whether it was so before the symbolism of chemistry and the notation of the infinitesimal calculus were incorporated in it*; for these are, so to speak, suburbs of our language. (And how many houses or streets does it take before a town begins to be a town?)

Our language can be seen as an ancient city: a maze of little streets and squares, of old and new houses, and of houses with additions from various periods; and this surrounded by a multitude of new boroughs with straight regular streets and uniform houses.

The question of language completeness (and thus the distinction between the linguistic and the non-linguistic) does not apply only to mathematical, chemical symbols, or emojis (Seargeant 2019; see Chapter 7). Emojis first gained momentum in 2011, to the point where they were used by 90 percent of the online population just only four years later, and the 'face with tears of joy' was even chosen by Oxford Dictionaries in 2015 as their 'word of the year' (3–4). But emojis are not merely supplementary to what is traditionally recognized as language. A single emoji can serve as a complete message, to convey the sender's joy or frustration, as when someone uses only a smiley face to indicate joy or positive feelings in general. Likewise, in response to a complaint, an emoji with a frown may convey concern or shared disappointment. Whether we want to treat mathematical and chemical symbols, and emojis, as linguistic or non-linguistic is itself ultimately a matter of how we decide to construct the linguistic assemblage. There is no prior non-assemblage basis on which any such decision or definition can be made.

Consider now the hashtag, which problematizes not just the issue of language completeness, but also claims about the abstract nature of language and its separability from communication. The arguments above about the boundary between language and non-language also apply to other symbols such as the hashtag. As we now see, the hashtag, when prefixed to phrases, also serves to problematize the boundary between a language and its users. Examples of hashtagged phrases include Urban Outfitter's '#UOPRIDE' and Wells Fargo Bank's "#TOGETHERisBEAUTIFUL', both used in support of San Francisco's Gay Pride Movement. The hashtag here is a metadata tag that is used in social media. Its purpose is to allow users to find the collection of messages that have been posted using that hash. Here, then, is a good demonstration of the materiality of language at work, where what is linguistically relevant is not just the phrase *per se*, but also the fact that it is being prefixed by a hash and thus the technological affordances and online intertextual opportunities that follow from being hashtagged. In other words, the hash here is not merely a symbol if by 'symbol' we mean an abstract conceptual signifier that exists above and beyond how it is used. Rather, the hash, when used as a hashtag, exists to provide a specific means by which users can discover and contribute to the circulation of phrases and the resulting posts. Qua hashtag, the hash works only when used in relation to social media platforms. Merely writing the hashtagged phrase on a piece of paper, for example, will not enable the same set of affordances.

The comparison with writing on paper provides further useful comparisons. Contrast, for example, the differences between writing with pen and paper versus writing on a computer or using a messaging app. In the case of the former, the writer will have to depend on their own understanding of spelling and grammatical conventions, or on someone else to check on the draft for errors and to perhaps make stylistic suggestions. In the case of the latter, especially since spellcheck and other proofing tools are now standard parts of a word processing software – and the user even has the option of specifying his or her preferred language (e.g. British English, US English, Catalan, Indonesian) so that the program automatically uses the dictionary, where available, of the selected language – it is possible to leave much of the correcting and cleaning up of a text to the program itself. In fact, there are constant advances being made in using AI to aid in message composition. Google's Gmail uses AI to highlight incorrect grammar with blue squiggly lines and a user can click on the highlighted text to access grammar suggestions from the program (Baca 2019). We have already seen in the preceding chapter that further advances mean that AI is not just limited to correcting the messages produced by human authors and principals. AI itself can act as author and principal, as demonstrated by GPT-3.

So, proponents of a 'linguistics of systems' approach may agree that the lexicon is never complete. But they might then argue that the abstract language system can be considered complete in terms of its structure. We know that the structure – if by this we mean the specific grammatical rules or conventions of a named language such as 'English' or 'Japanese' – can and does change in much the same way as the lexical inventory. And this is no surprise since named languages are (as noted in the discussion above about colonialism) themselves assemblages. Hence, the only other recourse for the argument that structure can be considered complete is to return the more abstract notion of structure, such as the ones proposed by Chomsky and Saussure. But we have seen that there are serious concerns about the plausibility of I-Language and *la langue* because of problems in (re-)establishing connections between actual communication and these highly abstract postulates. The plausibility of these postulates suffers even more once we bring in the use of automation. Certainly, the Chomskyan postulation of a species-specific biological I-Language cannot be coherently argued to exist in the many apps, programs and robots discussed in this book. In which case, either the use of language in automation is *not* language, which in this case merely serves to assert the claim that anything not found in human must by fiat be designated non-language, or such use is conceded to be language, which then begs the question of how such language might be possible when there presumably is no language faculty to license its manifestation.

The Saussurean concept of *la langue* perhaps fares somewhat better given that it is supposed to be an abstract system of signs internalized and shared by members of a community (Gasparov 2021). The first brings up the thorny but perhaps less polemical question of whether automated entities can be considered part of a community – a question that was discussed in the preceding chapter. The second raises the much more polemical question of whether the language and communication used by automation is internalized – and if so, in what sense? Saussure was himself rather unclear on how *la langue* actually related to *parole* beyond asserting (as does Chomsky) that the more abstract version makes the material manifestations possible. Automation can be said to have internalized *la langue* if we are prepared to forego human socialization as the only way in which *la langue* comes to be shared and to accept that programming, too, can lead to internalization – which is also controversial, to say the least. In this regard, it is worth noting, as Bakhtin (1986) does, that this insistence on separating language into *la langue* and *parole* provides no explanation for the fact that the meanings of words are subject to contestations and struggles, and these struggles in turn do lead to changes in *la langue*. So, whatever the process of internalization might be, it is the connection between *la langue* and *parole* that still remains to be resolved, and this is a conceptual gap that is not easily bridged.

Thus, the materiality of language, too often dismissed as E-Language or *parole*, and consequently also dismissed as being theoretically uninteresting or unimportant turns out to be not just difficult to ignore. Rather, it is where the linguistic action lies, so to speak, and where any fruitful attempt to understand the workings of language must begin. But language *qua* material phenomenon evinces changes to both its structure and lexical inventory. In what sense then, we should ask, can language be argued to be complete once attention is turned to the varied ways in which language is used in communicative practices?

Constructing but not quite Assembling

An interesting approach worth discussing at this point is Construction Grammar (CG) (Fillmore, Kay, and O'Connor 1988; Goldberg 1995; Lakoff 1987). CG does not assume that there is a language-specific faculty or language organ. Instead, CG treats language as something that is learned; language is 'CONSTRUCTED on the basis of the input together with general cognitive, pragmatic and processing constraints' (Goldberg 2005, 2; upper case in original).

Lakoff (1987, 463) emphasizes that CG draws on insights from other studies regarding human cognition, including what is known about prototypes and their effects on categorization, the fact that reasoning processes make use of metaphor and metonymy as well as cultural models, and that meaning is ultimately influenced by experiential factors such as bodily and other sensorimotor faculties. Hence, the willingness of CG to accommodate in its linguistic analyses the effects and processes associated with general cognition. Together, the individual constructions and the relationships between them constitute the grammar of the language that is constructed. Moreover, CG is 'flat' or non-derivational because it does not posit a strict separation of lexicon and grammar. Constructions are already surface-level phenomena, being pairings of form and meaning that have varying degrees of specificity (Goldberg 1995, 7). There is a continuum of constructions from the highly schematic to the much more lexically specific.

The constructional approach treats the grammar of a language as constituted by an inventory of constructions or form-meaning pairings, all of which are assumed to co-exist in a multi-dimensional network of inheritance relationships. Individual lexical items (such as *car* or *chair*) are constructions as are conventionalized linguistic collocations of varying sizes and specificity. The latter include formulaic expressions as well as more general phrasal and syntactic patterns (such as Determiner followed by Head Noun). For example, a morpheme like *pre-*, the word *avocado*, the covariational conditional *The Xer the Yer* (e.g. The more you think about it, the less you understand), and the ditransitive *Subj V Obj1 Obj2* (e.g. He baked her a muffin) are all examples of constructions, 'varying in size and complexity' (Goldberg 2005, 5). By looking at what constructions exist and how they combine, CG aims to account for the entire continuum of linguistic expressions associated with a named variety, ranging from those that are highly irregular to those that are more prosaic. So, in the language known as 'English', an expression such as 'What did Liza buy Zach?' might be said to involve a combination of the following constructions (10):

Liza, buy, Zach, what, do constructions
Ditransitive construction
Question construction
Subject-Auxiliary Inversion construction
VP construction
NP construction

CG accepts as constructions both form-meaning pairings with non-predictable properties as well as those that are completely predictable (Croft 2001; Goldberg 1995), pointing to psychological evidence that information about specific exemplars is stored alongside extracted generalizations (Barlow and Kemmer 2000; Bybee and Slobin 1982; Langacker 1987, 494; Ross and Makin 1999). And because CG takes seriously the ability of speakers to construe subtle differences in form and meaning, preference is given to *motivating* (Haiman 1985; Lakoff 1987) rather than predicting observed generalizations, and this sometimes entails drawing on functional or historical factors to explain why particular form-meaning correspondences happen to exist. Goldberg (2005, 17) gives the example of English words like *pants, trousers, khakis* and *leggings*; words that refer to 'lowertrunk-wear are grammatical plural'. Citing Langacker (1987), Goldberg (2005) points out that:

> ... this type of grammatical plurality is motivated by the fact that the referents involved all have bipartite structure. Lower-trunkwear all have two parts, one for each leg. Notice *skirt* and *wrap* are non-bipartite and as expected are also not grammatically plural.

Thus, CG acknowledges that it is also important to grapple with the question of how new constructions can come about. CG is not committed to the idea of language completeness and it relies on findings from a broad range of studies, including those dealing with category formation, grammaticalization, metaphor, and child language acquisition. This means that the linguistic assemblage postulated in CG does not eschew connections with other assemblages. Rather, its commitment to cognitive realism allows it to establish theoretical connections with research elsewhere, particularly research that focuses on general human cognitive processes. For example, learning strategies have been variously ascribed to a principle of contrast or synonymy avoidance (E. Clark 1993, 69), sensitivity to pre-emptive knowledge, or construal of semantic similarity (Childers and Tomasello 2001). Consequently, speakers are assumed to treat differences in form as guides to differences in meaning. Subtle differences in form help speakers to fine-tune the associated semantics or pragmatics. When speakers learn a construction such as the relative clause (Diessel and Tomasello 2005), they effectively learn the meaning that corresponds to a constructional pattern, and where relevant, they also learn the limits within which the pattern can be varied.

At the same, it has to be said that CG does not go quite far enough in embracing the implications of its commitment to cognitive plausibility. There are at least two reasons for this. First, there is a stance that might be described as weak autonomy, where the idea that there is a distinct language system is taken as a default rather than posited as an innate system. We see this in Goldberg's (2005, 3) reference to 'language system', and to 'language-internal generalizations' (2); by the latter she means to refer to the properties that characterize a group of related constructions belonging to the language system under investigation. For example, Goldberg discusses a variety of language-specific constructions, from languages such as French, Croatian, Maasai, Russian and, of course, English (8). But a speaker's knowledge of English or French, etc., also includes knowledge of what constructions are to be metalinguistically considered 'English' as opposed to 'French' or 'Russian'. That is, what a speaker knows about any given construction is not only its phonology, morphosyntax, semantics and pragmatics, but also what language name it is conventionally classified under. However, this metalinguistic issue is never really discussed in CG. But if CG accepts that 'language is learned as a type of categorization' (25), then the question of how specific constructions come to be metalinguistically categorized cannot be consigned as irrelevant. Furthermore, this is an issue that is even more pertinent once we acknowledge that speakers' experiences with language are increasingly multilingual. This means that the ongoing acquisition of newer constructions cannot be divorced from the question of how speakers decide or even contest whether a particular construction can be said to belong to a particular language over some other. That this question is never seriously addressed is attributable to the fact that CG tends to still operate under the assumption that the speaker is monolingual, and even where the speaker is acknowledged to be multilingual, this multilingualism is treated as one involving separate monolingual systems or multiple monolingualisms (Heller 2000).

Second, given that constructions are signs, there is the question of how the system of language constructions comes to be constituted in such a way that it is distinct from non-linguistic signs or other sign systems. For CG, much is made of the fact that constructions arise as a result of how speakers experience and construe the world around them (Lakoff 1987; Langacker 1987; Goldberg 1995, 7). Basic clause-level constructions are claimed to encode 'humanly relevant scenes', and argument structure is argued to be associated with our construal of 'experientially grounded gestalts, such as that of someone volitionally transferring something to someone else, someone causing something to move to change state, someone experiencing something, something moving, and so on' (Goldberg 1995, 5, 39). Given the multi-modal nature of any scene or gestalt, CG needs to address the question of how comes it that the system called 'language' then emerges separate from 'non-language'. It cannot, on pain of contradicting itself, appeal to some natural tendency to separate linguistic signs or constructions from non-linguistic ones. The upshot of all this is that greater attention needs to be given to how the relationship between language and non-language is itself constructed.

The key point to note here is that constructions are not innate but learned on the basis on speakers' encounters with relevant input and experiences, as well as general cognitive constraints on processing. But since the same experiences and general cognitive constraints are also said to apply to the learning of non-linguistic information, CG needs to say something about how linguistic and non-linguistic constructions come to be distinguished. Thus, even though the way in which language is understood within CG is certainly less abstract than, say, the way in which it has been conceptualized by the generative program, CG still does not go quite far enough in trying to address the wider and more fundamental question of how a language assemblage comes to be constituted. CG still takes as its starting point the idea of a language or a grammatical system, and then proceeds to focus on the inventory of construction 'within' the system. But it is precisely this 'within' that needs to be analysed because it is here that the boundary between the linguistic and non-linguistic is established or assembled.

Advancing the Study of Language and Communication

By way of closing this chapter, it is useful to ask the question of how advancements in the study of language and communication can be made, given the conceptual challenges raised by automation. Where a field like linguistics is concerned, it is important to avoid taking as axiomatic the idea that language exists as an autonomous system. Even a relatively catholic approach such as CG needs to start *not* with the idea of investigating the 'internal' workings of a language but with the acceptance that language itself is an assemblage that is put together in various ways, the specifics of which depend on the ideologies that inform our views about communicative practices. Importantly, this acceptance of language as assemblage would mean a shift in how we understand context (Canagarajah 2020, 301):

> ... many verbal resources relegated to context would actively mediate and shape communication; such resources [LW: including automation] would make context agentive and dynamic rather than being static or monolithic ...

This opens up exciting possibilities for advancements in linguistics. For example, it becomes conceptually feasible to attend to material calibration, that is, *the ways in which resources, such as activities and technologies, are – to varying degrees –*

assembled so as to bring about desired states of affairs. Some assemblages may be the result of relatively unplanned confluences of activities and technologies (even where such confluences are the results of historical trajectories of peoples, objects, and ideas as in the nexus analysis proposed by Scollon and Scollon [2004]). Others are deliberately designed in order to create as far possible specific affective regimes. Regardless, the term 'calibration' serves to highlight how various resources that constitute an assemblage are brought together so as to serve specific purposes, such as urban management, and thus adjustments and assessments might be made to these assemblages from time to time. As a simple illustration, consider (1).

(1) Please move to the rear [inside a public bus]

This relatively simple example brings out three key dimensions of material calibration: (i) the selection of activities and technologies, (ii) their spatial arrangement, and (iii) their temporal arrangement. The purpose of (1) is to encourage passengers to move to the rear of the bus so as to prevent crowding near the doors. Passengers sometimes congregate near the doors because it makes disembarkation easier. But this also can mean that the bus is below capacity since the empty spaces at the rear may remain unoccupied because they become less accessible to subsequent passengers. To aid in management, the driver may also have access to a camera that allows her to check if there is indeed unnecessary crowding near the doors. The bus driver may need to vocalize the request in (1) and thus may even be provided with a microphone. The sign itself will likely have been specially manufactured for just this specific purpose. This would have been reflected in the use of fabricated materials, as well as the print and color choice – all of which may semiotically reflect the corporate identity of the bus company. The manufactured nature of the sign, together with the provision of a microphone and a camera for the driver all point to careful consideration and investment by the bus company regarding the choice of activities and technologies.

And of course, the specific placement of the sign itself is important. The sign is typically placed near the doors of the bus, where crowding is likely to occur. Even something as mundane as positioning the camera and microphone to be within the driver's easy access involves placement considerations. Here, we have the second dimension of material calibration, that of its spatial arrangement. Finally, the installation of the sign, the camera and microphone represent also speak to a relatively high degree of permanence in the temporal arrangement. That is, resources that the bus company has committed towards the goal of encouraging passengers to move to the back constitute a fairly stable and long-term form of material calibration. There could be some misalignment of the resources if, for example, the sign were to be mistakenly placed right at the rear of the bus. Such a placement would make less sense since those passengers reading the sign would already have moved to the rear. Miscalibration can indeed occur, as when a sign is wrongly placed. For example, a customer may order a slice of pizza from a restaurant counter where two different types of pizza are displayed with identifying labels. But when the order arrives, it is not the pizza that the customer wanted, because the staff had wrongly aligned the labels with the pizzas that they were supposed to refer to. This is an error that is easily rectified because it simply requires switching the labels around. Things get more interesting and complex once when the materials involved (such as screwed-on signs and automated programs) are not as easily changed or moved around, unlike small cardboard labels.

Material calibration as a form of assemblage brings a new conceptual dimension to studies of linguistic landscapes, sometimes also referred to as semiotic landscapes. Such studies have seen a shift in emphasis from a reliance on quantitative methodologies that count the distributions of different languages in a given landscape (e.g. Backhaus 2007; Coluzzi 2009; Muth 2012) to a more phenomenological orientation that understands the landscape to be ideologically loaded and, moreover, is interested in how this ideological loading may be aimed at regulating the patterns of interactions of those individuals or groups that happen to be located within the landscape (Jaworski and Thurlow 2010; Shohamy and Gorter 2008; Wee and Goh 2019).

Viewing the landscape through the lens of materially calibrated assemblages provides a way to get a theoretical grip on the Internet of Things (IoT), for example. IoT refers to how physical objects, sensors, AI, and other technologies exchange data via various communication networks. Many cities are getting 'smarter/networked/connected' (where this emergence of 'smart' cities is itself just one aspect of the much more encompassing IoT). The result is a 'smart landscape', where temperature and lighting controls, crowd information, facial recognition software, and various security systems, increasingly converge to regulate access to and usage of features in the landscape. In addition to studies of how activities within the landscape are conducted, the concept can also potentially inform the development of policy guidelines and standards that are aimed at regulating both the activities and the construction of the landscape, especially where matters of privacy and personal security are implicated. That is, if linguistic landscape studies are to contribute broadly to scholarly discussions about the governance of urban spaces, they have to be able to theorize about attempts to link up infrastructure with computer technologies to improve the urban experience. Importantly, this would require not positing an autonomous view of language. Instead, as Gurney and Demuro (2022, 11, italics in original) point out, '[t]hrough agential realism, language would similarly constitute a *becoming* contingent on the intra-action of agents and apparatuses.'

A more fundamental implication for advancements in linguistics concerns our understanding of concepts such as language and agency. These concepts cannot be understood as abstract or essentialized phenomena that exist independently of their material manifestations. This is especially the case, if the insistence is that language and agency exist in an abstract realm or plane that only humans have access to. Human and non-human actors alike have to be treated as 'apparatuses', with their various activities contributing to the demarcation, emergence and identifiability of 'things' such as 'speaker' and 'language', whose relationships to one another can then be talked about (Barad 2003, 816). Barad emphasizes that (816):

Apparatuses are not inscription devices, scientific instruments set in place before the action happens, or machines that mediate the dialectic of resistance and

accommodation. They are neither neutral probes of the natural world nor structures that deterministically impose some particular outcome …
   Importantly, apparatuses are themselves phenomena.

'Phenomena', for Barad is not something that exists to be observed by a separately existing observer. Rather, it is a term for referring to whatever it is that we are interested in analysing or understanding *before* we start to impose structure and boundaries on it, and in so doing, establish 'differential boundaries between "humans" and "nonhumans," "culture" and "nature," the "social" and the "scientific"' (Barad 2003, 817).

   The presence of automation thus also raises important questions about accountability in language use and communicative effects, matters that are relevant to language policy. When automation is involved in the production of messages or when it is being used to police the communicative practices of people, then it behoves language policy scholars to start seriously asking questions about where and how to locate communicative agency and responsibility. Such questions cannot be dismissed as too philosophical or too abstract. Rather, they increasingly are consequential for what we understand by language policy. In this regard, as pointed out in the preceding chapter, the study of language policy has to be cognizant of the presence of posthumanist organizations.

Note

1 Note that this is not the same as the distinction between relative and absolute deterritorialization' (Deleuze and Guattari 1987, 142, 510). With the former, a newly constructed assemblage follows patterns that have already been conventionalized. With the latter, the new assemblage diverges from established patterns, resulting in novelties. It would, to be sure, be difficult to come up with an example of absolute deterritorialization that bears absolutely no similarity or relation to other assemblages. We are in fact looking at degrees of differences and similarities. And the specific makeup of an assemblage is not the same as the ideologies that give it coherence. One can in fact have an assemblage that bears strong similarity to an earlier assemblage while denying how those similarities came about (as in cases of plagiarism, where a new text ostensibly has strong similarities to an earlier text). The question then is whether the new text was constructed without any awareness of the earlier one (similarities are then coincidental) or whether it was constructed by carefully replicating the latter (copying). Conversely, one can imagine a student of poetry trying to write a sonnet (hence, relative deterritorialization) but being told by their teacher that there is no resemblance at all to what counts as a sonnet (hence, unintended absolute deterritorialization).

References

Books, Chapters, and Articles

Ahearn, Laura. 2001. "Agency." In *Key Terms in Language and Culture*, edited by Alessandro Duranti, 7–10. Oxford: Blackwell.

Ahmed, Sara. 2004. *The Cultural Politics of Emotion.* Edinburgh: University of Edinburgh.

Anderson, Stephen R. and David W. Lightfoot. 2004. *The Language Organ.* Cambridge: Cambridge University Press.

Austin, J.L. 1962. *How to do Things with Words*, edited by J.O. Urmson and Marina Sbisá. 2nd ed. Cambridge, MA: Harvard University Press.

Backhaus, Peter. 2007. *Linguistic Landscapes: A Comparative Study of Urban Multilingualism in Tokyo.* Clevedon: Multilingual Matters.

Bäckström, Stina. 2020. "A Dogma of Speech Act Theory." *Inquiry.* doi:10.1080/0020174X.2020.1724563.

Bakhtin, Mikhail. 1986. *Speech Genres and Other Late Essays*, translated by Vern W. McGee, edited by Caryl Emerson and Michael Holquist. Austin, TX: University of Texas Press.

Barad, Karen. 2003. "Posthumanist Performativity: Toward an Understanding of How Matter Comes to Matter." *Gender and Science* 28, no. 3: 801–831.

Barad, Karen. 2007. *Meeting the Universe Halfway: Quantum Physics and the Entanglement of Matter and Meaning.* Durham, NC: Duke University Press.

Barlow, Michael and Suzanne Kemmer, eds. 2000. *Usage-Based Models of Language.* Stanford, CA: Center for the Study of Language and Information.

Barthes, Roland. 1986. "The Death of the Author." In *The Rustle of Language*, translated by Richard Howard, 49–55. New York: Hill & Wang.

Bayat, Nihat. 2013. "A Study on the Use of Speech Acts." *Behavioral Sciences* 70: 213–221.

Benjamin, Geoffrey. 1976. "The cultural logic of Singapore's 'multiracialism'." In *Singapore: Society in Transition*, edited by Riaz Hassan, 115–133. Kuala Lumpur: Oxford University Press.

Bennett, Jane. 2010. *Vibrant Matter: A Political Ecology of Things.* Durham, NC: Duke University Press.

Blommaert, Jan. 2005. *Discourse.* Cambridge: Cambridge University Press.

Bonta, Mark and John Protevi. 2004. *Deleuze and Geophilosophy: A Guide and Glossary.* Edinburgh: Edinburgh University Press.

Bourdieu, Pierre. 1977. *Outline of a Theory of Practice.* Cambridge: Cambridge University Press.

Bryant, Melanie and Julie Wolfram Cox. 2014. "Beyond Authenticity? Humanism, Post-humanism and New Organization Development." *British Journal of Management* 25, no. 4 (October): 706–723.

Buchanan, Ray. 2013. "Conversational Implicature, Communicative Intentions, and Content." *Canadian Journal of Philosophy* 43, no. 5/6 (October–December): 720–740.

Bybee, Joan and Dan Slobin. 1982. "Rules and Schemas in the Development and Use of the English Past Tense." *Language* 58, no. 2 (June): 265–289.

Cameron, Deborah. 2000a. "Styling the Worker." *Journal of Sociolinguistics* 4, no. 3: 323–347.

Cameron, Deborah. 2000b. *Good to Talk?* London: Sage Publications.

Canagarajah, Suresh. 2007. "After Disinvention: Possibilities for Communication, Community and Competence." In *Disinventing and Reconstituting Languages*, edited by Sinfree Makoni and Alastair Pennycook, 233–239. Clevedon: Multilingual Matters.

Canagarajah, Suresh. 2010. "The Possibility of a Community of Difference." *The Cresset* LXXIII, no. 4: 18–30.

Canagarajah, Suresh. 2020. "English as a Resource in a Communicative Assemblage." In *Ontologies of English*, edited by Christopher J. Hall and Rachel Wicaksono, 295–314. Cambridge: Cambridge University Press.

Chen, Sibo. 2016. "Language and Ecology: A Content Analysis of Ecolinguistics as an Emerging Research Field." *Ampersand* 3: 108–116.

Cheong, Pauline Hope. 2020. "Religion, Robots and Rectitude: Communicative Affordances for Spiritual Knowledge and Community." *Applied Artificial Intelligence* 34, no. 5: 412–431. doi:10.1080/08839514.2020.1723869.

Childers, Jane B. and Michael Tomasello. 2001. "The Role of Pronouns in Young Children's Acquisition of the English Transitive Construction." *Developmental Psychology* 37, no. 6: 739–748.

Chomsky, Noam. 1976. *Reflections on Language*. New York: Pantheon.

Chomsky, Noam. 1986. *Knowledge of Language*. New York: Praeger.

Chomsky, Noam. 1993. *Language and Thought*. London: Moyer Bell.

Chomsky, Noam. 2001. *On Nature and Language*, edited by Adriana Belletti and Luigi Rizzi. Cambridge: Cambridge University Press.

Christian, Brian. 2011. *The Most Human Human*. London: Penguin.

Churchland, Paul. 1995. *The Engine of Reason, The Seat of the Soul*. Cambridge, MA: MIT Press.

Ciprut, Jose V. 2008. "Citizenship: Mere Contract or Construct for Conduct?" In *The Future of Citizenship*, edited by Jose V. Ciprut, 1–29. Cambridge, MA: MIT Press.

Clark, Billy. 2021. "Identity Inferences: Implicatures, Implications and Extended Interpretations." *Language and Literature: International Journal of Stylistics* 29, no. 4: 424–445.

Clark, Eve. 1993. *The Lexicon in Acquisition*. Cambridge: Cambridge University Press.

Clark, Herbert and Thomas B. Carlson. 1982. "Hearers and Speech Acts." *Language* 58, no. 2 (June): 332–373.

Clifford, James. 1988. *The Predicament of Culture*. Cambridge, MA: Harvard University Press.

Coluzzi, Paolo. 2009. "The Italian Linguistic Landscape: The Cases of Milan and Udine." *International Journal of Multilingualism* 6, no. 3: 298–312.

Cook, Vivian and Mark Newson. 1996. *Chomsky's Universal Grammar*. 2nd ed. Oxford: Blackwell.

Corti, Kevin and Alex Gillespie. 2015. "Revisiting Milgram's Cyranoid Method: Experimenting with Hybrid Human Agents." *Journal of Social Psychology* 155, no. 1: 30–56.

Coupland, Nikolas. 2007. *Style: Language Variation and Identity*. Cambridge: Cambridge University Press.

Crevier, Daniel. 1993. *AI: The Tumultuous History of the Search for Artificial Intelligence*. New York: Basic Books.

Croft, William. 2001. *Radical Construction Grammar*. Oxford: Oxford University Press.

Culler, Jonathan. 1986. *Ferdinand de Saussure*. Revised ed. Ithaca, NY: Cornell University Press.

D'Agostino, Fred. 1984. "Chomsky on Creativity." *Synthese* 58, no. 1: 85–117.

Darcy, Alison, Alan Louie, and Laura Weiss Roberts. 2016. "Machine Learning and the Profession of Medicine." *JAMA* 315, no. 6: 551–552.

Darcy, Alison, Jade Daniels, David Salinger, Paul Wicks, and Athena Robinson. 2021. "Evidence of Human-Level Bonds Established with a Digital Conversational Agent: Cross-sectional, Retrospective Observational Study." *JMIR Form Res* 5, no. 5: e27868. doi:10.2196/27868.

Das, Sukla. 1977. *Crime and Punishment in Ancient India*. New Delhi: Abhinav Publications.

DeLanda, Manuel. 2006. *A New Philosophy of Society: Assemblage Theory and Social Complexity*. London: Continuum.

Deleuze, Gilles and Felix Guattari. 1987. *A Thousand Plateaus*, translated by Brian Massumi. London: Athlone Press.

Demuro, Eugenia and Laura Gurney. 2021. "Languages/languaging as World-Making: The Ontological Bases of Language." *Language Sciences* 83 (January): 1–13.

Dennett, Daniel. 1971. "Intentional Systems." *Journal of Philosophy* 68, no. 4: 87–106. doi:10.2307/2025382.

Dennett, Daniel. 1987. *The Intentional Stance*. Cambridge, MA: MIT Press.

Diessel, Holger and Michael Tomasello. 2005. "A New Look at the Acquisition of Relative Clauses." *Language* 81, no. 4: 882–906.

Dosse, François. 1997. *History of Structuralism, Vols. 1 and 2*, translated by Deborah Glassman. Minneapolis, MN: University of Minnesota Press.

Dreyfus, Hubert L. 1972. *What Computers Can't Do*. New York: Harper & Row.

Du Bois, John W. 1992. "Meaning without Intention: Lessons from Divination." In *Responsibility and Evidence in Oral Discourse*, edited by Jane H. Hill and Judith T. Irvine, 48–71. Cambridge: Cambridge University Press.

Duranti, Alessandro. 1992. "Intentions, Self, and Responsibility: An Essay in Samoan Ethnopragmatics." In *Responsibility and Evidence in Oral Discourse*, edited by Jane H. Hill and Judith T. Irvine, 24–47. Cambridge: Cambridge University Press.

Eckert, Penelope. 2008. "Variation and the Indexical Field." *Journal of Sociolinguistics* 12, no. 4: 453–476.

Eckert, Penelope. 2012. "Three Waves of Variation Study: The Emergence of Meaning in the Study of Sociolinguistic Variation." *Annual Review of Anthropology* 41: 87–100.

Eisenstadt, Shmuel N. 2002. "Some Observations on Multiple Modernities." In *Reflections on Multiple Modernities*, edited by Dominic Sachsenmaier, Jens Riedel, and Shmuel N. Eisenstadt, 27–41. Leiden: Brill.

Eliade, Mircea. 1959. *The Sacred and the Profane: The Nature of Religion*, translated by Willard R. Trask. Orlando, FL: Harcourt, Inc.

Elliott, David J., Marissa Silverman, and Wayne D. Bowman. 2016. "Artistic Citizenship." In *Artistic Citizenship*, edited by David J. Elliott, Marissa Silverman, and Wayne D. Bowman, 3–21. Oxford: Oxford University Press.

Fairclough, Norman. 2001. *Language and Power*. 2nd ed. Essex: Longman.

Farías, Ignacio. 2010. "Introduction." In *Urban Assemblages*, edited by Ignacio Farías and Thomas Bender, 1–24. London: Routledge.

Fillmore, Charles J., Paul Kay, and Mary Catherine O'Connor. 1988. "Regularity and Idiomaticity in Grammatical Constructions: The Case of Let Alone." *Language* 64, no. 3 (September): 501–538. doi:10.2307/414531.

Firth, J.R. 1935. "The Technique of Semantics." *Transactions of the Philological Society* 34, no. 1: 36–72.

Firth, J.R. 1968. "Ethnographic Analysis and Language with Reference to Malinowski's Views." In *Selected Papers of J. R. Firth 1952–1959*, edited by Frank R. Palmer, 137–167. Bloomington, IN: Indiana University Press.

Fiske, Amelia, Peter Henningsen, and Alena Buyx. 2019. "Your Robot Therapist Will See You Now: Ethical Implications of Embodied Artificial Intelligence in Psychiatry, Psychology, and Psychotherapy." *Journal of Medical Internet Research* 21, no. 5: e13216. doi:10.2196/13216.

Foley, William. 1997. *Anthropological Linguistics*. Oxford: Blackwell.

Ford, Richard T. 2005. *Racial Culture: A Critique*. Princeton, NJ: Princeton University Press.

Gal, Susan. 1989. "Lexical innovation and loss: The use and value of restricted Hungarian." In *Investigating Obsolescence: Studies in Language Contraction and Death*, edited by Nancy C. Dorian, 313–331. Cambridge: Cambridge University Press.

Gasparov, Boris. 2021. "Ferdinand de Saussure." *Oxford Bibliographies*, last modified April 21, 2021, accessed August 5, 2022. doi:10.1093/OBO/9780190221911-0106.

Giddens, Anthony. 1987. *Social Theory and Modern Sociology*. Cambridge: Polity Press.

Gladden, Matthew. 2016. *Sapient Circuits and Digitalized Flesh: The Organization as Locus of Technological Posthumanization*. Indianapolis, IN: Defragmenter Media.

Godfrey-Smith, Peter. 2013. "Quine and Pragmatism." In *A Companion to W.V.O. Quine*, edited by Gilbert Harman and Ernie Lepore. Wiley Online Library. doi:10.1002/9781118607992.ch3.

Goffman, Erving. 1974. *Frame Analysis: An Essay on the Organization of Experience*. New York: Harper & Row.

Goffman, Erving. 1981. *Forms of Talk*. Pennsylvania, PA: University of Pennsylvania Press.

Goldberg, Adele. 1995. *Constructions: A Construction Grammar Approach to Argument Structure*. Chicago, IL: University of Chicago Press.

Goldberg, Adele. 2005. *Constructions at Work*. Oxford: Oxford University Press.

Goodwin, Charles and Marjorie Harness Goodwin. 2003. "Participation." In *A Companion to Linguistic Anthropology*, edited by Alessandro Duranti, 222–244. Oxford: Wiley.

Gordon, W. Terrence. 2004. "Langue and Parole." In *The Cambridge Companion to Saussure*, edited by Carol Sanders, 76–87. Cambridge University Press (online). doi:10.1017/CCOL052180051X.006.

Grandy, Richard E. and Richard Warner. 2020. "Paul Grice." In *The Stanford Encyclopedia of Philosophy* (Summer 2020 Edition), edited by Edward N. Zalta. https://plato.stanford.edu/archives/sum2020/entries/grice.

Green, Mitchell. 2021. "Speech Acts." In *The Stanford Encyclopedia of Philosophy* (Fall 2021 Edition), edited by Edward N. Zalta. https://plato.stanford.edu/archives/fall2021/entries/speech-acts.

Grice, H.P. 1957. "Meaning." *Philosophical Review* 67, no. 3 (July): 377–388. www.jstor.org/stable/2182440.

Grice, H. P. 1975. "Logic and Conversation." In *Syntax and Semantics Volume 3: Speech Acts*, edited by Peter Cole and Jerry L. Morgan, 41–58. New York: Academic Press.

Grice, H.P. 1989. *Studies in the Way of Words.* Cambridge, MA: Harvard University Press.

Grünthal, Riho, Sami Honkasalo, and Markus Juutinen. 2019. "Language sociological trends in South African Ndebele communities: A pilot survey." *Studia Orientalia* 120: 17–62.

Gurney, Laura and Eugenia Demuro. 2022. "Simultaneous Multiplicity: New Materialist Ontologies and the Apprehension of Language as Assemblage and Phenomenon." *Critical Inquiry in Language Studies* 20, no. 2: 127–149. doi:10.1080/15427587.2022.2102011.

Haggerty, Kevin D. and Richard V. Ericson. 2003. "The Surveillant Assemblage." *British Journal of Sociology* 51, no. 4: 605–622.

Haiman, John. 1985. *Iconicity in Syntax.* Cambridge: Cambridge University Press.

Haleem, Abid, Mohd Javaid, and Ravi Pratap Singh. 2022. "An era of ChatGPT as a significant futuristic support tool: A study on features, abilities, and challenges." *Bench-Council Transactions on Benchmarks, Standards and Evaluations* 2, no. 4 (October): 100089. doi:10.1016/j.tbench.2023.100089.

Han, Fook Kwang, Warren Fernandez, and Sumiko Tan. 1998. *Lee Kuan Yew: The Man and His Ideas.* Singapore: Singapore Press Holdings.

Hansen, Maj-Britt Mosegaard and Marina Terkourafi. 2023. "We need to talk about Hearer's meaning." *Journal of Pragmatics* 208 (April): 99–114. doi:10.1016/j.pragma.2023.02.015.

Haraway, Donna. 2016. "A Cyborg Manifesto." Originally published in *Socialist Review* 15, no. 2 (1985): 65–107. Accessed via http://ebookcentral.proquest.com/lib/warw/detail.action?docID=4392065.

Harris, Roy. 1988. *Language, Saussure and Wittgenstein: How to Play Games with Words.* London: Routledge.

Harrison, K. David. 2007. *When Languages Die: The Extinction of the World's Languages and the Erosion of Human Knowledge.* Oxford: Oxford University Press.

Haverkate, Henk. 1984. *Speech Acts, Speakers and Hearers.* Amsterdam: John Benjamins.

Hazard, Sonia. 2013. "The Material Turn in the Study of Religion." *Religion and Society* 4, no. 1: 58–78.

Heller, Monica. 2000. "Bilingualism and Identity in the Post-Modern World." *Estudios de Sociolingüística* 1, no. 2: 9–24.

Henrich, Joseph, Steven J. Heine, and Ara Norenzayan. 2010. "The weirdest people in the world?" *Behavioural and Brain Sciences* 33, no. 23: 61–83.

Hill, Jane. 2008. *The Everyday Language of White Racism.* Oxford: Wiley.

Hill, Michael and Kwen Fee Lian. 1995. *The Politics of Nation Building and Citizenship in Singapore.* London: Routledge.

Hinzen, Wolfram. 2006. *Mind Design and Minimal Syntax.* Oxford: Oxford University Press.

Holston, James. 1998. *Cities and Citizenship.* Durham, NC: Duke University Press.

Holtgrewe, Ursula, Christian Kerst, and Karen Shire, eds. 2002. *Re-organising Service Work: Call Centres in Germany and Britain.* Aldershot: Ashgate.

Hultgren, Anna Kristina. 2009. "Linguistic Regulation and Interactional Reality: A Sociolinguistic Study of Call Centre Service Transactions." PhD dissertation, University of Oxford. https://oro.open.ac.uk/47572.

Hutchinson, Sue, John Purcell, and Nick Kinnie. 2000. "Evolving High Commitment Management and the Experience of the RAC Call Centre." *Human Resource Management Journal* 10, no. 1: 63–78.

Janssens, Leen and Walter Schaeken. 2016. "'But' Implicatures: A Study of the Effect of Working Memory and Argument Characteristics." *Frontiers in Psychology* 7: 1520. doi:10.3389/fpsyg.2016.01520.

Jaworski, Adam and Crispin Thurlow, eds. 2010. *Semiotic Landscapes: Language, Image, Space*. London: Continuum.

Kachru, Braj. 1995. "Transcultural Creativity in World Englishes and Literary Canons." In *Principle and Practice in Applied Linguistics: Studies in Honour of H. G. Widdowson*, edited by Guy Cook and Barbara Seidlhofer, 271–287. Oxford: Oxford University Press.

Kachru, Braj. 1997. "World Englishes and English-Using Communities." *Annual Review of Applied Linguistics* 17: 66–87.

Kecskes, Istvan. 2010. "The Paradox of Communication." *Pragmatics & Society* 1, no. 1: 50–73.

Kerruish, Erika. 2021. "Assembling Human Empathy towards Care Robots: The Human Labor of Robot Sociality." *Emotion, Space and Society* 41 (November): 100840.

Kim, Youjeong and S. Shyam Sundar. 2012. "Anthropomorphism of computers: Is it mindful or mindless?" *Computers in Human Behavior* 28, no. 1: 241–250.

Kobis, Nils and Luca D. Mossink. 2021. "Artificial Intelligence Versus Maya Angelou: Experimental evidence that people cannot differentiate AI-generated from human-written poetry." *Computers in Human Behavior* 114: 106553.

Lakoff, George. 1987. *Women, Fire and Dangerous Things: What Categories Reveal About the Mind*. Chicago, IL: University of Chicago Press.

Langacker, Ronald. 1987. *Foundations of Cognitive Grammar: Theoretical Prerequisites, Vol. 1*. Stanford, CA: Stanford University Press.

Langlotz, Andreas. 2015. "Language, Creativity and Cognition." In *The Routledge Handbook of Language and Creativity*, edited by Rodney Jones, 40–60. London: Routledge.

Larsen-Freeman, Diane. 2008. *Complex Systems and Applied Linguistics*. Oxford: Oxford University Press.

Latour, Bruno. 1986. "Visualisation and Cognition: Drawing Things Together." In *Knowledge and Society: Studies in the Sociology of Culture, Past and Present* Vol 6, edited by Henrika Kuklick, 1–40. Stamford, CT: Jai Press.

Latour, Bruno. 1993. *We Have Never Been Modern*, translated by Catherine Porter. Cambridge, MA: Harvard University Press.

Latour, Bruno. 1999. *Pandora's Hope: Essays on the Reality of Science Studies*. Cambridge, MA: Harvard University Press.

Lee, K. C. 1983. *Language and Education in Singapore*. Singapore: Singapore University Press.

Levinson, Stephen. 1992. "Activity Types and Language." In *Talk at Work: Interaction in Institutional Settings*, edited by Paul Drew and John Heritage, 66–100. Cambridge: Cambridge University Press.

Maffi, Luisa. 2001. *On Biocultural Diversity: Linking Language, Knowledge, and the Environment*. Washington, DC: Smithsonian Institution Press.

Makoni, Sinfree and Alastair Pennycook. 2005. "Disinventing and (Re)Constituting Languages." *Critical Inquiry in Language Studies* 2, no. 3: 137–156.

Makoni, Sinfree and Alastair Pennycook, eds. 2007. *Disinventing and (Re)Constituting Languages*. Clevedon: Multilingual Matters.

Manning, Philip. 1992. *Erving Goffman and Modern Sociology*. Stanford, CA: Stanford University Press.

Manning, Paul and Ilana Gershon. 2013. "Animating Interaction." *Journal of Ethnographic Theory* 3, no. 3: 107–137.

Marston, Sallie, John Paul Jones III, and Keith Woodward. 2005. "Human Geography without Scale." *Transactions of the Institute of British Geographers* 30, no. 4: 416–432.

Mendes, Alexander. 2020. "Verdant Vernaculars: Corsican Environmental Assemblages." *Journal of Linguistic Anthropology* 30, no. 2: 156–178.

Meyer, John W. and Brian Rowan. 1991. "Institutionalized Organizations: Formal Structure as Myth and Ceremony." In *The New Institutionalism in Organizational Analysis*, edited by Walter W. Powell and Paul J. DiMaggio, 41–62. Chicago, IL: Chicago University Press.

Milroy, James and Lesley Milroy. 1998. *Authority in Language*. 3rd ed. London: Routledge.

Mühlhäusler, Peter. 2000. "Language Planning and Language Ecology." *Current Issues in Language Planning* 1, no. 3: 306–367.

Muth, Sebastian. 2012. "The Linguistic Landscapes of Chişinău and Vilnius: Linguistic Landscape and the Representation of Minority Languages in Two Post-Soviet Capitals." In *Minority Languages in the Linguistic Landscape*, edited by Durk Gorter, Heiko F. Marten, and Luk Van Mensel, 204–224. Basingstoke: Palgrave Macmillan.

Nass, Clifford and Youngme Moon. 2000. "Machines and Mindlessness: Social Responses to Computers." *Journal of Social Issues* 56, no. 1: 81–103.

Nettle, Daniel and Romaine, Suzanne. 2000. *Vanishing Voices: The Extinction of the World's Languages*. Oxford: Oxford University Press.

Normand, Claudine. 2004. "System, Arbitrariness, Value." In *The Cambridge Companion to Saussure*, edited by Carol Sanders, 88–104. Cambridge: Cambridge University Press.

Norris, Christopher. 2004. "Saussure, Linguistic Theory and Philosophy of Science." In *The Cambridge Companion to Saussure*, edited by Carol Sanders, 219–239. Cambridge: Cambridge University Press.

Oishi, Etsuko. 2006. "Austin's Speech Act Theory and the Speech Situation." *Esercizi Filosofici* 1, no. 1: 1–14.

Orman, Jon. 2008. *Language Policy and Nation-Building in Post-Apartheid South Africa*. Dordrecht: Springer.

Pearce, Kevin J. 2009. "Media and Mass Communication Theories." *Encyclopedia of Communication Theory*, edited by Stephen W. Littlejohn and Karen A. Foss, 623–627.

Pennycook, Alastair. 2018. *Posthumanist Applied Linguistics*. London: Routledge.

Pettit, Philip. 1975. *The Concept of Structuralism: A Critical Analysis*. Dublin: Gill and Macmillan.

Pullum, Geoffrey K. 1999. "African American Vernacular English is Not Standard English with Mistakes." In *The Workings of Language*, edited by Rebecca S. Wheeler, 39–58. Westport, CT: Praeger.

Purcell, Mark. 2002. "Excavating Lefebvre: The Right to the City and its Urban Politics of the Inhabitant." *GeoJournal* 58 (October): 99–108.

Quine, Willard Van Orman. 1953. *From a Logical Point of View*. Cambridge, MA: Harvard University Press.

Rabinowitz, Neil, Frank Perbet, H. Francis Song, Chiyuan Zhang, S.M. Ali Eslami, and Matthew Botvinick. 2018. "Machine Theory of Mind." *Proceedings of the 35th International Conference on Machine Learning*, PMLR 80, 4218–4227. https://arxiv.org/pdf/1802.07740.pdf.

Rampton, Ben. 2006. *Language in Late Modernity*. Cambridge: Cambridge University Press.

Rappa, Antonio. 2000. "Surviving the Politics of Late Modernity: The Eurasian Fringe Community of Singapore." *Southeast Asian Journal of Social Science* 28, no. 2: 153–180.

Récanati, Francois. 1993. *Direct Reference: From Language to Thought*. Oxford: Blackwell.

Reeves, Byron and Clifford Ivar Nass. 1996. *The Media Equation: How People Treat Computers, Television, and New Media Like Real People and Places*. Cambridge University Press.

Rocha, Zarine L. and Brenda S.A. Yeoh 2020. "Measuring Race, Mixed Race, and Multiracialism in Singapore." In *The Palgrave International Handbook of Mixed Racial and Ethnic Classification*, edited by Zarine L. Rocha and Peter J. Aspinall, 629–647. Palgrave Macmillan.

Rosaldo, Michelle Z. 1982. "The Things We Do with Words: Ilongot Speech Acts and Speech Act Theory in Philosophy." *Language in Society* 11, no. 2: 203–237.

Rose, Nikolas. 1998. *Inventing our Selves: Psychology, Power and Personhood*. Cambridge: Cambridge University Press.

Ross, Brian and Valerie S. Makin. 1999. "Prototype versus Exemplar Models." In *The Nature of Cognition*, edited by Robert J. Sternberg, 205–241. Cambridge, MA: MIT Press.

Sarangi, Srikant. 2000. "Activity Types, Discourse Types and Interactional Hybridity." In *Discourse and Social Life*, edited by Srikant Sarangi and Malcolm Coulthard, 1–27. Harlow: Pearson.

Saul, Jennifer. 2010. "Speaker-Meaning, Conversational Implicature and Calculability." In *Meaning and Analysis: New Essays on Grice*, edited by Klaus Petrus, 170–183. London: Palgrave Macmillan.

de Saussure, Ferdinand. 1983. *Course in General Linguistics*. Chicago, IL: Open Court.

Scollon, Ron and Suzanne Wong Scollon. 2004. *Discourses in Place: Language in the Material World*. London: Routledge.

Scott, W. Richard. 2001. *Institutions and Organizations*. Thousand Oaks, CA: Sage Publications.

Scott, W. Richard. 2004. "Institutional Theory." In *Encyclopedia of Social Theory*, edited by George Ritzer, 408–414. Thousand Oaks, CA: Sage Publications.

Searle, John R. 1969. *Speech Acts*. Cambridge: Cambridge University Press.

Searle, John R. 1980. "Minds, Brains and Programs." *Behavioral and Brain Sciences* 3, no. 3: 417–457.

Searle, John R. 1992. *The Rediscovery of the Mind*. Cambridge, MA: MIT Press.

Seargeant, Philip. 2019. *The Emoji Revolution*. Cambridge: Cambridge University Press.

Sellars, Wilfrid. 1963 [1956]. "Empiricism and the Philosophy of Mind." In *Science, Perception and Reality*, 127–196. London: Routledge/Kegan Paul.

Shankar, Shalini and Jillian R. Cavanaugh. 2017. "Toward a Theory of Language Materiality: An Introduction." In *Language and Materiality: Ethnographic and Theoretical Explorations*, edited by Shalini Shankar and Jillian R. Cavanaugh, 1–28. Cambridge: Cambridge University Press.

Shapin, Steven and Simon Schaffer. 1985. *Leviathan and the Air-Pump: Hobbes, Boyle and the Experimental Life*. Princeton, NJ: Princeton University Press.

Shohamy, Elana, and Durk Gorter, eds. 2008. *Linguistic Landscape: Expanding the Scenery*. New York/London: Routledge.

Shyam Sundar, S. and Clifford Nass. 2000. "Source Orientation in Human-Computer Interaction: Programmer, Networker, or Independent Social Actor." *Communication Research* 27, no. 6: 683–703. doi:10.1177/009365000027006001.

Silverstein, Michael, 2003. "Indexical order and the dialectics of sociolinguistic life." *Language and Communication* 23, no. 3: 193–229.

Sperber, Dan and Deirdre Wilson. 1995. *Relevance: Communication and Cognition*. 2nd ed. Oxford: Blackwell.

Spence, N.C.W. 1957. "A Hardy Perennial: The Problem of La langue and La parole." *Archivum Linguisticum* 9: 1–27.

Stanlaw, James. 2020. "Ecolinguistics." In *The International Encyclopedia of Linguistic Anthropology*, edited by James Stanlaw, 1–2. doi:10.1002/9781118786093.iela0110.

Stroud, Christopher. 2001. "African Mother-tongue Programmes and the Politics of Language: Linguistic Citizenship Versus Linguistic Human Rights." *Journal of Multilingual and Multicultural Development* 22, no. 4: 339–355.

Tomasello, Michael. 2003. *Constructing a Language*. Cambridge, MA: Harvard University Press.

Tomasello, Michael. 2010. *Origins of Human Communication*. Cambridge, MA: MIT Press.

Tomasello, Michael. 2014. "The ultra-social animal." *European Journal of Social Psychology* 44, no. 3: 187–194.

Trovato, Gabriele, Cesar Lucho, Alvaro Ramón, Renzo Ramirez, Laureano Rodriguez, and Francisco Cuellar. 2018. "The creation of SanTO: a robot with 'divine' features." *2018 15th International Conference on Ubiquitous Robots*, Honolulu, HI, 437–442. doi:10.1109/URAI.2018.8442207.

Turing, Alan. 1950. "Computing Machinery and Intelligence." *Mind* LIX, no. 236: 433–460. doi:10.1093/mind/LIX.236.433.

Turner, Bryan S. 1993. "Outline of a Theory of Human Rights." *Sociology* 27, no. 3: 485–512.

Vasil, Raj K. 1995. *Asianising Singapore*. Singapore: Heinemann Asia.

Watson, Vanessa. 2009. "Seeing from the South: Seeing from the South: Refocusing Urban Planning on the Globe's Central Urban Issues." *Urban Studies* 46, no. 11: 2259–2275.

Wee, Lionel. 2002. "When English is not a Mother Tongue: Linguistic Ownership and the Eurasian Community in Singapore." *Journal of Multilingual and Multicultural Development* 23, no. 4: 282–295.

Wee, Lionel. 2005. "Class-inclusion and correspondence models as discourse types." *Language in Society* 34, no. 2: 219–238.

Wee, Lionel. 2010. *Language Without Rights*. Oxford: Oxford University Press.

Wee, Lionel. 2014. *The Language of Organizational Styling*. Cambridge: Cambridge University Press.

Wee, Lionel. 2015. "Mobilizing Affect in the Linguistic Cyberlandscape: The R-word Campaign." In *Conflict, Exclusion and Dissent in the Linguistic Landscape*, edited by Rani Rubdy and Selim Ben Said, 185–206. Basingstoke: Palgrave Macmillan.

Wee, Lionel. 2016. "Are there zombies in language policy?" In *Sociolinguistics: Theoretical Debates*, edited by Nikolas Coupland, 331–348. Cambridge: Cambridge University Press.

Wee, Lionel. 2021a. *The Communicative Linguistic Landscape*. London: Routledge.

Wee, Lionel. 2021b. *Posthumanist World Englishes*. Cambridge: Cambridge University Press.

Wee, Lionel and Robbie B. H. Goh. 2019. *Language, Space and Cultural Play: Theorizing Affect in the Semiotic Landscape*. Cambridge: Cambridge University Press.

Weir, Kirsten. 2015. "Robo Therapy: A New Class of Robots Provides Social and Cognitive Support." *American Psychological Association* 46, no. 6: 42. www.apa.org/m onitor/2015/06/robo-therapy.

Widdowson, Henry. 2019. Creativity in English. *World Englishes* 38, no. 1–2: 312–318.

Wimmer, Heinz and Josef Perner. 1983. "Beliefs About Beliefs: Representation and Constraining Function of Wrong Beliefs in Young Children's Understanding of Deception." *Cognition* 13, no. 1: 103–128.

Wise, J. Macgregor. 2005. "Assemblage." In *Gilles Deleuze: Key Concepts*, edited by Charles J. Stivale, 77–87. Montreal/Kingston: McGill/Queen's University Press.

Wittgenstein, Ludwig. 1958. *Philosophical Investigations*. 2nd ed. Wiley: Blackwell.

Young, William. 2019. "Reverend Robot: Automation and Clergy." *Zygon* 54, no. 2: 479–500.

Zucker, Lynne G. 1987. "Institutional theories of organization." *Annual Review of Sociology* 13: 443–464.

Newspapers, Magazines, and Webpages

Acante Solutions Limited. 2019. "McDonald's Touchscreen Kiosks." *Acante*, accessed October 27, 2021. https://acante.co.uk/2019/01/29/mcdonalds-touchscreen-kiosks-case-study.

App Store. n.d. *"foodpanda: Food and Groceries."* Accessed July 10, 2023. https://apps.apple.com/us/app/foodpanda-food-delivery/id758103884.

Baca, Marie. 2019. "People Do Grammar Bad. Google's AI is Hear Too Help." *Washington Post*, August 26, 2019. www.washingtonpost.com/technology/2019/08/26/people-do-grammar-bad-googles-ai-is-hear-too-help.

Bateman, Sophie. 2020. "World's Religions Embracing AI 'God Robots Capable of Performing Miracles'." *The Daily Star*, July 26, 2020, accessed July 14, 2022. www.dailystar.co.uk/news/world-news/worlds-religions-embracing-ai-god-22406074.

Baylor Institute for Studies of Religion. 2022. "How Safe Are Congregations and Clergy from Automation?" *Religion Watch* 34, no. 8 (June 8, 2022). www.religionwatch.com/how-safe-are-congregations-and-clergy-from-automation.

Becker, Sam. 2023. "AI-powered digital colleagues are here. Some 'safe' jobs could be vulnerable." *BBC Worklife*, November 30, 2023, accessed February 1, 2024. www.bbc.com/worklife/article/20231128-ai-powered-digital-colleagues-are-here-some-safe-jobs-could-be-vulnerable.

Choi, Yejin. 2023. "Why AI Is Incredibly Smart and Shockingly Stupid." *TED Talk*. April 28, 2023, accessed May 1, 2023. www.youtube.com/watch?v=SvBR0OGT5VI.

Chong, Siow Ann. 2021. "The AI Robot Therapist Will See You Now." *The Straits Times*, November 12, 2021. www.straitstimes.com/opinion/the-ai-robot-therapist-will-see-you-now.

Christian, Alex. 2023. "ChatGPT: How generative AI could change hiring as we know it." *BBC*, April 24, 2023, accessed May 1, 2023. www.bbc.com/worklife/article/20230419-chatgpt-how-generative-ai-could-change-hiring-as-we-know-it.

Computer History Museum. n.d. "About." *CHM*. September 1, 2023, accessed October 17, 2023. https://computerhistory.org/about.

Cullins, Ashley and Katie Kilkenny. 2023. "As writers strike, AI could covertly cross the picket line." *The Hollywood Reporter*, May 3, 2023, accessed October 29, 2023. www.hollywoodreporter.com/business/business-news/writers-strike-ai-chatgpt-1235478681.

Estrada, Zac. 2018. "Mercedes Uses Its New Car to Launch Yet Another Voice Assistant." *The Verge*, January 10, 2018, accessed September 27, 2019. www.theverge.com/2018/1/10/16872494/mercedes-voice-assistant-infotainment-ux-ces-2018.

Flood, Alison. 2021. "'A Box of Light': AI Inspired by British Verse Attempts to Write Poetry." *The Guardian*, March 20, 2021, accessed July 5, 2022. https://amp.theguardian.com/books/2021/mar/20/a-box-of-light-ai-inspired-by-british-verse-attempts-to-write-poetry.

Fontanella-Khan, Amana. 2020. "A robot wrote this entire article. Are you scared yet, human?" *The Guardian*, September 8, 2020, accessed October 21, 2023. www.theguardian.com/commentisfree/2020/sep/08/robot-wrote-this-article-gpt-3.

Frankiewicz, Marcin. 2023. "ChatGPT for collaborative innovation: Accelerating cross-industry solutions and partnerships." *TS2*, April 30, 2023, accessed May 1, 2023. http s://ts2.space/en/chatgpt-for-collaborative-innovation-accelerating-cross-industry-solutions-and-partnerships.

Galeon, Don. 2017. "Our Computers are Learning How to Code Themselves." *Futurism*, February 24, 2017, accessed September 13, 2019. https://futurism.com/4-our-computers-are-learning-how-to-code-themselves.

Google Play. "Bang & Olufsen." Accessed October 31, 2022. https://play.google.com/store/apps/details?id=com.bang_olufsen.OneApp.

GPT-3. 2020. "A Robot Wrote This Entire Article. Are You Scared Yet, Human?" *The Guardian*, September 8, 2020, accessed September 16, 2020. www.theguardian.com/commentisfree/2020/sep/08/robot-wrote-this-article-gpt-3?CMP=fb_a-technology_b-gdntech.

Grayson, Kent. 2016. "Cultivating trust is critical – and surprisingly complex." *KelloggInsight*, March 7, 2016, accessed November 8, 2023. https://insight.kellogg.northwestern.edu/article/cultivating-trust-is-critical-and-surprisingly-complex.

Hart, Matthew. 2020. "Google's New AI Helps You Write Poetry Like Poe." *Nerdist*. November 24, 2020, accessed July 5, 2022. https://nerdist.com/article/google-ai-writes-poetry-like-legendary-poets.

Indeed Editorial Team. 2021. "What is an app? Types of apps and examples." *Indeed*. July 24, 2021, accessed October 29, 2021. www.indeed.com/career-advice/career-development/what-is-an-app.

International Ecolinguistics Association. n.d. "About." Accessed October 30, 2023. http://ecolinguistics-association.org.

Joshi, Naveen. 2022. "How Robotics Can Automate Religious Rituals." *Allerin*, June 8, 2022. www.allerin.com/blog/how-robotics-can-automate-religious-rituals.

Lamadrid, Amanda 2022. "AI wrote a Cobra Kai script and it's more absurd than you can imagine." *ScreenRant*, September 22, 2022, accessed September 23, 2022. https://screenrant.com/cobra-kai-ai-script-parody-video.

Lamb, Robert. 2015. "Echoborg: The Computer Controls You." *Stuff to Blow Your Mind* (podcast), August 11, 2015, accessed May 20, 2017. www.stufftoblowyourmind.com/podcasts/echoborg-the-computer-controls-you.htm.

Lee, Don. 2019. "Desperate for Workers, Ageing Japan Turns to Robots for Healthcare." *The Star*, August 10, 2019, accessed November 13, 2021. www.thestar.com.my/tech/tech-news/2019/08/10/desperate-for-workers-ageing-japan-turns-to-robots-for-healthcare.

Leong, Chee Seng. 2019. "McDonald's Kiosk Ordering System: A UX case study." *UX Collective* (publication/blog), September 9, 2019, accessed October 27, 2021. https://uxdesign.cc/mcdonalds-kiosk-ordering-system-ui-ux-case-study-fe7b3693f12c.

Lerman, Anthony. 1996. "The Holocaust heritage." *The Independent*, December 3, 1996, accessed October 1, 2018. www.independent.co.uk/news/uk/the-holocaust-heritage-1312777.html.

Maruf, Ramishah. 2022. "Google fires engineer who contended its AI technology was sentient." *Egypt Independent*, July 26, 2022, accessed November 9, 2023. https://egyptindependent.com/google-fires-engineer-who-contended-its-ai-technology-was-sentient.

McFarland, Alex. 2023. "5 Best Deepfake Detector Tools & Techniques (November 2023)." *Unite.ai*, November 1, 2023. www.unite.ai/best-deepfake-detector-tools-and-techniques [page updates regularly].

News Reporter. 2019. "Elvis Presley's Hair Sells for $15,000." *NME*, October 19, 2019, accessed June 14, 2022. www.nme.com/news/music/elvis-presley-34-1316944.

Nolan, Beatrice. 2023. "More than 200 books in Amazon's bookstore have ChatGPT listed as an author or co-author." *Business Insider*, February 23, 2023, accessed May 1, 2023. www.businessinsider.com/chatgpt-ai-write-author-200-books-amazon-2023-2.

Patterson, Dan. 2023. "ChatGPT's intelligence is zero but it's a revolution in usefulness, says AI expert." *Innovation*, March 31, 2023, accessed May 1, 2023. www.zdnet. com/article/chatgpts-intelligence-is-zero.

Samuel, Sigal. 2020. "Robot Priests Can Bless You, Advise You, and Even Perform Your Funeral." *Vox*, January 13, 2020. www.vox.com/future-perfect/2019/9/9/2085175 3/ai-religion-robot-priest-mindar-buddhism-christianity.

Simpson, Dave. 2014. "Interview: Gary Numan and Mary Vango: How we made Are 'Friends' Electric?" *The Guardian*, February 18, 2014. www.theguardian.com/music/ 2014/feb/18/how-we-made-are-friends-electric-gary-numan.

Singapore Government. 1997. "Speech by Mr Abdullah Tarmugi, Minister for Community Development, at the Sikh Community National Day Dinner on Saturday, 30 Aug 97 at 7.30pm at Singapore Khalsa Association, 2 Tessensohn Road." Press release. August 30, 1997, accessed April 12, 2023. www.nas.gov.sg/archivesonline/data/p dfdoc/1997082-12.htm.

Sky News. 2023. "Deepfake Audio of Sir Keir Starmer Released on First Day of Labour Conference." *Sky News*, October 9, 2023, accessed October 30, 2023. https://news.sky. com/story/labour-faces-political-attack-after-deepfake-audio-is-posted-of-sir-keir-starmer-1 2980181.

Stokel-Walker, Chris. 2023. "AI Safety: How Close Is Global Regulation of Artificial Intelligence Really?" *BBC Future*, November 8, 2023. www.bbc.com/future/article/ 20231107-why-global-regulation-of-artificial-intelligence-is-still-a-long-way-off.

Sullivan, Will. 2023. "The Beatles Release Their Last Song, 'Now and Then,' Featuring A. I.-Extracted Vocals From John Lennon." *Smithsonian Magazine*, November 3, 2023, accessed November 5, 2023. www.smithsonianmag.com/smart-news/the-beatles-relea se-their-last-song-now-and-then-ai-john-lennon-180983188.

Tearle, Oliver. 2021. "A Summary and Analysis of Roland Barthes' 'The Death of the Author'." *Interesting Literature*, accessed June 19, 2023. https://interestingliterature. com/2021/10/barthes-death-of-the-author-summary-analysis.

Telefónica. n.d. "What is a deepfake and how to detect it?" *Telefónica* (blog), accessed October 5, 2023. www.telefonica.com/en/communication-room/blog/what-is-a -deepfake-and-how-to-detect-it.

Tenbarge, Kat. 2023. "YouTube Will Tell Users When Content Was Created With AI." *NBC News*, November 15, 2023. www.nbcnews.com/tech/tech-news/youtube-will-te ll-users-content-was-created-ai-rcna125080.

Time Out Group. 2016. "Los Angeles area guide: From Santa Monica to Downtown LA and more." *Time Out*, accessed January 25, 2021. www.timeout.com/los-angeles/fea tures/33/los-angeles-area-guide.

TODAY. 2019. "Meet Woebot, the therapy robot who's ready to listen." 15 January 2019, accessed November 27, 2021. News video. www.youtube.com/watch?v=XXArF d24JJE.

Today Online. 2023. "Did a Computer Write This? Book Industry Grapples With AI." *TODAY*, October 28, 2023. www.todayonline.com/world/did-computer-write-book-industry-grapples-ai-2288346.

UNESCO. n.d. "Safeguarding Cultural Heritage." UNESCO Office in Venice. Accessed September 29, 2018. www.unesco.org/new/en/venice/culture/safeguarding-cultura l-heritage.

US Weekly. 2017. "Jennifer Aniston Blasted for Using the Word 'Retard'" *US Weekly*, October 15, 2017, accessed February 1, 2024. www.usmagazine.com/celebrity-news/ news/jennifer-aniston-blasted-for-using-the-word-retard-2010198.

Webber, Alex. 2021. "Sermon-Giving 'Robotic Priest' Arrives in Poland to Support Faithful During Pandemic." *The First News*, October 29, 2021, accessed June 10, 2022. www.thefirstnews.com/article/sermon-giving-robotic-priest-arrives-in-poland-to -support-faithful-during-pandemic-25688.

Woollaston, Victoria. 2023. "The surprisingly subtle ways Microsoft Word has changed how we use language." *BBC Future*, October 25, 2023, accessed October 28, 2023. www.bbc.com/future/article/20231025-the-surprisingly-subtle-ways-microsoft-word- has-changed-the-way-we-use-language.

Writers Guild of America West. 2023. "Summary of the 2023 WGA MBA." *Writers Guild of America West*, accessed October 29, 2023. www.wga.org/contracts/contracts/m ba/summary-of-the-2023-wga-mba.

Yen, Zhi Yi. 2023. "Club-wielding woman in China assaults hospital robot." *Mothership*, April 30, 2023, accessed May 2, 2023. https://mothership.sg/2023/04/china-woma n-attack-hospital-robot.

Yeung, Jessie and Gawon Bae. 2022. "Forever young, beautiful and scandal-free: The rise of South Korea's virtual influencers." *CNN*, August 17, 2022, accessed September 23, 2022. https://edition.cnn.com/style/article/south-korea-virtual-influencers-beauty-so cial-media-intl-hnk-dst/index.html.

Zarka, Lisa. 2018. "The Rise of the Robot Therapist." *The Bold Italic*, November 14, 2018, accessed November 27, 2021. https://thebolditalic.com/the-rise-of-the-robot- therapist-459b20f770a9.

Index

For Product Safety Concerns and Information please contact our EU
representative GPSR@taylorandfrancis.com Taylor & Francis Verlag GmbH,
Kaufingerstraße 24, 80331 München, Germany

Printed and bound by CPI Group (UK) Ltd, Croydon, CR0 4YY
08/06/2025
01897008-0018